The Art of Hypnotherapy

Part II of "Diversified Client-Centered Hypnosis"

(based on the teachings of Charles Tebbetts)

by

C. ROY HUNTER, M.S., C.Ht.

KENDALL/HUNT PUBLISHING COMPANY
4050 Westmark Drive   Dubuque, Iowa 52002

Other books by Roy Hunter:
The Art of Hypnosis: Mastering Basic Techniques
Master the Power of Self-Hypnosis
Success Through Mind Power
HypnoCise

DEDICATION & ACKNOWLEDGEMENTS

This second volume, just like the first, is dedicated to all those who believe in the benefits of *diversified client-centered hypnotherapy* to facilitate positive change.

We all owe a debt of gratitude to Charles Tebbetts for his tireless dedication to the art of hypnotism, evidenced by his many years of teaching and practicing; but additional gratitude is in order for his wife, Joyce Tebbetts, who worked behind the scenes for so many years to support her husband's important work. Certainly her efforts helped a great deal in promoting competent hypnotherapy training.

While Charlie was living, I expressed my appreciation to both Mr. and Mrs. Tebbetts for their support in my teaching The Charles Tebbetts Hypnotism Training Course. Joyce has continued that support by putting her blessing on this book, for which I am grateful.

I also wish to acknowledge Tacoma Community College for allowing me to teach hypnotherapy during the pioneer years of our profession, while our future was still uncertain. In my opinion, this courage and foresight of an established educational institution is worthy of national recognition.

And again, my deepest gratitude goes to Jo-Anne, my loving wife, for her willingness to share so many hours of my time with all of you who read this book.

> Roy Hunter
> *... in memory of Charles Tebbetts*
> *Memorial Day, 1994*
> *Revisions completed 2/29/2000*

Table of Contents

Table of Contents (cont.)

Table of Contents (cont.)

Table of Contents (cont.)

Table of Contents (cont.)

Preface

by Joyce Tebbetts

My husband devoted his life to hypnotism. He loved helping people, and he loved teaching others how to help people through hypnotherapy. Since I worked with him for many years, I feel qualified to give my opinion on the contents of this book, for which I have nothing to say but praise.

When Charlie passed away, he was still doing what he loved. We were at the annual convention of the National Guild of Hypnotists, where he was preparing to teach parts therapy to other hypnotherapists; and when he found himself unable to teach his workshop, he asked Roy Hunter to teach it in his behalf. I sat next to Roy's wife as he honored my husband by teaching in a way that I believe would make Charlie proud. And I told this to the Hunters in my hotel room later that night.

The confidence Charlie felt in choosing Roy Hunter to continue teaching his methods in hypnotherapy speaks for itself. Roy has been teaching our course since 1987. In a letter I wrote to him last January, I said, "You are the only one I'd pick out for teaching it if I had to do so." I believe him to be the most qualified to carry my husband's torch.

I highly approve of Roy's additions to some of the topics of importance. I feel that reading this book opens the door to a more complete understanding of hypnotherapy in every aspect.

I am delighted that he has written this book in a way that honors my husband's name and perpetuates his teachings into the next century. It is very gratifying to me personally to know that Charlie will continue to touch people's lives.

Joyce Tebbetts, C.Ht.
(Mrs. Charles Tebbetts)

Chapter 1

Introduction to Hypnotherapy

Increasing numbers of people around this planet want answers.

Not only do they want answers to life, they want to know how they can reach their own goals and bring their dreams into reality. Untold numbers of men and women spend countless sums of dollars annually--seeking professional help just in overcoming undesirable habits alone.

Why Is Hypnotherapy the Answer?

Charles Tebbetts began the first chapter of his hypnotherapy text book, *Miracles on Demand* (2nd edition), with these words:

Millions of people are suffering mental anguish and are striving unsuccessfully to find help. Hypnotherapy is the answer for most of them because it is short-term, safe, practical and effective.

SPECIAL NOTE: All quotes throughout this book from *Miracles on Demand* are taken from the 2nd Edition, which is out of print *(see NOTICE at end of this chapter).*

With the advent of the fast-food society, increasing numbers of people are looking for faster methods of achieving their desires than in the past. There is far greater interest in alternative therapies than ever before; and while this makes some people vulnerable for the "quick fix" artists out to make a fast buck, the upside is the most favorable public acceptance of hypnotherapy than we have seen in centuries--and possibly in the entire history of the human race.

Yet with this widespread awareness of the emergence of the artistic group of professional hypnotherapists, we have a few highly educated people with advanced degrees and restrictive health care licenses trying to stop the growth of the hypnotherapy profession. They claim that only those with post graduate degrees should be allowed to use hypnosis. These elite would like to preserve the secrets of hypnosis for themselves, just as the secrets of trance induction have been jealously guarded by an elite few throughout history since the dawn of time. They would limit the ability of the public to choose their practitioners, even though many of them learned their hypnosis skills from some of the very same professionals whom they attack!

As with any profession, including medicine and psychology, we must endure a few who seem self-centered and greedy. Hypnotherapy is no exception, and has its share of practitioners more skilled in marketing than in hypnotherapy; but some psychologists are too quick to throw us all out as they apparently ignore the many good results obtained by many dedicated hypnotherapists. (They conveniently overlook the fact that many people spend years in psychological treatment with little or no improvement!)

Many highly educated counselors, psychotherapists, and psychologists received only miminal specific training in the art of hypnotherapy--just as many hypnotherapists have only minimal training in psychology. There is need for both fields, and much need for building bridges of mutual support and cooperation. Our country is laced with experienced and properly trained hypnotherapists who DO know how to competently use a variety of beneficial techniques. These professionals are quite willing to call in psychologists or physicians when appropriate.

The question, then, is not in what academic degrees the hypnotherapist does or does not have. Rather, how thorough was the specific training in the art of hypnotherapy?

Mr. Tebbetts believed that some of the most simple hypnotic techniques could result in some of the most profound benefits when done properly. He did not require his students to have advanced degrees; but he took great care in how he taught these techniques, because my late teacher felt strongly that we should know enough about hypnosis to fit the technique to the client rather than to try to fit the client to the technique. Why? Read on....

The Biggest Hypnotic Secret Revealed

As modern science brings technological enlightenment to this world, it's high time to bring hypnosis out of the dark ages and shine the light of truth on its secrets. Let's rip away once and for all the shroud of mysticism that has surrounded this art for so many centuries. Let's begin by exposing the biggest secret of all: the power is NOT in the hypnotist, it is in the *client*--the person who is guided into hypnosis!

Charles Tebbetts, who became a legend in the hypnotherapy profession while still living, revealed this secret of hypnosis at the start of every session he did with these words: "All hypnosis is self-hypnosis." (I expanded on this in my first volume, *The Art of Hypnosis*.) Mr. Tebbetts believed that the hypnotist or hypnotherapist was simply a guide (or artist) facilitating the client's inborn ability to change as desired, because all the power is already inside the mind of the person experiencing hypnosis.

Most certainly if it were the hypnotist that had the power, it stands to reason that very intensive (and expensive) training would be vital before turning a new hypnotist loose on any trusting person entering the trance state--especially if the person in trance was powerless to refuse suggestions. Yet that is simply not the case, unless the person entering hypnosis was tricked into believing that he/she was under the control of the hypnotist. Even in such a case there are limits to the suggestions such a person would accept.

Charles Tebbetts: a Master Teacher

Charles Tebbetts spent all of the last years of his life teaching hypnotherapy. He kept his students in "hands-on" training for 150 hours, and then required that they pass both a written and practical exam, successfully demonstrating the art of hypnosis prior to certification. He believed that hypnosis could be learned and used effectively by almost any mature adult with average intelligence and education, provided he/she was honest, ethical, had a sincere desire to help others, and was willing to invest enough time practicing to master the art. (My own experience validates his opinions.)

During the decades when hypnosis was shunned by both the medical profession and the mental health field, Mr. Tebbetts successfully used hypnotherapy to help people get results. He invested over six decades of his life practicing and studying hypnosis, and eventually opened his legendary hypnotherapy training institute in the Pacific Northwest--where this author had the privilege of learning the art of hypnosis. Indeed, Charles Tebbetts directly touched the lives of thousands of people, and indirectly touched the lives of my own clients through his teachings--as well as the lives of clients reached by his former students.

My mentor, honored for lifetime achievement by the International Hypnosis Hall of Fame, believed that too many people spent too much money and too much time trying to deal with causes of their problems on a cognitive level rather than at a subconscious level where one can obtain results. Let me quote his own words, taken from the preface of his book, *Miracles on Demand:*

...I have helped thousands of people improve the quality of their lives through my knowledge of hypnotism and my understanding of human behavior. Although I have studied psychology in depth in college courses, I am more concerned with beneficial results than with interesting theories.

He goes on to say:

I feel a glow of pleasure and satisfaction when someone stops me on the street and says, "You're the man who changed my life!" Of course, he did it himself, but I feel fortunate in possessing the knowledge that enabled me to help him.

This author, who prefers to write in the first-person format, discovered by experience how that "glow of pleasure" feels some years back when one of my former clients came up to me in a public place and introduced me to her sister with the words, "This is the man who gave my life back to me!" Yet I agree with my former mentor and teacher. This woman already had the power to give herself a better life. All I did was use the client-centered techniques taught by Charles Tebbetts to help her unlock the power of her own mind--but I was still moved emotionally by this woman's gratitude for my part in her personal growth. My *master teacher* indirectly helped give this woman her life back by teaching me what he knew.

One of my main goals in writing this book is to organize and preserve the essence of what my late mentor taught, updated with my own professoinal experience and some techniques learned elsewhere. I have successfully used my mentor's techniques since training under him personally in 1983. In addition, I enjoyed both the privilege of knowing Charles Tebbetts as a personal friend and a mentor. My hypnosis course, based on his teachings, is now called *Diversified Client-Centered Hypnosis.*

Learn the Art of Hypnosis First

All hypnotherapy employs hypnosis; but hypnosis is not hypnotherapy except when certain techniques are used to help a client with self-improvement. For example, one does not need to know the art of hypnotherapy in order to be a good stage hypnotist.

Before practicing any of the techniques taught in this book, one should first master a variety of basic hypnosis techniques with confidence and competence. Even the best hypnotherapy techniques could prove ineffective if a client's depth of hypnosis is so light that he/she lets the conscious mind get in the way and resists guidance.

Before my own students are exposed to the techniques presented in these pages, they have completed the same training detailed in *The Art of Hypnosis,* the first part of what used to be called the Charles Tebbetts Hypnotism Training Course. There will be references that will make more sense to the reader who has the first volume of my book to refer to, so I hope it is already in your library. If you have not had formal training in the art of hypnosis, it is my very strong professional opinion that you should *obtain professional hypnosis training* before even attempting the techniques presented in this second volume! Even if you have a doctorate in medicine or psychology, hands-on training can really make a difference, because there is *no substitute for practice* to master an art with confidence and competence.

I am not a scientist, and I will not to be one. There are physicians, psychiatrists and psychologists who have done some profound research with medical applications of hypnosis; but how competent would some of these same scientists be at helping a smoker quit smoking without weight gain? ...at helping a smoker quit smoking yet still be comfortable around others who smoke, or even help a smoker who does not choose to quit but would like to greatly reduce the number of cigarettes smoked? ...or at helping an overweight person reduce without creating aversion to sweets? ...at helping a salesman reach sales quota? ...or simply helping a bowler improve his/her average? ...or helping a person stop biting fingernails without aversion suggestions? ...or helping someone forgive and release a deceased parent? ...etc., etc., etc. Do the scientists practice hypnotherapy full-time, or only occasionally while they practice medicine or psychology as a primary main vocation?

Also, do all those who genuinely help their clients or patients with hypnosis seek to help the person become *self-empowered* with the realization that all hypnosis is guided self-hypnosis? Or are there still some hypnotists out there who treat people more like "subjects" who become *bound* by their suggestions?

Who Should Teach Hypnosis?

Charles Tebbetts said numerous times that there is no substitute for practice to develop confidence and competence with the art of hypnosis. In my opinion, this is even *more* true for those who wish to teach the art of hypnotherapy.

If you have purchased this book because you believe you need more training, how can you determine whether or not your prospective trainer is your wisest choice?

Professional experience is vital

First of all, ask your prospective hypnotherapy teacher whether or not he/she practices hypnotherapy on a full-time or part time basis, and for how many years. This is far more important than his or her academic credentials.

In my opinion NO ONE should teach hypnosis unless he or she has at least two or three years of full-time experience *exclusively* doing hypnotherapy--or a minimum of five years of part time experience in those techniques that are taught! (Some therapists are VERY competent at hypnotherapy, but inadequate at marketing, so they work two jobs.) No matter what the person's academic credentials--or other professional experience--there is *no substitute for hypnotherapy experience* when it comes to teaching hypnotherapy (with allowances for certain specialty courses).

I would far rather see someone teaching basic hypnotherapy with two years' full-time experience in the profession than an instructor with a doctorate degree who only occasionally uses hypnosis in his or her practice of medicine or psychology--except for medical and/or other specialized applications of hypnosis. (Even with all my years of full-time experience in the practice of hypnotherapy, I do not consider myself to be qualified to teach a specialty course on medical applications of hypnosis! I only touch on it in my course on advanced techniques, encouraging interested students to pursue additional studies.)

Those newly certified hypnotherapists who jump right into teaching hypnosis a few weeks after their certification course are jeopardizing the credibility of our profession. *Pay your dues and get your experience first!* This is important for both students and their future clients--AS WELL AS for personal long-term professional credibility and survival. You can far more adequately answer student questions when you have your own client experiences to draw upon--and you will learn far more about hypnotherapy from actual *experience* than from any text book, training manual, trainer or instructor, provided you made a wise choice in your initial training.

What about length of training?

Secondly, find out the *length* of the training. Is it a one-weekend certification course? If so, *forget it* unless it is a promoted and represented as an *introduction* with additional training required prior to certification. Even training in basic hypnotherapy (for those not previously trained in the art of hypnosis) should span at least 100 hours to cover adequately what you need to know when you are out on your own, regardless of your other professional experience.

Charles Tebbetts required 150 hours of training for full certification for most of his students, but allowed those with backgrounds in psychology and/or counseling to take their certification exams after 100 hours if they so chose. Also, my teacher exclusively taught subject matter that was *directly* related to the art of hypnotherapy. He did not believe we needed hundreds of hours of classes on theories or on topics that have nothing to do with the practice of hypnotherapy. If you choose to specialize in certain areas, then you might seek additional professional training in those specific fields.

Will you learn client-centered techniques?

Thirdly, find out whether or not the techniques taught are client-centered and the classes student-centered. Will you learn hypnotherapy techniques that you must use on every single client? There is no hypnotic technique I know of that will work on all of the people all of the time. Charles Tebbetts taught what I call *diversified client-centered hypnosis*. If your class offers only a basic modality, consider investing in additional workshops as you are able.

Other important concerns

Furthermore, does the prospective instructor hold himself or herself up as some *guru* or expert who frowns on all other techniques except the ones he/she teaches? Is this person the self-appointed director of a hypnosis association that he/she thinks is the *only* one you should belong to? If the answer to ANY of these questions is "yes," you might consider looking elsewhere for your training.

Also important: has the instructor submitted his/her entire course outline to one or more nationally recognized hypnotherapy associations for approval? If so, this is a plus. (Several associations, including the International Medical and Dental Hypnotherapy Association, have credentialed my course, whether taught by me, or taught by another instructor using my copyrighted instructor's training manual. Not only have I submitted my material to several different hypnotherapy associations, I submitted it to the entire profession by writing these books! Also, my course is now offered in several colleges, including a fully accredited college.)

Finally, find out whether or not the instructor teaches that all hypnosis is self-hypnosis. This truth must be taught to the general public as well as to the student of hypnosis!

Truth Removes Fear

Many of my clients who have been previously hypnotized complain that they either felt like the hypnotist was in control, or felt like they were not the least bit hypnotized. They often seemed surprised when I explained that hypnosis--as I use it--is guided self-hypnosis. Some of them had been afraid of hypnotherapy for quite some time even though hypnotized previously.

Even now there are still tens of millions of Americans who erroneously believe that a person in hypnosis is a *subject* who has placed himself/herself under the "power" or control of the hypnotist. Many medical writings spread this belief by labeling the person in hypnosis as a *subject*. This very word is misleading, as it gives the impression that the person in hypnosis is *"subject"* to the power of the hypnotist. That simply is not the case unless the person in hypnosis is tricked into believing that he/she is giving up control--and then he/she might respond according to the false belief system held at the time unless holding on to a strong emotioal objection to a suggestion. It's time for us to tell the truth about hypnosis-- and we can begin by changing the language.

In my first book I explained my view that a hypnotherapist using non-medical applications of hypnosis should use the word *client* or *participant,* while the word *patient* may be used with medical applications of hypnosis-- unless the person being hypnotized is the subject of an experiment.

Using more respectful terms for those experiencing hypnotherapy is, in my opinion, an important step in removing the fear from hypnosis; and we can further diminish people's fears by revealing to them the fact that *they are the ones with the power.* We are only the artists--or tour guides--trained to guide them on their journey.

The Purpose of This Book

My goal in the first book, *The Art of Hypnosis,* was to present the basic hypnosis techniques similar to those taught by Charles Tebbetts just as I present them to my classes at Tacoma Community College in Tacoma, Washington. My students must learn how to induce and deepen hypnosis as well as how to manage the hypnotic state with both confidence and competence before learning hypnotherapy.

My goal in this second book is to present the same *client-centered* techniques that my own students learn so that they can effectively work with the majority of clients who seek help. Once one finally masters the art of hypnosis, how can hypnotic techniques be used to help people achieve goals? How can we facilitate *diversified client-centered hypnosis?*

The second part of my three-quarter course presents the meat of client-centered hypnotherapy techniques. The student learns how to use hypnosis for habit control and motivation--such as smoking cessation and weight management. I also present a class on dealing with simple phobias as well as a class on a more thought-provoking use of hypnosis. This book contains the entire content of Part II, as well as most of the contents of the third part blended in as appropriate.

The third part of the course shows how my mentor applied advanced techniques in some of the more specialized areas, including the legendary parts therapy of Charles Tebbetts. For example, I will not use hypnosis to help a client manage pain unless referred by his/her physician; but how can hypnotherapy help the client who has the appropriate written referral from his/her examining physician??? It's a good idea to know more than one technique if your client walks in with the appropriate referral--because if the technique you use first does not work, what do you do next?

Some actual case histories are presented to my class. My students enjoy the privilege of viewing videotapes of Mr. Tebbetts doing parts therapy while he was living. I also have several guest presenters discuss other specialized areas, so that the student who is interested in specializing has enough information to become motivated to seek more training in his/her area(s) of interest. Since those portions of the third part remain subject to change, I simply encourage the serious student of hypnotherapy to seek specialized training in those fields in which he/she desires to specialize.

With my professional hypnotherapy experience dating back to 1983, I feel qualified to share from my own experiences what might and might not be effective. You will read about some of my successful clients; and in addition, I'm willing to share some of my mistakes (as well as the mistakes of others) so that you will not have to re-invent the wheel.

There are so many effective techniques that no one book could adequately cover them all; but those taught by Charles Tebbetts brought him legendary fame while he was still living. Just as he taught his students much more "how to" rather than theory, my teaching style is more "how to" than academic.

Also, many text books are written in pedantic styles that make for difficult reading. I appreciated the easy-to-read style that my former mentor used, and shall attempt to do likewise. Thus, I present these techniques in a simple and logical way, just as I teach the course. I invested over seven years and several thousand hours in organizing the teachings of Charles Tebbetts into what I believe to be a clear, easy-to-understand, logical learning sequence.

Rather than doubling the size of this book with volumes of outside research, let me simply encourage you, the reader, to do whatever independent research you desire. Several associates who evaluated the first drafts of chapters in this book asked me to refrain from inserting boring references just to satisfy the scientific minds, because they believe it would make the book more difficult to read and comprehend.

How effective are the techniques taught by Charles Tebbetts? Once you've mastered the *art of hypnotherapy,* find out for yourself.

By learning enough techniques to be able to adapt flexibly to your client, you will be practicing *diversified client-centered hypnosis.* It is my belief that you will discover something very important: results speak louder than books.

Before getting into the rest of this book, however, allow me to honor the request of one of the hypnotherapy associations endorsing my course by listing the names and addresses of those who have given their approval of my course as of the date this book was first sent to the publisher:

Hypnotherapy Associations Recognizing This Course:

These are listed in alphabetical order...

The International Medical and Dental Hypnotherapy Association
4110 Edgeland, Suite 800
Royal Oak, MI 48073-2251
(800) 257-5467

The International Society for Professional Hypnosis
PO Box 452
North Haven, CT 06473
(203) 239-7046

National Assocation of Transpersonal Hypnotherapists
PO Box 249
Goshen, VA 24439
(540) 997-0325

*National Guild of Hypnotists
PO Box 308
Merrimack, NH 03054-0308
(603) 429-9438
*Certification granted to my personal students, but only granted to students
of other instructors on an individual basis unless the instructors meet certain
NGH requirements.

National Society of Clinical Hypnotherapists
31916 University Circle
Springfield, LA 70462
(225) 294-2129

Washington Hypnosis Association
PO Box 445
Kelso, WA 98626
(360) 425-6878
NOTE: Other state associations have also given endorsement.

SPECIAL NOTICE about *Miracles on Demand*:

I wish to express my deepest gratitude to the copyright owner for granting
permission to use numerous quotations from that book in this text. Both Charles
and Joyce Tebbetts granted me pemission, both verbally and in writing, to use any
and all materials written by Charles Tebbetts; however, the additional authorization
given proved vital in clarifying potential misunderstandings. If my mentor's
important book again becomes available for distribution, I will be very happy to
recommend it to my students.

Chapter 2

The Preinduction Interview

One of the most important qualities of a good therapist is the ability to put one's self in the place of the client and have genuine understanding and empathy.

According to Charles Tebbetts, this feeling--when genuine--is actually picked up by the client subconsciously, and is an important part of building rapport (*Miracles on Demand*, 2nd Edition, p.214). While rapport is vital throughout the entire therapy process, it begins before hypnosis--and is the first of four main objectives of the pre-induction interview. The other three objectives are: allay fears, build mental expectancy, and gather information.

This chapter will limit itself to the teachings of Mr. Tebbetts, expanded by my own experience. The reader interested in additional research may invest the necessary time to learn about established methods used (S.O.A.P., etc.) in other health care professions; but I wish to present this topic here adapted for hypnotherapy primarily as I do for my own classes. Let's begin our discussion with the first objective of the pre-induction interview of the intake session.

Objective #1: Building and Maintaining Rapport

Rapport begins the moment of first contact--whether in person or by phone.

How do you answer the telephone? Do you project a willingness to be a good listener? Or do you try as quickly as possible to get the prospective client into your office so the clock can start ticking? Perceptive people on the other end of the telephone may discern your attitude by listening to your tone of voice. Of course, there must be a balance, as experienced therapists know that some people can and will take advantage of your time if you let them.

The second part of building rapport begins the moment the client steps into the office. What kind of image do you project? We can project a professional image both by our appearance as well as the appearance of the office.

By dressing professionally we convey an unspoken message that the client will be treated professionally. Personal grooming is also important. For example, a man with long hair and/or an excessively long beard could easily lose rapport within seconds. Furthermore, excessive makeup, strong breath, and/or strong perfume or cologne could make both men and women uncomfortable. Much more could be said about personal image, but this book is not the place for it. If you have questions, invest some time and/or money with an image consultant.

The office should be pleasant but professional. If there are religious and/or metaphysical pictures or symbols around (such as crystals and/or crucifixes), some people will immediately become uncomfortable. Unless you are working primarily within your church or within a certain group of people, be extremely careful about how you decorate your office. This is even more important if you are taking the risk of working out of your home--which is already two strikes against you.

My first exposure to a hypnotherapist took me to a private home. When the door opened, a seductively-dressed woman took me down to a candle-lit basement filled with new-age pictures. I had already decided against hypnosis even before meeting her husband, who appeared dressed in a robe that made him look like a sorcerer from the days of King Arthur! Over a year passed before I even considered hypnotherapy again. Fortunately someone changed my opinion of hypnosis, or you wouldn't be reading this book right now.

Even though my own example was extreme--and, I hope, very rare--I have been in several hypnotherapy offices that would immediately tarnish rapport in the minds of many prospective clients.

So now you've introduced yourself and invited your client to be seated in a comfortable environment... What next?

Take a few minutes to get acquainted. My mentor taught us that part of building rapport was in making friends with the client--because a client who likes his/her therapist will be much more comfortable and responsive to therapy. Be balanced in this. Getting too friendly in a personal way could easily give the wrong image. Be professional, but be yourself.

We should also respect the client's pocketbook and limit the amount of "small talk" so that we may get to the task we are paid for. This also includes taking the phone off the hook (or having a silent answering service) unless expecting an urgent call--in which case the client should not be charged for the time until after the call.

The last part of rapport is *ongoing*. We should maintain rapport throughout the entire session and/or series of sessions by being good listeners as well as by doing for the client what we would want done if the roles were reversed. By all means let's remain ethical, making ethics second nature. (If you have any questions about ethical conduct, refer to Chapter 9 of my first volume of this major work, *The Art of Hypnosis*.) Remember that it is much easier to maintain rapport than it is to try to regain it if lost.

Now let's discuss the second important objective of the pre-induction interview: *allaying fears*.

Objective #2: Allaying Fears

Many clients have entered my office with fears, whether expressed or unexpressed. What were they afraid of?

A smoker confessed to me that she had two fears. First, she was afraid that she couldn't be hypnotized, thus wasting her money. Second, she was also afraid that hypnosis would indeed work, and she feared the thought of never having another cigarette again in her life!

Some people have fears of being alone with a member of the opposite sex. I invite my clients to bring friends or relatives with them if they wish--and this seems to alleviate those fears. Very few clients actually do bring other persons with them; but just knowing they have the option to do so seems to help them feel more secure. There are some hypnotherapists who will not do a session alone with a member of the opposite sex, while others make tapes of the sessions and/or keep the door open throughout. You are free to choose your own precautions for both your own peace of mind as well as that of your clients.

Some people have expressed or unexpressed fears of hypnosis itself. They are afraid of losing control of their minds and/or revealing personal secrets. Before addressing the latter fear, let's discuss the former one.

Effective use of suggestibility tests is essential in minimizing fears of hypnosis as well as in building mental expectancy. If you have *The Art of Hypnosis,* you may wish to re-read Chapter 4 at this time, as the suggestibility tests are too important to omit in the intake session.

I also reveal to my clients the fact that all hypnosis is really guided self-hypnosis--or *guided daydreaming.* Some might ask whether this could reduce the response of clients who wish to be hypnotized. Perhaps yes; but am I really doing clients a favor if helping them means taking their power away and making those people already caught in a victim trap become subjects of unethical hypnosis??? If people want me to rescue them instead of helping them to greater self-empowerment, what role might they take if I fail to rescue them to their own satisfaction?

Unless I believe that my clients realize I'm only a guide, or an artist facilitating their own abilities to change, I will not take their money--instead, I recommend that they seek other professional help.

I explain to my clients that one of my goals is to help them *claim the power of choice* by teaching them how to get the subconscious to accept the choices of the conscious mind, or to attain their ideal empowerment.

Furthermore, by explaining that *imagination is the language of the subconscious,* I teach clients how to communicate with their own subconscious minds! The suggestibility tests effectively demonstrate this important fact, so I end the demonstration by saying, "Your fingers [or arms] did not move because I told them to; they moved because of what you imagined!"

If a client is afraid of revealing secrets, I explain that I cannot make him/her reveal anything against his or her will. Furthermore, in Washington State, hypnotherapists must abide by the terms of the Uniform Disciplinary Code, which requires hypnotherapists to maintain client confidentiality. Even if your state does not have such a requirement, most professional hypnosis associations have this requirement in their codes of ethics.

Here are some words of Charles Tebbetts about allaying fears (p. 215, *Miracles on Demand,* 2nd Edition):

> *The usual fears expressed by clients who are not familiar with hypnotism are that they will reveal their secrets, that they will be unable to come out of the*

trance, and that they will be made to do things they don't want to do. Contrary to average beliefs, these fears are all unfounded. Although the conscious, analytical mind is dormant during hypnosis, it is always functioning. A person can choose to lie when deeply hypnotized, and will not reveal any information he doesn't want others to know. He can remember things he couldn't remember consciously, but he chooses what he wishes to tell. He can come out of hypnosis at any time he wishes, and if he chooses to remain hypnotized, he will eventually go to sleep and awaken as usual. He will also refuse to do anything that he doesn't want to do. He will do things while in hypnosis that he wouldn't do otherwise, but only those things that he doesn't mind doing.

Objective #3: Building Mental Expectancy

Remember the roles of belief, imagination, conviction and expectation? These are the ingredients of the hypnotic formula. (Refer to Chapter 2 of *The Art of Hypnosis.*)

The advantage of having been in the profession for several years is that I can draw upon the successes of other clients whose circumstances resemble those of the person consulting me for the first time. When I did not have this advantage, I drew upon the experiences of Charles Tebbetts and other veteran hypnotherapists to help my clients believe that hypnosis could help them too. To benefit my readers, I have threaded some of my own case summaries throughout this book as well as some case summaries of my late mentor; so you might enjoy these same benefits if you are new in the profession.

Another part of building mental expectancy lies in your own level of expertise and confidence. There is no substitute for practice to develop that confidence and competence; so if you have learned hypnosis simply out of a textbook or a weekend seminar, do a favor for both yourself and your clients and seek more training. (Refer to the section in the first chapter entitled, "Who Should Teach Hypnosis?" to find out how to choose wisely.)

Once again, I must also emphasize the value of suggestibility tests as a vital part of building mental expectancy. Read the words of Charles Tebbetts about this important objective (p. 216, *Miracles on Demand,* 2nd Edition):

> *The fact that the client chose to come to you suggests that he recognizes you as a hypnotist. Your own confidence in your ability to guide him into hypnosis is your greatest asset for building the client's expectancy. The statement, "If you can follow my simple directions, no power on earth can prevent you from becoming hypnotized," suggests to the client that you are capable of doing your part and that it is up to him to do his. **Inform him that all hypnosis is self-hypnosis,** and that you are an expert in guiding him into the trance state. Always project the attitude that a good hypnotist never fails. It is only the subject [client] who can fail.* (Emphasis mine.)

Objective #4: Gathering Information

It would be pointless to begin hypnotherapy without finding out what the client wishes to accomplish. This seems very basic--yet it is so important that I must share a personal experience with my readers.

A woman who was at least 100 pounds overweight entered my office after I had been in the profession for about two years. She told me that she had been heavy all her life, and had gone up and down like a yo-yo. She answered every question I had asked her about her weight--including how much she weighed--and told me that she had great resentment towards society's attitude against fat people. She *resented people who even hinted* that she should lose weight, and had not tried to reduce in over six years. When I asked her why she finally decided to use hypnosis to deal with her weight, she cleared her throat and exclaimed, "I came here to quit smoking!" Even though she accepted my apology, I wanted to crawl under the carpet. Needless to say, I shall always remember this lesson!!!

Never assume. Ask your client what goal he/she hopes to accomplish through hypnotherapy before you put your foot into your mouth; and if the problem is beyond your area of competence, refer him/her elsewhere.

If it is a medical problem, avoid crossing the invisible line. You cannot diagnose illness or disease unless licensed to do so; and you should avoid medical applications of hypnosis without the appropriate medical referral (unless you are a licensed physician). Even if you are an ordained minister incorporating hypnotherapy into prayer and/or pastoral counseling, at least advise people that pain is a warning that something is wrong with the body and suggest that they consider appropriate medical examination to deal with the cause of the pain.

Assuming you can help, proceed to gather whatever relevant information is necessary for you to help the client. This includes history and development of the problem or bad habit he/she might wish to change, as well as other relevant factors. Information from the client might also help you determine which induction is best.

We should ask whether or not the client has ever been professionally hypnotized--and if so, which induction was used. Also ask when, how and why, as well as whether or not the hypnosis was helpful.

If you plan to use of guided imagery techniques, it's very important to know whether your client *visualizes or not*--and whether or not there are any phobias. For example, do not take a client down an imaginary elevator as a deepening technique if he/she is afraid of elevators! Likewise, let's avoid guiding someone to the beach if he/she is afraid of the ocean, etc., etc. Ask the *client* to *tell you* where his/her peaceful place might be. One of my students liked boats, so she had another student imagine being in a boat. He literally got seasick, and went outside to lose his dinner!

If you intend to use any touch techniques, you should first find out whether your client is comfortable being touched. Also, if you plan on using eye-fixation inductions, perhaps you'd better find out whether your client is sensitive to light. If so--or if he or she is not visual--he/she just might prefer another induction type.

There are other questions that may or may not be appropriate depending on the client objectives, such as questions about marital status, family background and/or medical background. I used to ask every client about marital status until one woman took it the wrong way. This taught me that sometimes it's not just what you ask, it's how and when you ask. If you tend to sometimes put your foot in your mouth, you may ask your client to complete a written form with written answers to these questions.

Many therapists consider a lengthy written survey the professional thing to do. Some people hate writing, so Charles Tebbetts believed that these questions should be asked verbally. I believe the therapist should be free to make a choice--but even if most questions are answered verbally, there should still be some sort of written disclosure and/or client information sheet which your client completes. Washington State has a state law *requiring* a written disclosure be completed and signed by both therapist and client--with the client retaining a copy. Such disclosure must contain fee structure, disclosure about therapist's training, education and experience, estimated number of sessions (where known), and certain other information specified by the state. Even if not required, disclosure is professional.

Remember to maintain rapport even while gathering information. Some people may be reluctant to answer questions of a personal nature even though they relate to therapy. On page 214 of *Miracles on Demand*, my mentor wrote:

> *Even after you have gained rapport, the client will often hold back consciously from disclosing vital information about the true nature of the problem. She may indulge in superficial conversation, appearing very friendly and cooperative. Or she may describe her problem fully, stating all the facts as she perceives them, completely isolating herself emotionally from the story she is telling. She may lie persistently as a means of defense.*

You may or may not perceive this at the time; but competent use of client-centered hypnotherapy techniques may help your client in spite of pre-induction resistance so long as the client is sincere in the desire to be helped.

That brings up the most important part of the therapy process... *Your client must choose to change!* Also, I urge you to know whether your client is making the free choice to change before you begin hypnotherapy.

The Importance of Choice

If I believe that a client is only seeing me because his or her spouse manipulated the appointment, I will not accept the money.

Since all hypnosis is self-hypnosis, I cannot force clients to quit smoking. I can only help them help themselves by making them aware of the benefits of hypnosis, and determining whether or not the benefits of overcoming the problems are important enough for a *commitment* to change!

I inform them that hypnosis will not make them quit smoking, but it can make the decision easier once they make the commitment to change.

Both before and during the client's first hypnotic trance, I will ask for confirmation that it is the client's own free choice to change. If this is not the case, then I'm not the right professional for that client.

Several years ago a woman set up an appointment for her husband to quit smoking, and she came with him to the first session. Within minutes of the pre-induction interview, it became apparent that he came under protest--so I asked him whether or not it was *his choice* to become a non-smoker. He asked his wife to wait for him in the lobby; and as soon as she had left the room he informed me that her nagging had kept him smoking for the last several years. When I informed him that I could only help him if he was making the choice of his own free will, he signed the disclosure and gave me a check. Other clients have seen me as a result of his success!

The Four Hypnotherapeutic Steps to Facilitate Change

Let's assume you've completed the four objectives of the pre-induction interview. The client's goal is within your training and qualifications, and the client is ready to make a change. What next?

Charles Tebbetts taught that there are four main therapeutic steps to facilitate change--helping a client remove problems--and he described them in the very first chapter of *Miracles on Demand* (2nd Edition).

I discussed them briefly in Chapter 12 of *The Art of Hypnosis;* but I feel it's necessary to discuss them again here because of their importance to the hypnotherapeutic process:

1. Post-hypnotic suggestion and imagery

With a strong motivating desire, post-hypnotic suggestion

(direct or indirect) may be sufficient. Without a strong desire, either the conscious or the subconscious may easily block the suggestions. (This is further evidence that the person in hypnosis is not under the control of the hypnotist!) When a person uses only this first step alone with post-hypnotic suggestion (or affirmations), it is what Charles Tebbetts used to call *band aid therapy*--because often the improvement is only temporary. Our 19th Century pioneers of hypnosis called it *prestige suggestion.*

Various imagery techniques and/or metaphors can also be used in conjunction with fulfillment of a goal to strengthen this step. For example, positive feelings associated with the fulfillment of a desired goal can be induced in hypnosis by progressing a person forward in time in the imagination. This will be discussed in the next chapter on my *benefits approach*, which is designed to increase the motivating desire through emotion; but a strong emotional desire at a subconscious level to retain a problem may necessitate the next three hypnotherapeutic steps. When the other three steps are used, the first step becomes the last step, emphasizing step #4.

2. Discovering the cause

If subconscious resistance exists, there is a reason, whether from the past or the present. Although certain hypnotherapy techniques may sometimes gain release without the client ever consciously knowing the cause(s), Charles Tebbetts taught that if the problem (or symptoms) resulted from a childhood perception of a past event, hypnotic recall of the event(s) can provoke the *emotional feelings* associated with the event(s) and bring them into awareness--resulting in an emotional discharge. This is called an abreaction; and this is easily accomplished in hypnosis, because we are dealing with the emotional rather than the intellectual mind. Once the emotional energy is brought into awareness, it can be redirected and/or released in a positive way.

Many techniques may help uncover the cause(s) of resistance, whether the cause lies in the client's past or in the present--including techniques which may not result in regressions. Sometimes the subconscious can discover and release a cause without emotional discharges, such as with an overweight client of mine whose subconscious indicated that she would keep snacking until she started creating some "fun time" for herself. She had to make an agreement with herself in order to be released from the problem. If the cause is an unresolved issue from the client's *present*, then the client may have to make some decisions at a conscious level--and sometimes the hypnotherapist may need to refer that client to cognitive counseling or other professional help.

3. Release

After the relationship of the symptom to the cause(s) is established emotionally as well as intellectually, we may use one or more hypnotherapy techniques to facilitate forgiveness and/or release from the cause(s) of a problem.

If the cause(s) resulted from perceptions of *past events,* not only does this involve forgiving, or at least *releasing* others who might have *victimized* the client, it also includes forgiving one's self for participating and/or carrying grudges, etc. If we hold a grudge against someone who hurt us, *we* are the ones in bondage to the grudge. We can still protect ourselves without staying angry. Whether the client's memories are real memories, false perceptions, or a combination of both, they can still be forgiven and/or released in a therapeutic way without the necessity of "confronting" another relative for what might not have been an accurate perception in the first place. (Chapter 7 contains more on forgiveness.)

Numerous techniques, including but not limited to guided

imagery, can be used to facilitate release.

4. Relearning (new understanding)

Numerous client-centered techniques can be used to *facilitate adult understanding at a subconscious level, where it gets results.* The goal is to help a client create a more mature understanding (or new perception) of the problem, including its cause(s) and solution(s). Sometimes it is sufficient simply to have the *subconscious* relearn; however, the client-centered techniques taught by Charles Tebbetts often result in total conscious recall of the entire hypnotic process.

Note that many qualified and trained counselors employ hypnosis to discover causes; but instead of completing the vital third and fourth hypnotherapeutic steps, they often try to deal with those causes at a conscious level--and have sometimes needlessly kept clients in therapy for months or years!

Each of these four steps could also be considered as *therapy objectives,* with each one serving as a stepping stone towards the next step. Although the first step may be sufficient for some of the people some of the time, if the problem remains, consider the accomplishment of ALL FOUR steps as your *prime hypnotherapeutic goal.*

As you read this book, you may wish to consider how each technique presented can help accomplish one or more of these four steps. References will be made frequently to these important hypnotherapeutic objectives. In my opinion, all hypnotic techniques revolve around one or more of these four very important objectives. I suggest that you *memorize* them and make them an integral part of your therapy.

Now where do I personally begin? For habit control and motivation, I begin with the first step by intensifying the motivating desire; and the next chapter describes how.

Chapter 3

The Benefits Approach

As Charles Tebbetts taught, post-hypnotic suggestion alone may be sufficient when the motivating desire is strong. Also, Ormond McGill, a good friend of mine who is an expert in the art of hypnosis and author of numerous books, teaches that any suggestion charged with emotion has a far greater impact on the subconscious. (LeCron and Bordeaux also realized this when they wrote Chapter 5 of *Hypnotism Today* in the earlier part of the 20th century.)

In light of this, I've taken what I learned from my former teacher and mentor and combined it with my extensive experience in professional sales, and developed what I call the *benefits approach*. It is based on a simple concept. Once we fall in love with the *benefits* of change, it's much easier to pay the price of change. I call this process *selling success to your subconscious*.

The Subconscious Resists Force

When is the last time you refused to buy a product or service because somebody tried to force you to buy?

Will-power and self-discipline come across to the subconscious like a high-pressure sales pitch. That's why so many smokers find their new-year's resolutions literally going up in smoke. Also, that's why diets work on the body but not the mind.

Any person competently trained in professional sales knows that people buy benefits rather than price. I explain this during a client's intake (pre-induction) interview. I go on to explain that even if the price is right, we all still tune into mental station **WII-FM**, and I sometimes write these letters on my white board for clients to see. These call letters stand for: "*W*hat's *I*n *I*t *F*or *M*e?"

In other words, before the subconscious mind will buy the price of change, the benefits of change must be identified and effectively communicated to the subconscious.

Identifying the Benefits

Before I ever guide my clients into hypnosis, I ask them a simple question: "Let's assume you've already achieved your goal... what's in it for you?" I then proceed to write down their personal benefits on a form that I provide to them at the conclusion of the session. Meanwhile, I use their listed benefits during the session itself.

I suggest that you take whatever time is needed to help your client identify his or her *personal benefits* of change if he/she is seeing you for habit control or motivation. The reason is that it means more to clients if *they tell you* rather than if you tell them. This is salesmanship.

For example, most clients may tell you that better health is a benefit of quitting smoking; but if you tell your prospective client that he/she should list better health, you might unintentionally push the wrong button if that person is in excellent health and went through some aversion program which tried to scare him or her into quitting with gross pictures of diseased lungs, etc. While one client may enjoy having more money to spend after quitting, another client may think nothing of burning up $2000 a year in smoke!

If your client does need prodding, discuss some key benefits that others have given you, and ask whether that benefit is of personal importance--then take your client's word for it. Don't push.

In addition, I suggest you provide assistance to keep the

language positive.

For example, if a smoker says, "I won't be short of breath," I write down *longer winded.* If a smoker or overweight person says, "I won't get so tired all the time," I write down *more energy.* Why do I do this?

The reason is that I want clients imagining the *benefits* rather than the problems. This is very important, because the *language of the subconscious is imagination*--but more about this in a moment.

Let's talk about a hidden purpose for asking our clients what their benefits are for habit control and motivation: *it is easier to determine whether the desire to change is genuine!* If they cannot get involved in the desire to enjoy the benefits, then they probably are not ready to make a change. Some people are manipulated into hypnosis by nagging relatives, etc.; and this will usually show up when they start discussing benefits (if not sooner). If this is the case, perhaps you'd better ask your prospective client to give further consideration before beginning hypnotherapy, or refer him/her elsewhere as appropriate.

But let's assume that typical client benefits are identified...now what?

I ask my clients which one or two would be the most important--and put an asterisk (*) by the selections. Then I emphasize--as mentioned above--that imagination is the language of the subconscious, and that emotion is its motivating power or energy.

Explain the Role of Imagination

If we have effectively helped a client respond to one or more suggestibility tests, it is easy to refer back to how the subconscious responded to what was imagined. The imagination is our own private rehearsal room of the mind, where we have total power to do anything we wish. If my client loves

Star Trek, I tell him/her that the imagination is the holodeck of the mind, where the desired reality can be programmed.

I discuss this analogy with my client before hypnosis begins, and go on to explain the importance of vividly imagining each of the benefits as I suggest them--because if I ask clients to imagine looking at reflections of themselves at their ideal weight, but they imagine eating cookies, guess what the subconscious buys!

It's *positive imagining* that gets results--not just positive thinking, which can be neutralized by a negative imagination.

Why do I say this? Well, I remember all-too-well a time in my life when I believed in positive thinking and found that my life got worse in spite of the daily use of affirmations. By imagining sales turning sour, even my best efforts were fruitless--destroying ten years of successful sales experience for me. Until hypnotherapy made a difference, I kept doing the very thing I did not want to do.

Haven't you ever wondered why so many people do things they tell themselves not to do? Remember that the subconscious is like the child inside each of us. While the conscious mind could engage in volumes of theories and/or techniques to try to force the subconscious mind into success habits, we still tend to do whatever we *consistently imagine* ourselves doing. If you don't believe this, try telling a ten-year old who is perfectly content at play that he/she cannot have any freshly-baked chocolate-chip cookies! By telling that child what you do not want him or her to do, you've actually increased the desire to do that very act--because of what that child now imagines doing. It does not take a psychologist to understand this.

The ex-smoker who keeps imagining lighting up will consistently have the urge to do so--and will find it difficult or impossible to avoid backsliding. Likewise, the person on a diet who keeps imagining the taste of chocolate will find a way to get it.

The imagination can make or break one's success; so it is my opinion that one of the most valuable things I can do for my clients is to teach them how to use self-hypnosis to control what they imagine. This becomes very self-empowering; but if my clients learn self-hypnosis, then why do they need hypnotherapy?

Self-hypnosis is like a muscle. I can move a chair, but I can move a couch more easily if someone is on the other end helping me lift. So I give my clients that initial mental lift, and teach them to continue imagining benefits long after they leave my office. If the motivating desire is strong enough, the benefits approach is very powerful.

What About the Price of Change?

Most clients know the price of change--they just don't know how to get the subconscious to cooperate. (By "price" of change, I do *not* mean the cost of the sessions!)

For example, a smoker wishing to quit smoking must avoid buying cigarettes for the rest of his/her life. Since it's easier to *replace* habits than it is to try to erase them, I suggest that my clients replace the breath of smoke with a breath of air--which has no calories and no side effects.

People wishing to reduce also can easily tell me what changes of habit would make a difference in their weight, such as resigning from the clean plate club, drinking water instead of snacking, etc. The challenge is in getting the subconscious to accept those changes. Note: if you facilitate weight management sessions, remember to avoid giving nutritional advice unless you are qualified to do so!

Doing Hypnotherapy: Benefits Approach

So now my client and I are ready to begin, and I've asked the magic question. (The magic question is "Are you ready to be hypnotized?" Refer to Chapter 4 of *The Art of Hypnosis*.)

After the appropriate induction and deepening techniques, I project my client forward in time, doing what could be called a hypnotic progression. Using the listed benefits as my guide for programmed imagery, I then ask my client to vividly imagine--with as many of the five senses as possible--enjoyment and appreciation of each of his/her benefits.

I go through the benefits one by one, suggesting that clients imagine situations where they enjoy each particular benefit. My clients are asked to imagine a sense of appreciation for these benefits--and to imagine them so *vividly* that they feel as though they currently enjoy success. This helps to enhance the motivating desire, facilitating subconscious acceptance of the post-hypnotic suggestions for success (to strengthen the first hypnotherapeutic step as described in Chapter 2).

Each client imagines *emotional feelings* associated with fulfillment of the desired goal. This positive emotional desire to enjoy the benefits creates an energy that may propel the client into success. Some clients actually get so emotionally involved with success that the positive feelings linger long after they leave my office.

So what makes the *benefits approach* effective?

When someone falls in love with the benefits of success, that person will usually find a way to pay the price of change. In short, I am teaching my clients to use selling skills on their own subconscious minds--because the subconscious is one tough customer that doesn't want to be forced to buy. Yet just as we have all paid more than we thought we should for a product once we bonded emotionally with it, the subconscious is capable of doing more than we think when energized with the power of positive emotion!

For emphasis, let me repeat: emotion is the motivating energy of the subconscious. In other words, *emotion is the motivating power of the mind.*

What Are Typical Client Benefits?

Since some clients may desire some prompting by asking what benefits others give, let's look at the more common benefits given for habit control and motivation:

Smoking cessation

Typical benefits for smokers wishing to quit are: better health, more energy, longer winded, clear throat and lungs, more money, cleaner environment (residence, car, clothes, etc.), greater social acceptance, pride of success, better parental example, greater professional image, better self-image, better sense of taste and/or smell, freedom (from the habit), and whiter teeth. There are other, less common benefits that I list upon request, but I will not use them for prompting.

We must also remember to use positive words. For example, people often say, "Save money." During childhood, how did you feel if you suddenly found some money to spend and one of your parents told you to save it instead? So I list *more money.* It's a little more negative if someone says, "I won't have smoker's cough every morning." We may simply list *clear throat and lungs.* If they say that they won't be ostracized any longer, we can list *greater social acceptance.*(Note deliberate avoidance of the words *peer pressure!*)

Weight management

Typical benefits for weight management are: better health, more energy, more physically active, more mobility, more attractive, greater freedom, more choices in clothes, happier spouse, pride of success, greater social acceptance, better self-image, better professional image, and just feeling good. Some clients actually list *more sexy* or *better sex life* as a benefit; but I do NOT prompt a client with any benefit related to sex.

Also notice that I do weight management, not weight loss. We have been programmed to try to find what we lose! So I recommend that my clients release, discard, reduce, donate, take off, get rid of, or throw out excess weight--and start talking about weight reduction instead of weight loss.

Sales motivation

Typical benefits for reaching sales quotas are: greater income, more vacations, new car, new home, pride of success, peace of mind, better self-image, more free time, greater freedom. At this point, however, I must say from experience that no one can empathize totally with a salesperson experiencing a slump more than someone with sales experience. If you have not had previous professional sales experience, please be ready to refer a slumping salesperson to a hypnotherapist who does!

What Do You Say?

The best way for me to answer this question is to provide two actual scripts: one for smoking cessation and another for weight management. You will find them in the next chapter. You may change the wording as appropriate--but keep the language positive, emphasizing the desired results. (Refer to Chapter 8 of *The Art of Hypnosis.*)

After Hypnosis

People are often surprised at how good they feel. Every person hypnotized will not necessarily respond to the degree you might wish. Be aware that there is NO technique that will work with all the people all the time; however, most of my clients enjoy their progressions into the benefits.

After a very brief discussion about the session, each client leaves the office with a hypnosis tape and the list of personal benefits. I recommend a brief review of the benefits just prior to the client listening to the hypnosis tape, in order to remember to vividly imagine them while listening.

You may wish either to record the individual session for your client, or make generic tapes for smoking cessation and/or weight management, etc. (Or you may wish to buy mine at wholesale!)

Also, be certain to schedule the next appointment before the client leaves your office. I write the day and time down on one of my business cards and hand it to my client. In addition, I frequently give two or three extra business cards as well, asking my clients to share me with their friends.

I thank them for choosing me as their hypnotherapist, and send them on their way.

The Next Session — *Stress Mgmt*

The second time clients come, I check their progress and often spend some time teaching stress management as discussed in Chapter 10 of *The Art of Hypnosis*. Why?

First, smokers often light up when stress buttons get pushed. An ounce of prevention is worth a pound of cure--so I almost always include a session on stress management when people see me for smoking cessation. Secondly, many people who have weight problems tend to eat more when stressed--so the majority of clients seeing me for weight management also have one session on managing stress.

If someone convinces me that he/she has very little stress, and no desire to learn self-hypnosis, then I may skip this session and be flexible to the client's wishes. Also, I frequently find clients who feel so stressed that they wish to begin with the stress management and wait until the second or third session for the *Benefits Approach*. Again, let's adapt to each client's individual needs.

Mapping the Motivation

So we've completed the hypnotic progression and the session on stress management. Where do we go next?

Although it may be professional for you to help the client with any appropriate hypnotherapeutic techniques within your training and experience, you might wish to consider spending the third session mapping the motivation. This survey of subconscious motivation is described in detail in Chapter 15; however, since it is optional (and original) for use at your discretion, I will not devote further space to it this early in the text. Instead, I'll conclude this chapter by explaining why I start with the *Benefits Approach* for habit control and motivation rather than diving right into the subconscious to look for the cause.

Why Not Begin with Advanced Techniques?

Frequently the *Benefits Approach* is sufficient for smoking cessation when combined with stress management and motivation mapping, although weight management clients often need other techniques in later sessions to help them discover and release subconscious resistance. However, even those who might need regression therapy and/or *parts therapy* are left with good first impressions of hypnosis--which may benefit them greatly if it becomes necessary to use advanced techniques.

Going forward in time with a hypnotic progression triggering positive emotions is much more enjoyable than a regression back into past negative feelings--and some people are more apt to talk about pleasant and enjoyable experiences, which creates good public relations for hypnotherapy.

In short, I believe it is an excellent starting point--and then we may adapt from there based on the degree of client response.

Chapter 4

Scripts for Progressions

The scripts for smoking cessation and weight management are presented in a chapter by themselves for your easy reference. They utilize hypnotic progressions and the *benefits approach* described in Chapter 3 (which I suggest you read thoroughly if you have not already done so).

Become familiar with both the wordings and approaches before using them. What to say is in **bold** print. Pauses are indicated by three dots (...), but you can feel free to pause at other places instead if you prefer. (Pauses can add emphasis to hypnotic suggestions, making them more powerful.) Do NOT read out loud what is *[bracketed and italicized]*. Also, **know** what is in the *italicized* instructions!

You may paraphrase in your own personality and style, using my wording simply as a guide. Let the scripts serve the therapist, not vice versa. I tell my students that scripts are like bicycle training wheels: they provide valuable assistance to the beginner. When you master the art of hypnosis, you can grow beyond the need to depend exclusively on scripts. That being said, I use them occasionally with some of my clients some of the time; but I will vary them as necessary to adapt individually to each client.

If you modify any hypnosis script, keep the wording positive, affirming the desired result (refer to Chapter 8 of *The Art of Hypnosis*, or Chapters 15 & 16 of my book, *Master the Power of Self-Hypnosis*). Since imagination is the language of the subconscious, remember to give suggestions that make it easy to imagine the solutions rather than the problems.

Benefits Approach for Non-Smoking

Use appropriate induction and deepening...

Now imagine this is one year from today, and you have already been a totally tolerant non-smoker for one year. Your lungs reward you for the fresh air you give them and you love how you feel--physically, mentally, and emotionally.

Make sure your client's list of benefits is within easy reach. At this time, suggest all the client's stipulated benefits in ways which make him/her feel good, incorporating as many of the five senses as possible. Use programmed imagery. Help the client to establish a positive emotion towards the benefits.

Now imagine your MOST IMPORTANT BENEFIT SO VIVIDLY that you feel as though you already enjoy success. *[Slowly!]* Imagine your benefits . . . SO VIVIDLY . . . that you feel . . . as though . . . you already . . . enjoy . . . SUCCESS! If you choose these benefits for yourself, then indicate that choice right now by moving one of your index fingers.

Wait up to a minute for the ideomotor response, then repeat the suggestion if necessary. If client fails to give an ideomotor response after two attempts, then you might have to use another hypnotherapy technique--or you may consider awakening first and asking the client to reconfirm whether he/she is ready to quit totally, or wishes to simply control the habit--in which case you need to deal with the request appropriately.

Once you have the appropriate ideomotor response, then continue...

You have used your power of choice to choose your benefits. The terms are so simple... you simply use that same power of choice to choose one deep breath any time an old light-up trigger occurs, allowing one deep breath to become a totally satisfying replacement for yesterday's fair-weather friend. The physical replacement for yesterday's breath of smoke is one deep breath of air. The mental replacement for yesterday's urge is your new friend, FREEDOM to focus your mind or imagination on whatever you choose, because you love your power of choice.

You LOVE your power of choice. And like a muscle that's used becomes stronger with use, your power of choice becomes stronger with use. Imagine using that power of choice right now by imagining a situation that used to trigger a light-up. Now take a deep breath and RELAX... CHOOSE something fun, enjoyable, beautiful, or pleasant to imagine. Indicate you have successfully done that by moving a finger.

Wait for response.

Very good. Like a muscle that's used becomes stronger with use, your power of choice becomes stronger with use. And every time you take that deep breath, it becomes easier and easier to choose the deep breath instead of the old slave master.

You are a non-smoker now, because the BENEFITS are so satisfying, and you LOVE your power of choice! Now once again imagine another old light-up trigger. As you do, take a deep breath and RELAX. Now imagine something fun, enjoyable, beautiful or pleasant. As you do, you are already practicing your ability to use your new power and friend, FREEDOM, to be a non-smoker.

When you use your power of choice to focus your mind on whatever you choose, yesterday's urges are simply forgotten... fading away into the mists of time, vanishing into the fog of forgetfulness, replaced with your new friend, FREEDOM... to focus your mind, thoughts or actions on WHATEVER YOU CHOOSE, whether at work or play, at home or away from home, alone or with others. You have the power of choice. You LOVE your power of choice, and it was YOUR CHOICE to become a non-smoker... and it is YOUR CHOICE to put your mind or imagination on

WHATEVER YOU CHOOSE. And YOUR DECISION is bringing you the benefits you have chosen...

At this time, suggest all the client's stipulated benefits once again, in ways that makes him or her feel good. Help to establish a positive emotional attraction towards the benefits.

Now imagine your MOST IMPORTANT BENEFITS SO VIVIDLY that you feel as though you already enjoy success. *[Speak slowly and with feeling!]* Imagine your benefits... SO VIVIDLY... that you feel as though you already... enjoy . . . SUCCESS!

You have chosen the benefits because you absolutely deserve them. KNOW that you deserve the benefits. You LOVE your power of choice--and every day it becomes easier and easier for you automatically to take that deep breath at times you used to light-up. And as you do, you feel more and more like a non-smoker with each passing day, as the deep breath becomes a TOTALLY satisfying replacement for yesterday's fair-weather friend. Your new friend, FREEDOM, becomes so much more satisfying that you simply allow your subconscious to accept that you are now a non-smoker simply because you chose to be, and you love your power of choice.

And now, as I give you some silence, once again imagine your success SO VIVIDLY that all of these ideas and suggestions simply go deeper and deeper into your subconscious, becoming a part of you simply because you choose them. And when you again hear my voice, it will be almost time to come back.

After a brief silence, tell client to remember what was rehearsed in imagination, and then awaken properly.

Benefits Approach for Weight Management

Use appropriate induction and deepening...

Now imagine you are already at your ideal, healthiest body weight. You LOVE how you look and feel. Imagine standing in front of a mirror seeing a reflection of yourself wearing the size clothes you choose to wear. These clothes LOOK good, and they FEEL good, and they fit well on you. Now imagine doing something you totally enjoy doing at your ideal weight. Just BE THERE in your mind... and ENJOY.

Make sure your client's list of benefits is within easy reach. At this time, suggest all the stipulated benefits in ways that make him/her feel good, incorporating as many of the five senses as possible. Use programmed imagery to help establish a positive emotional desire for the benefits.

Now imagine your MOST IMPORTANT BENEFITS SO VIVIDLY that you feel as though you already enjoy success. *[Slowly!]* Imagine your benefits... SO VIVIDLY... that you FEEL as though you already... enjoy... SUCCESS! If you choose these benefits for yourself, then indicate that choice right now by moving one of your index fingers.

Wait up to a minute for the ideomotor response, then repeat the suggestion if necessary. If the client fails to give an ideomotor response after two attempts, then you may have to use parts therapy and/or regression, etc., to discover and remove the subconscious resistance. Awaken first if you have not explained regressions or parts therapy so the first impression of hypnosis is a positive one.

You have used your power of choice to choose your benefits. The terms are so simple. You simply use that same power of choice to choose what goes into your mouth... when, where, and how much. YOU decide what goes into your mouth... when, where, and how much. And you have an increasing satisfaction from the right amounts of those foods which help you reach your ideal, healthiest body weight. And you make wise choices about your health and eating habits. Also, whenever you choose water or a non-caloric beverage to satisfy an in-between meal snack urge, you are TOTALLY satisfied -- physically, mentally, and emotionally, because YOU CHOSE....

You LOVE your power of choice. And like a muscle that's used becomes stronger with use, your power of choice becomes stronger with use. Imagine using that power of choice right now to choose water or a non-caloric beverage. And when you've successfully practiced this imagery in your mind, indicate by moving your finger.

Wait for response.

Very good. Like a muscle that's used becomes stronger with use, your power of choice becomes stronger with use. And every time you make a wise choice, it becomes even easier to make wise choices -- because the BENEFITS are so satisfying, and you LOVE your power of choice!

If client indicates he/she eats too fast, SLOWLY read next paragraph... otherwise, skip it.

Also, whenever you eat, you . . . eat . . . S L O W L Y . . . enough . . . to . . . E N J O Y . . . the FLAVOR . . . of each bite. And when you have had enough food to give your body nourishment, you are satisfied -- physically, mentally, and emotionally. And every day it becomes easier for you to be TOTALLY self-motivated to do those things that help you reach your ideal body weight, because you love the benefits.

If client indicates he/she always cleans plates, read next paragraph... otherwise, skip it.

You eat... S L O W L Y . . . enough to... LISTEN to your body and FEEL your satisfaction. You allow your physical and emotional appetites to harmonize. And when you have had enough to eat, you simply take your thumb or finger and do a PUSH-AWAY. Simply push your plate ever so slightly away from you -- pushing away the excess food and the excess pounds -- pound after pound. You release the excess food and you release the excess pounds -- pound after pound -- until you reach your ideal body weight.

Now imagine you are already at your ideal, healthiest body weight. You LOVE how you look and feel. Imagine standing in front of a mirror seeing a reflection of yourself wearing the size clothes you choose to wear. These clothes LOOK good, and they FEEL good, and they fit well on you. Now imagine doing something you totally enjoy doing at your ideal weight. Just BE THERE in your mind -- and ENJOY.

At this time, once again use programmed imagery of all the client's stipulated benefits in ways that establish and strengthen positive emotional desires to enjoy the benefits. Give positive suggestions for feeling good about self as well as for the benefits.

Now imagine your MOST IMPORTANT BENEFITS SO VIVIDLY that you feel as though you already enjoy success. *[Speak lowly and with feeling!]* Imagine your benefits SO VIVIDLY... that you FEEL... as though you already ENJOY... SUCCESS! You have chosen the benefits because you absolutely deserve them. KNOW that you deserve the benefits. You LOVE your power of choice -- and every day it becomes easier and easier for you to be TOTALLY self-motivated to do those things which help you reach and maintain your ideal, healthiest body weight. And like a muscle that's used becomes stronger with use, your power of choice becomes stronger with use -- giving you a GREATER STRENGTH OF WILL THAN YOU HAVE EVER KNOWN BEFORE.

And now, as I give you some silence, once again imagine your success SO VIVIDLY that all of these ideas and suggestions simply go deeper and deeper into your subconscious, becoming a part of you simply because you choose them. And when you again hear my voice, it will be almost time to come back.

After silence, tell client to remember what was rehearsed in imagination -- and then awaken properly.

Notice that the script for weight management does not address the issue of exercise, nor does it specify which particular foods to eat or avoid. This puts the responsibility on the client to make those decisions, and to obtain whatever professional and/or medical advice is appropriate for decisions concerning health. I take the position of informing my client that I am not qualified to give a medical opinion on which exercises are appropriate for the body--and that if there are any questions, it would be wise to seek advice from the appropriate source. I also let my clients know that I am not a nutritional consultant. Furthermore, I believe it is both risky and unprofessional for any hypnotherapist to give nutritional or medical advice unless qualified and licensed to do so.

Notice that the script for smoking cessation gives a new response of a deep breath of air as a replacement for lighting up a cigarette when old "triggers" occur. The next chapter discusses anchoring and triggers, which we should overview before getting into the meat of the hypnotherapy techniques taught by Charles Tebbetts.

Chapter 5

Anchoring and Triggers

Therapists frequently talk about anchoring and triggers. Something seen, heard, felt, tasted or smelled can act as a "trigger" to activate a memory, attitude, desire, emotion, and/or a physical response--depending on what was "anchored" into it.

Some confusion exists regarding the difference between an anchor and a trigger. We may remember it more easily by comparing a trigger to the "execute" button to activate a computer program. Installing the program corresponds to anchoring, which becomes active every time designated triggers execute (or trigger) the program. A common example is a smoker lighting up every time he/she gets into an automobile. Often the act of starting the engine triggers the urge to smoke, even if no cigarettes are available.

Since habits that clients wish to change are usually kept active by triggers, hypnotherapists need to have at least a basic understanding of what they are. Let's briefly summarize the various types of triggers and how they might influence our lives.

Triggers of Habit

How often do we find ourselves doing something almost as though on "automatic pilot" without consciously thinking about it? Most of these actions are the results of learned habits. We find ourselves subconsciously stopping at red lights, braking and accelerating automatically, picking up the phone and answering appropriately whether at work or home, flushing the toilet without thinking about it, tying our shoes while thinking about something else, etc., etc.

For the most part, it's really wonderful that we can learn to respond automatically to triggers--because this makes doing many of life's mundane chores much simpler by freeing our minds to think about whatever else we choose. The exceptions, of course, help justify the existence of the hypnotherapy profession.

For the smoker trying to quit, "old light-up triggers" can be very frustrating. Most smokers tend to reach for a cigarette without consciously choosing one whenever putting the key into the ignition, or picking up a telephone, or picking up a beverage cup, etc. Usually the habitual response to a trigger of habit was anchored into the subconscious through repetition. Since nature tends to dislike a vacuum, I usually recommend a new habit to replace an old one.

For example, the smoker learns to take one deep breath of air in response to a light-up trigger, because one deep breath has no calories and no side effects. The overeater often snacks as though on automatic pilot during breaks at work, or while reading or watching television, etc. A small amount of water may be used instead of a snack.

I inform my clients that it is easier to replace an unwanted habit than it is to erase it. In other words, changing the response to a trigger is usually more successful than trying to erase the trigger altogether. If the motivating desire is strong enough, the first hypnotherapeutic step may be sufficient to accomplish this. If memories, attitudes or emotions are anchored into the habit as well, then more needs to be done.

Anchored Memories

Memories, whether pleasant, neutral or unpleasant, can be triggered by certain events that are similar to what might have happened during the time those memories were created.

For example, a unique fragrance of perfume or cologne can trigger the memory of a past romance. Also, a certain song can bring back the memory of a special prom during high school or college, or the memory of a deceased friend or loved one. "You Light Up My Life" is a song that always reminds me of a close friend who was like a brother to me. He was killed in a plane crash, and I heard that song at his funeral.

The memory may be anchored gradually over a period of time (such as in the example of a unique fragrance); or the memory may be anchored during one emotional event, such as the example of my friend's funeral.

Memories associated with a particular trigger can be quickly recalled even at a conscious level unless those memories were suppressed--in which case there may be emotions attached to those memories.

Anchored Attitudes and Desires

Attitudes linked to certain anchored memories can also come into conscious awareness when the memory is triggered.

For example, a non-smoker might have unpleasant memories of working in an environment with an inconsiderate smoker, and consequently feels prejudice against all smokers whenever seeing another person light up. Or a person taken advantage of by a car mechanic might afterwards become suspicious whenever taking the car in for repairs.

Desires can be triggered as well, such as the desire either an adult or a child can have for candy immediately upon seeing another person eat some--or simply by passing a vending machine at the office. Hence someone who overeats may be vulnerable to snacking without consciously deciding to eat.

Just as with memories, the trigger could either be anchored gradually over a period of time, or suddenly with a single emotional event. This could be important to know if you are using regressions to look for causes of certain attitudes and/or desires.

With smokers, we must not only help our clients deal with the habitual responses to "old triggers," we must help them overcome the urges as well--and become released from the desire to smoke. With overeaters, abstinence is not an option! Since we must all still eat, there are frequently many more subconscious dynamics involved than simple desires anchored into the sight of certain foods. Some of those dynamics relate to anchored emotions.

Anchored Emotions

Emotional experiences are very powerful. When an emotional state of mind is anchored into the subconscious with an event, the same emotions can easily surface by any type of trigger that reminds the subconscious of that same event. Repeat events can cause further sensitization of the subconscious, such as in the case of phobias. For example, simply *seeing* a dog could cause an emotional reaction in a person who was viciously attacked by one--even if the attack was years in the past.

In my case, I do not have a phobia of dogs; yet there is a strong dislike because of a neighbor's dog that used to run up to my bicycle and bite at my ankle when I was in grade school. There may come a time when I choose to deal with this; but I refuse to learn to like dogs just because others tell me to. In spite of my personal dislike, the part of me wanting to be a good parent allowed my children to have a dog--which I treated well in spite of my personal feelings.

Generally an emotion is anchored suddenly--and the subconscious sensitized to the trigger--with the impact of an intense emotional event, although further sensitization over repeated events can increase the power of the emotional impact on the subconscious. If the client even *fantasizes* the trigger while in the hypnotic state, there may be a spontaneous regression back to a sensitizing event--resulting in an emotional reaction. Regression therapy can uncover both the memories and the emotions anchored to those memories so that the client can then be released (covered in Chapter 7). Other techniques can also be used to uncover sources of emotional resistance to change, as will be discussed in the next chapter of this book.

Anchoring and Hypnotherapy

Frequently our clients need to be released from negative anchors. This chapter, however, was not written to teach you how to deal with those triggers. Its primary objective is to acquaint you with them so that the chapters that follow will make more sense, as most hypnotherapy involves release from negative anchoring.

We also need to realize that positive anchoring can take place during hypnotherapy as well as in real life. For example, a sense of inner peace can be anchored into the act of taking one deep breath, so that it becomes a trigger for becoming calm. Chapter 10 of *The Art of Hypnosis* shows how to help a client practice this for managing stress. Also, Chapter 14 of this book reveals a powerful way to help a client create a trigger for success, or maximum performance.

There are other occasions when it might be in a client's best interest to use positive anchoring, or to turn a negative trigger into a trigger for a positive response--such as in suggesting that what used to trigger a need for a cigarette now triggers one releasing deep breath of air. Additionally, there is one trigger that I strongly recommend for any client experiencing advanced hypnotherapeutic techniques...the peaceful place trigger. The best way to anchor this trigger into the subconscious is to establish a peaceful place.

Peaceful Place (or Safe Place)

Almost every one of my clients will spend at least part of one session in his/her private, peaceful place (also called the "safe place"). Often it's helpful during regression therapy to allow a client to return to his or her peaceful place momentarily. We may employ open screen imagery or programmed imagery to accomplish this objective.

Open screen imagery allows the client to create the peaceful (or safe) place with total freedom to imagine sights, sounds, and feelings that are comfortable, safe, peaceful and beautiful. The other method would be to have the client describe an ideal peaceful place before hypnosis ever begins; then we may use programmed imagery to help the client fantasize being at peace in the place previously described.

The next step is to have the client take a deep breath and think the word "relax" while exhaling--thus anchoring the peaceful place into the trigger of the deep breath. Note that touching the thumb and finger together can become an alternative (or additional) trigger. Let the client practice this while in trance. Step your clients through this exercise so that you may enable them to use the peaceful place trigger at will. I call this the *peaceful place meditation.*

There are numerous benefits to the client for creating this trigger, both during and after hypnotherapy itself. Teach your clients how to do the peaceful place meditation on their own. They may use self-hypnosis to reinforce their peaceful place triggers.

Now that we've overviewed anchoring and triggers, let's get into the meat of diversified client-centered hypnotherapy.

Chapter 6

Hypnotic Uncovering Techniques

So your client is not responding sufficiently to the benefits approach, or is seeing you with a situation that calls for techniques to get immediately to the cause of a problem-- now what? Since the hypnotherapist cannot diagnose a client's problem (unless licensed and trained to do so), what can we do to help the person who wants help?

It's time to consider one or more of what Charles Tebbetts called *hypnotic uncovering techniques*. They are designed to help the client uncover the source of his or her subconscious resistance to change. This is the second major therapeutic step summarized at the end of Chapter 2--and relieves the therapist from the task of having to look for the problem on a cognitive level, or trying to diagnose.

The title for this chapter was used by Mr. Tebbetts for the second chapter of *Miracles on Demand*--where he described some of the available techniques (especially those which he believed to be the most effective). Out of respect for my former teacher and mentor, I chose that same title for this chapter. Now let's find out how hypnotherapy might help discover the cause of a problem.

Does the Client Know the Cause of a Problem?

Charles Tebbetts believed strongly that the client was far more able to disclose the real cause of his/her problem than an outside person simply diagnosing (if the cause is not organic). He believed that even when the client could not identify the cause at a cognitive level, the answer was still inside the mind of that very same client--buried deep inside the subconscious. This opinion is shared by many in the hypnotherapy profession. On page 9 of the 3/94 edition of the *Journal of Hypnotism,* Garrett Oppenheim, PhD, writes:

> *I have often expressed the belief, shared by many of my colleagues, that each of our patients has, in his unconscious or inner mind, the answers he is looking for. I explain that my task as a hypnotherapist is to unlock the door to that inner mind so that he may find his own true answers.*

Mr. Tebbetts started out by just asking the subconscious questions to get it to reveal the cause of a problem. Sometimes the client will verbalize the cause(s). But what if the client fails to give verbal answers to questions, or fails to go deep enough for us to believe the answers? Sometimes ideomotor responses might provide more accurate answers.

Ideomotor Responding

When a client responds to yes/no questions by finger and/or thumb movement, it is called *ideomotor responding.* This can often be a good starting point for determining which therapy technique to use if the preinduction interview leaves you uncertain--or if the client fails to respond to the technique that you might normally use for another client with a similar problem.

The theory is that people may often be prone to allow more accurate information to come from the subconscious mind through ideomotor responses than through verbal answers. Since the conscious intellect can filter and/or embellish easily if a person is only in a light or medium trance depth, there is greater likelihood of accuracy when the answer comes more spontaneously from the inner mind. In fact, I have frequently seen clients answer "no" verbally while moving the "yes" finger. There is still no guarantee that total truth will always emerge, as people can lie with finger responses while under hypnosis if they really want to. (Lest anyone debate this point, I have personally done so when asked to indicate seeing something that I could visualize! I am not a good visualizer--but I don't like to argue during hypnosis. I'd rather just move on with the trance.)

There may also be times when ideomotor responding is preferable to hypnotic regression, such as is explained by Mr. Tebbetts on page 25 of *Miracles on Demand:*

> *Occasionally, age regression fails because the client has built an impenetrable wall of defense around the regressed material to protect her from the painful feelings she experienced when the event occurred. Information may be obtained by the use of ideomotor signals without asking the client to suffer the memory of the traumatic event.*

If you as a therapist choose ideomotor responding rather than regression therapy (due to lack of training in regressions and/or any other reason), realize that your client still could regress and remember past pain if there is no wall of defense to prevent it. If this happens, the client would most likely have an abreaction--and you need to be prepared to deal with what emerges.

Before using the ideomotor responding technique, we must take a moment to establish which responses will indicate "yes" and so on. When I studied under Charles Tebbetts in 1983, he taught that the therapist should be the one to determine which finger/thumb movement should indicate the "yes" and "no" responses as well as the "I don't know" response. In the two pages following the last quote from my mentor's book, he discussed two methods and theories about how and why to do this, but I now believe the *client should make those choices.* Why? ...because if a client is asked by one therapist to raise the left index finger for "yes" after another therapist has established that same finger as a "no" response, there is a greater possibility of miscommunication-- and all the left-brain/right-brain theories go right out the window. Also, to avoid inappropriate leading (or projecting your own opinions into the client), *use a monotone voice!* Here is what I say and do:

> **In a moment I'm going to ask you some questions. If the answer is "yes," would you please indicate by moving a finger. Please move the "yes" finger now.**
>
> *Wait for response, and make a note of it.*
>
> **If I ask you a question and "no" is the answer--that's "N.O."** *[spell it out]*--**would you please move a different finger or thumb. Please indicate the N.O. response now.**
>
> *Wait for response, and make a note of it.*
>
> **If I ask you a question and the answer is either "I don't know" or "I don't want to say," you may move a different finger or thumb. Please indicate that response now.**
>
> *Wait for response, and make a note of it. Now you are ready for therapeutic questions.*

My logic in allowing a third response to indicate either "I don't know" or "I don't want to say" is for the client's benefit. People are often afraid of revealing secrets during hypnosis, and may resist even if they understand the ethics of client confidentiality. Just knowing that they have the option of the third answer makes the probability of truth far greater when they give the actual "yes" or "no" responses!

So which questions did Mr. Tebbetts ask? This was answered in the last three pages of the first chapter of his textbook--and is the next logical discussion in this chapter.

Seven Psychodynamics of a Symptom

On page 18 of *Miracles on Demand*, Charles Tebbetts describes what he referred to as the seven psychodynamics of a symptom. Although he admitted verbally that there may be some problems with unique causes, he believed that most causes of problems could be categorized into one or more of the psychodynamics that he taught. Here are his own words:

> *The belief systems and their resulting feelings cause the client to choose adjustive behavior. The symptoms may vary in intensity according to the client's ability to tolerate his environment. There are a number of psychodynamics of a symptom, and the therapy procedure depends upon the therapist's understanding of the client's reasons for having chosen it. You may ask him to respond verbally (while hypnotized) and explain what purpose the symptom is serving, or if he refuses to speak, you may ask him to respond with yes/no ideomotor signals. Ask him if it is serving more than one function, and then proceed to inquire which of the following behavior sets represent his symptom.*

I have personally observed Mr. Tebbetts going through every one of the psychodynamics with a client before determining which therapy technique to use; and more than one of them may contribute to the same problem. They are presented here as he taught them to his students. If you wish, list the psychodynamics on a sheet of paper for prompting during the finger response questioning. Some potentially helpful therapy techniques are presented as well for your consideration. Use the index if desired to locate the page numbers, as some techniques are discussed more than once in this book. Also, remember to fit the technique to the client rather than the other way around. If your chosen technique fails to obtain the desired results, use another one.

1. Self-punishment

Sometimes the subconscious indulges in self-punishment in order to remove feelings of guilt or to avoid possible punishment from a higher authority. For example, a professional person I worked with who was approaching burnout was also allowing others take advantage of him, creating a need to *work even harder* in order to please his firm and his family as well as to give to charity. His subconscious said it was punishing him for having been greedy and selfish with money during his teens.

Any number of techniques may be useful to release someone from self-punishment--whether or not they are covered in this book. The primary objective is to help a client forgive himself/herself and internalize release from the real or imagined past mistakes. With release confirmed, additional techniques may be employed to help facilitate new understanding at a subconscious level (refer to steps 3 & 4 in the last section of Chapter 2 of this book). Verbalizing is often very effective for relearning. If there is resistance of the suggestions to forgive self and quit the self-punishment, regression and/or parts therapy might be helpful to find out why.

2. Past experience

A past event which was painful and/or incorrectly perceived by the subconscious could have a lasting effect, such as with a person afraid of dogs because of an attack during childhood. Even though the perception of all dogs being vicious is incorrect, once that idea is accepted emotionally, the subconscious acts on that idea in spite of all logical evidence otherwise. (There is more on this in the chapter on phobias!)

Regression therapy is frequently the most helpful, as well as other techniques as appropriate, with the objective of accomplishing all four therapy steps described in the last section of Chapter 2. (Chapter 7 is devoted entirely to regression therapy.) When a client had been victimized, Mr. Tebbetts frequently accomplished the last two hypnotherapeutic steps with Gestalt during the hypnotic regression. Open screen imagery and/or silent abreaction may also be used for reframing the event.

3. Internal conflict

The symptom prevents the carrying out of a tabu desire. For example, one might stay heavy to minimize being tempted into sexual contact with others--such as an overweight military man who told me under hypnosis that his weight protected him from cheating on his wife. He had not responded to the benefits approach because of this internal conflict.

Parts therapy is frequently the fastest way to resolve internal conflicts--and the therapist is well advised to be prepared to *deal with what emerges!* (Hopefully this book will help you become better prepared.) Other techniques as appropriate can also be used--with or without parts therapy. The third and fourth hypnotherapeutic steps are the primary objectives, although the session should conclude with appropriate direct or indirect suggestion for resolution after agreements are verbalized during parts therapy. Study Chapter 8 of this book thoroughly before even attempting parts therapy!

4. Body language (unresolved present issue)

According to Mr. Tebbetts, this symptom represents psychosomatic illness (hives, migraine headaches, etc.) or a symptom produced by the subconscious in a way that says, "I don't like what you are doing." The subconscious seeks the attention of the conscious mind. My mentor called this "body language" but I prefer to call it *unresolved present issue.*

Once the real problem is discovered, we can then choose

whatever technique best fits the situation. In many instances, client awareness is sufficient--as a decision must be made at a conscious level on how (or whether) to resolve an issue. Often a few ideomotor questions followed by imagery and appropriate direct or indirect suggestion may suffice.

There may be times when other hypnotherapeutic techniques are immediately useful; but if in doubt, awaken your client and discuss the situation before proceeding. In some cases, a client may need *traditional counseling.* On occasion I find that an overweight client needs a marriage counselor, as the weight is a symptom of unresolved marriage problems.

One of my clients who answered "yes" to this psychodynamic while in the hypnotic state said that she would not stop snacking until she resolved a personal issue which she had been procrastinating dealing with. She already knew what the issue was--even though she did not know consciously that it related to her snacking--and she had to make a conscious decision to resolve it. It was totally up to her when and how to create resolution, and her decision required no further hypnotherapy. In fact, she did not even reveal to me what her unresolved issue was; however, she did thank me for helping her to realize why she had been unable to reduce.

Also, I saw Mr. Tebbetts work with a woman whose subconscious indicated that a skin problem on her hands was because of an unresolved issue with her son. When she resolved the issue, her skin problem cleared up!

Verbalizing is often sufficient, followed by imagery and post-hypnotic suggestion. Additionally, if needed, a very wide range of techniques can be used effectively--depending on the client's needs or wishes. (Refer to Chapter 9.) If parts therapy has revealed this psychodynamic, it might be appropriate to call out the conscious mind to get involved in the solution--and proceed as appropriate. (Again, become very familiar with Chapter 8!)

5. Secondary gain

The symptom offers a reward or the hope of a reward. The reward, if not yet history, is insufficient to justify the suffering caused by the symptom. Mr. Tebbetts devoted the entire fourth chapter of *Miracles on Demand* to a diabetic named Bruce who saw him after a written referral from a physician. I saw one of these sessions, and remember a hypnotized Bruce saying that he wanted to gain more love and attention from his parents. Several years later he met me for breakfast and informed me that he was still taking far less insulin than before his sessions with Mr. Tebbetts.

In many cases, the secondary gain might be *protection,* such as a person staying overweight in order to protect against attracting the wrong kind of person for a relationship.

Parts therapy can be very effective with secondary gain, as this is similar to internal conflict. Regression therapy to the event where the "gain" originated is another option. Once the secondary gain is identified, the feeling connection (or affect bridge technique, discussed later in this chapter) may be used to go back to its origin. Also, a client whose secondary gain was love, pity and/or attention from a parent can often be released through *Gestalt* therapy during hypnotic regression. (This valuable technique is covered in a subsection of "Abreactions and Emotional Clearing" in Chapter 7.)

Verbalizing may be sufficient for some clients; but if the subconscious is slow to reveal just what the secondary gain really is, then you may use age regression.

6. Identification

The client may be identifying with a hero or loved one. Several years ago a smoker who failed to respond to the benefits approach told me under hypnosis that he wanted to

be like John Wayne--his childhood idol. This new understanding made him laugh loudly during hypnosis, exclaiming
that it was silly to emulate a dead man--and he was finally
able to replace smoke with fresh air.

The primary objective is the fourth therapy step--to
facilitate adult understanding at a subconscious level (end of
Chapter 2). *Any number of techniques* can help accomplish
this, as long as the client is willing to change.

7. Imprint or attribution

An imprint is a belief that was implanted in a client's
mind, usually by an authority figure. Charles Tebbetts
defined this as an imprint back in 1983, but refers to this as
attribution on page 19 of *Miracles on Demand:*

> *A client might have been told that he has an Irish
> temper, or that he is a hot-blooded Italian who flares up
> easily. These are attributions given to children by
> authority figures. "You're just like your father,"
> programmed into a child's mind will result in behavior
> similar to his father's. If his father displayed self-destruc-
> tive or self-limiting behavior, the child may do the same
> as a result of attribution.*

The best technique depends on what the imprint is as well
as when and how it was imprinted into the mind. It could
necessitate regression therapy, but this is not always true.
Also, more questioning may be necessary, whether by
ideomotor responding or by verbal responses from the client,
in order to determine the most appropriate technique.

Mr. Tebbetts went on to explain that a good hypnotherapist deals with causes rather than symptoms, so the
first goal is to uncover the cause. On the same page as the
above quote, there are some more profound words of wisdom from the grandmaster of hypnosis:

Good hypnotherapy is a matter of probing, trial and error, the ability to recognize pay dirt when you find it and the ability to move smoothly from one method to another if the first is not getting results.

Let me repeat for emphasis: when using ideomotor responding, remember to use a monotone to avoid leading the client into conclusions. Now let's look at other uncovering techniques.

Age Regression

The words of my mentor best summarize age regressions, taken from page 22 of *Miracles on Demand:*

Age regression is the most common uncovering technique used in hypnotherapy. It is one of the fastest and surest ways to uncover repressed material and is often successful on the first session.

The next chapter deals with regression therapy in much more detail, since it may be used both for uncovering and releasing both problems and their causes--so I will save the discussion on how to facilitate hypnotic regression until then, except for another uncovering technique that almost always results in a regression.

The Feeling Connection(Affect Bridge Technique)

Charles Tebbetts taught and used a very effective uncovering technique, which he called *the feeling connection* (many therapists call this the affect bridge technique). The objective is to use an emotional feeling as a bridge through time to regress a client back to the origin of an emotional problem.

He would ask the hypnotized client to feel whatever emotion was associated with a problem, and then suggest that he/she feel that emotion again and then go into his/her body and pinpoint the place where he feels it (chest, throat, stomach, etc.). Then he would count forward with suggestions to let the emotions grow stronger as he counted forward from one to ten, saying words such as the following:

> **Number 1, go deeper into the feeling. 2, let the feeling grow stronger with each number. 3, stronger and stronger. 4, powerful. 5 and 6, feeling the emotion more and more with every number you hear. 7, 8, 9, 10! Feel it so totally that it's a relief to go back in time to the first time you felt this way. Going back as I count back 10-9-8, farther back. 7-6-5, way back. 4-3-2, back to the very first time you felt that way. ONE!**

> *Snap finger quickly (or tap client with finger) and continue immediately...*

> **Be there. Make a report. What's happening?**

He believed that the main advantage of this technique was that it facilitated the ability to deal with feelings rather than ideas. It provides a quick way to connect the client to a past event by using emotion as the bridge through time-- hence the names *feeling connection* or *affect bridge*. (I personally omit asking the client to pinpoint a place in the body where the emotion is felt in order to avoid any possibility of creating a physical pain.)

Although very effective, the feeling connection may not always be all that is necessary to discover and release a problem. Read the words of Charles Tebbetts on page 24 of *Miracles on Demand:*

> *This is a rapid method of getting to the source of a problem, but more uncovering is often necessary. It may take you to the symptom-producing event, but not to the sensitizing event which could have occurred years earlier. In one case, the client's fear of height seemed to have*

started at the age of eleven when his family took an excursion to the roof of an unusually high building to observe the view. When they reached the roof, his mother remarked jokingly, "I hope we don't have an earthquake right now!" The boy froze and refused to move from the center of the roof. He experienced fright closely related to panic. Later the fear of height generalized over the years to a fear of driving across bridges. The event recalled was the symptom-producing event, but we later discovered that the original sensitizing event occurred at the age of four, when he had fallen down the basement stairs.

What is not recorded here in my mentor's book is the fact that the person with the fear of bridges was a hypnotherapy student who was hypnotized in front of the class. Although the first use of the feeling connection resulted in the student's regression to the top of the Empire State Building, his fear remained until another hypnotic uncovering technique regressed him back to the original sensitizing event--which he released effectively. I'll always remember how happy he was when he came to class a couple weeks later and told all of us that he had driven across the Tacoma Narrows Bridge. He got a round of applause!

Dream Interpretation

Mr. Tebbetts spent one entire class on this topic during my schooling--which included a videotape of Fritz Perls doing dream therapy.

On page 28 of *Miracles on Demand*, he discusses how Ann Boyne organized Fritz Perls' dream theories into a very effective uncovering technique--and that the subconscious is speaking to us in symbols, and that the meaning can become clear through hypnosis. He goes on to say:

Perls believes that all dreams are the product of the dreamer, and Ann believes that they are efforts of one part of the client to communicate with another part or the total of the parts.

A formal induction is often unnecessary because most clients will go into a trance while reliving a dream. Tell the client to be in the dream and describe her feelings. If she says, "I was standing on a dark corner," correct her and ask her to say, "I am standing." Tell her to be there, and feel the feeling of being there. As she relives the dream and describes it, her trance will deepen.

Dream therapy never intrigued me enough to utilize; but Richard Zarro of Futureshaping Technologies, Inc. (in Woodstock, N.Y.) has researched dreams considerably.

Parts Therapy

No chapter discussing the hypnotic uncovering techniques taught by Charles Tebbetts would be complete without mentioning his legendary *parts therapy*--which can be used for uncovering, releasing, and all four of the hypnotherapeutic steps mentioned in Chapter 2 of this book. This technique requires an entire chapter to describe adequately, so I have devoted Chapter 8 exclusively to parts therapy; and since it often results in spontaneous regression, the chapter on regression therapy comes first.

One Final Caution!

When uncovering subconscious causes, remember to stay objective! Eager therapists, if tempted to form a preconceived opinion about the cause(s) of a problem, can unwisely project that opinion into the client's trance state, resulting in the client "validating" that opinion with false perceptions or false memories! Read Chapter 7 *thoroughly*.

Regression Therapy

What do we do when regression therapy is appropriate for a client?

There are four phases of regression therapy. The first is client preparation, normally done during the pre-induction interview and/or the previous sessions. The second phase is guiding the client back into time in his/her mind--like imaginary time travel--in order to discover the cause(s) of a problem. (We also need to know how to keep a client in the regression once we discover the primary cause, and we need to understand the difference between leading and guiding.) The third phase is the handling of abreactions--the actual emotional clearing or releasing--followed by the fourth, subconscious re-learning. Before exploring these phases in order, however, let's discuss how a person untrained in regression therapy may facilitate a spontaneous regression.

Handling Undesired Spontaneous Regression

Suppose you do not have adequate training in regression therapy, or you simply do not wish to use regression therapy for a particular client. How can you safely deal with the unplanned regression?

First of all, you need to recognize what is happening. The client may not inform you that he/she is experiencing a regression, but an unexpected display of emotions is a good clue! Since stopping the emotional discharge abruptly is insensitive and unwise, you may attempt to lessen the intensity with a suggestion such as:

Imagine you are looking at the scene as though watching a movie.

Allow the client to remain in the abreaction (emotional discharge) for a brief moment, until the emotional discharge starts subsiding. Then continue with words such as:

Let the scene fade away now. When you are ready, you may choose another appropriate time and place to deal with that issue. For now, just clear your mind, and go to your SAFE PLACE. Take a deep breath, go deeper into relaxation, and enjoy this pleasant, relaxed feeling... deeper and deeper...

Give client a moment to enjoy the peaceful place. If you have not established one yet, take client to a happy time or a happy vacation spot. Then help your client create a safe place.

Are you now ready to continue with this session?

Wait for response. If there is none, wait 10-20 seconds and repeat the question, asking for an ideo-motor response.

If appropriate, you may use whatever client-centered techniques are within the scope of your training to have the client imagine or reframe his/her desired outcome--such as open screen imagery. You may find it helpful to read the chapter section entitled, "Silent Abreaction (Reframing)" found in Chapter 9.

In some situations, you may simply wish to give some positive suggestions for feeling good, and for making wise decisions about physical, mental and emotional health. Depending on what the situation is, as well as what is discussed in post-hypnosis discussion, you might need to refer the client either to another hypnotherapist (who is trained in regression therapy), or suggest cognitive counseling with an appropriate professional.

If you know anyone using hypnosis who does not have training in regression therapy, feel free to photocopy the first two pages of this chapter--and give this information to that hypnotist (or therapist). Or better yet, encourage that person to buy this book!

Discussion with Client Before Regression

This first phase of regression therapy could become just as important as the regression itself...as without it, we might not attain the desired results.

First of all, let's realize that hypnosis will not guarantee client veracity; so enough rapport and trust must be built during the previous sessions and/or the pre-induction interview to make it as easy as possible to tell the truth.

Explaining the role of imagination is, in my opinion, just as valuable for regressions as it is for progressions. Also, helping to build the client's belief and expectation before we use hypnosis may help convince him/her of the potential benefits. (Review Chapter 2 if necessary.)

If there is any reason to consider regression therapy, I briefly describe a hypnotic regression before I ever hypnotize a client. I explain that in the imagination there is only NOW. Whether we are fantasizing tomorrow, remembering yesterday, or thinking about today, our subconscious reacts as though our fantasy is happening in the *here and NOW*-- whether it is a real memory, an embellished memory, or a fantasized event. In that sense, the imagination is like a time machine, allowing one to re-live the past, reframe the past, or create a desired future with as many of the five senses as desired. (For someone who loves *Star Trek*, we might say that the imagination is the holodeck of the mind.) When appropriate, I remind the client of confidentiality to help facilitate more comfort with the idea of revealing the past.

I want the client to realize that my objective is neither to prove nor disprove whether perceptions are valid memories or fantasies, because we respond to subconscious perceptions as though they are real. My job is to simply help facilitate release and new understanding for healing. Perceptions of details of the past could be different than the reality, so one should carefully consider any potential consequences of laying blame on others. In light of this, there must be a willingness to release the past and heal, or I might decline to initiate a regression. Remember that we cannot force someone to change--so if we encounter resistance, or if the client indicates consciously that an abuser is a present threat, suggest other professional help. Also remember the words of Charles Tebbetts: *"You could resist if you wanted to, but that's not why you're here..."*

Now let's assume the client is ready and the therapist is ready. How do we help people use the imagination to take a journey back through time?

Regression Techniques

A regression becomes more powerful if re-lived in the present tense inside the imagination rather than simply remembered with the logical mind. Be aware of the fact that even someone who is not normally visual could be very visual during an intense regression--but that does *not* mean you can now use visualization techniques in future sessions with that person! Additionally, a person who is normally visual might have difficulty describing what was seen during a childhood trauma if the sense of hearing and/or physical pain dominated the awareness at the time. (Note that none of the regression techniques detailed here incorporate imagery, although there are excellent imagery techniques. Tad James, PhD, describes some valuable techniques in his book *Time-Line Therapy and the Basis of Personality*.)

Since the probability of success increases with the depth of hypnosis, it's wise to take as much time as is needed to deepen appropriately. Furthermore, resistance to remembering unpleasant feelings may keep the client stuck in the present, and/or result in emergence from trance--so as with the art of hypnosis itself, it's a good idea to know more than one technique.

Here are several that Charles Tebbetts taught:

Simple age regression

Regression by age (as well as by calendar years) is summarized on pages 22-23 of *Miracles On Demand*.

Counting backwards by age presumes you know at least the approximate age of the client--because the *first age mentioned* must be *younger* than the present age! This technique has been used by Hollywood as well as those untrained in any other techniques--nonetheless it can be effective with some people.

This sample script assumes that the client has not disclosed the particular event(s) which caused the problem. After deepening to at least a medium level of trance, say words such as:

Now take a deep breath and go deeper and deeper into a deep, pleasant, hypnotic sleep...

Speak very slowly and softly. Take a long, deep breath before each sentence and "sigh" the words as though you were sleepy.

You are drifting back in time. Just imagine you're going back in time to when you were 40... *[provided client is over 40!!!]* **Going back... 35... farther back... 30... Let the years fade away... 25... 20... 19... 18... 17... 16... 15...**

If you know the correct age you wish to investigate, keep counting backward until you reach it--otherwise continue with wording similar to what follows:

Stop me when we get to a very important year... 14... 13... 12... Stop me when something very relevant to that problem happens... 11... 10... You feel your body getting smaller... 9... Your arms and legs become shorter... 8... going back to a very important age... 7... 6... 5... very small now... 4... even younger... something important happens... BE THERE!

If client stops you and speaks, listen and proceed accordingly. If he/she displays emotion, or starts to speak and pauses, stop the script and say:

Make a report. WHAT'S HAPPENING?

If the client does not stop you after you get to the end of the script, continue:

Now you are 4 and getting even smaller... 3... a very early age... you are a toddler... something very important happens... tell me about it...

Something very important happens--BE THERE! What's happening?

If there is no answer, tap gently on the forehead or the back of the hand and say with more authority:

Answer quickly now--the first thing that comes to your mind--inside or outside?

As soon as client answers, continue with:

Are you alone or with others?

Wait for response. Client may start describing detail at this point. If so, LISTEN to the dialogue and deal with what emerges. If the response is "With others," ask who; but if the response is simply the word "Alone," continue with:

What do you see, hear, or feel?

Mr. Tebbetts taught that even if the client answers one of these last three questions just to satisfy the suggestion, it is most likely the correct one for uncovering the repressed material. He believed that this line of questioning leads to a report that makes it more apparent which questions to ask next as the story unfolds.

WARNING!!! Be careful to *avoid leading* the client with your own projections or opinions of what might have happened. See the section in this chapter entitled, "Guiding vs. Leading." Even a therapist doing cognitive counseling could unintentionally cause his or her client to create false memories by asking leading questions when the client enters a spontaneous trance state. (Refer to the last section of Chapter 9 for comments about spontaneous trance!)

Regression by calendar years

This technique is very similar to age regression, except that the count is by the year rather than by the age.

After deepening to at least a medium level of trance, say words such as:

> **Now as you take a deep breath and go deeper and deeper into a deep, pleasant, hypnotic sleep...**
>
> *Speak very slowly and softly. Take a long, deep breath before each sentence and "sigh" the words as though you were sleepy.*
>
> **You are drifting back in time. Just imagine you're going back in time to 1999... 1998... 1997... 1996... 1995... 1994... Going back... 1993... 1992...** *[you may count the first few years by fives if the client is over 40]* **Going back... 1991... farther back... 1990... Let the years roll backward, going back in time... 1989... Stop me when we get to a very important year.... [etc.]**

Continue counting the years backward in a similar manner, using the same phrases described with the simple age regression technique. Also, you may follow the same line of questioning as previously described.

Pleasant place

If the client fails to regress, we may consider the advice of Charles Tebbetts written on page 23 of *Miracles On Demand*:

> *Another choice might be to first take the client back to some pleasant scene in her childhood and progress forward or backward from there.*

Simply suggest going back to a very happy time out of childhood. This can be a very happy birthday party, a wonderful holiday or vacation experience, etc. Once there, we may simply ask the client to describe what is happening, or what can be seen, heard, and felt. Then we may move either forward or backward to a very relevant event. This technique might not be effective with clients who experienced a very sad childhood.

The feeling connection (affect bridge technique)

This technique is discussed in Chapter 6, in a chapter section on the *feeling connection*. This can be a very effective way of starting a hypnotic regression--but may or may not uncover all of the relevant events.

Specific event

The following advice is also written on page 23 of *Miracles On Demand*:

> *If you have gained relevant information in your pre-induction interview, you may regress the client to a certain date and time. You may even allow her to relive her birth experience if birth trauma is a suspected cause of the problem.*

When a client knows exactly which event he/she wishes to regress to, we may go straight to the start of the event rather than going through age regression or regression by years-- provided the client responds appropriately. We may ask what he/she can see, hear and feel.

Sometimes a client might need to remember a specific event from the more recent past, such as a store owner who told me she could not remember where she put her deposit of the daily receipts. (She had seen a shady character loitering in her store, and hid the money so well that *not even she* could find it!) During the pre-induction interview, I asked her when she last remembered having the envelope. After appropriate deepening, I took her to the very same place of her last conscious memory, and asked to re-live everything in her imagination just as it was happening. To her surprise, hypnosis helped her remember exactly where she decided to stash the cash! A later phone call from an excited client confirmed that she found her money.

If the specific event is from childhood and the client resists the regression, we might need to change to one of the other techniques to guide him/her into the past. We should pay close attention, however, to the way the client responds. Talking in the past tense indicates he/she is remembering rather than regressing.

Keeping Client in the Regression

Once a client gets to the relevant event, we must do our best to help the client re-live the event as though it is currently happening in the imagination. Why? Because it's much easier to help clear the emotion if the event is *re-enacted in the imagination* rather than simply remembered with the conscious mind.

Ask, "What's happening NOW?" If the client stays in a "left-brain" mode of remembering, he/she may even bounce out of hypnosis if we do not react quickly. If this starts to happen, then simply suggest:

Re-experience it in your imagination as though it is happening NOW. Feel the experience and make a report.

If a client still resists responding in the present tense, then we may employ further deepening and use another regression technique. In some rare instances, I've actually had to awaken my client from hypnosis and re-explain both the role of imagination and the importance of cooperation.

In a recent session of regression therapy, my client kept remembering rather than regressing even after two different regression techniques--and then opened his eyes and said, "It's not working!" I reminded him to go into his feelings and re-live the scene in his imagination, then asked him to close his eyes. After a couple more deepening techniques, the feeling connection (which he originally resisted) finally got him totally into a past emotional event--and we were able to proceed with the therapy. Also, let's remember that emotional energy can temporarily cause a visual person to be auditory or kinaesthetic, etc., or even cause a non-visual person to remember vivid visual details of a past trauma...so be ready to adapt accordingly.

So let's now assume our textbook client is finally in a regression and responding appropriately, just as the man mentioned in the above paragraph. Now what?

Guiding vs. Leading

Although many clients will immediately jump into descriptions of events, some may require *guiding*--especially if the regression is to remember forgotten details when the specific goal is for conscious memory rather than for release and emotional clearing. But in either case, it is vitally important that we understand the difference between guiding questions and leading questions. (Warning: before using any forensic applications of hypnosis, seek specialized training! See my comments about forensic hypnosis in Chapter 17.)

Questions that are *leading* the client into preconceived conclusions are very dangerous, and can result in creating fantasies that the client can mistake for real memories! This is called *false memory syndrome*. For example, let's assume a client is describing a scolding from a parent. A *guiding* question would be non-specific, such as asking, "What's happening now?" or "What do you see, hear or feel?" An improper *leading* question would be, "Does Daddy spank you?" The way this latter question is phrased will very likely cause the client to fantasize a spanking even if it never took place!

The danger of false memories

The danger of false memory syndrome is very real! This is why there are problems in a court of law if a witness has been hypnotized to remember a crime. If said hypnotist is not *extremely careful* in how the questions are asked, the memories could easily be embellished and/or distorted in a way that could damage other people greatly.

The biggest danger is in how the questions are phrased. This determines whether they become *leading* instead of guiding. DO NOT suggest what *you* believe is happening-- rather, let the client tell you his or her perception! Memories can become distorted even by a seemingly innocent question like: "Is your father sitting at the table with you?" It's almost like the law of reversed effect: if I tell you *not* to imagine a dog, did you imagine seeing one? Or did you hear the barking instead? Or did you imagine petting a dog? See how easy it is to create fantasy? During a hypnotic regression, the fantasy can easily become mixed with reality.

Increasing numbers of families are being divided because of false accusations made by people "remembering" past abuses--which may never have taken place. Some of these

memories may simply be *perceptions* of childhood events--
which may be distorted far beyond the actual truth. The
client may literally not know the difference between fantasy
and reality; and additional sensitizing events throughout the
years may have further distorted perceptions of past events.
Add to this the danger of a therapist asking leading questions
to "prove" his or her preconceived opinion that a client was
sexually abused. By planting seeds in the subconscious, the
client could actually become convinced that the imagined
sexual abuse was real. Does this sound far fetched? Many
therapists and psychologists have made this very mistake!

Now let's get back to the example of a client describing
being scolded by his or her father. A very appropriate *guiding*
question would be: "What happens next?" or "What is your
father doing now?" ...and wait for the response. But a *leading*
question such as "Is your father molesting you?" could result
in a fantasized event that never happened.

One of my clients informed me that she had unwisely
chosen to confront her father after some sessions with a
psychotherapist. She was asked if she could remember being
sexually abused as a child; and then hypnosis was used to
"dig up" memories to validate the therapist's opinion. Her
loving father had given her many fatherly hugs; and during
an improperly facilitated hypnotic regression, the
psychotherapist asked, "Can you feel your father getting
sexually aroused while he is hugging you?" This very inappropriate leading question created a false memory. It amazingly did not cause serious damage in this particular case, but
it could have resulted in family division and/or a lawsuit.

The best way to avoid the temptation to lead a client is to
be extremely careful to remain *objective* and *unattached to
the outcome!* By "diagnosing" ahead of time, and then asking
questions during a hypnotic regression to validate that diag-
nosis or opinion, a therapist could easily end up talking

about the case in a court of law. This is one very important reason for the hypnotherapist to refrain from diagnosing.

Even during a cognitive therapy session a client might easily enter a *spontaneous* trance. If the hypnotic state is not recognized by the therapist, leading questions could plant seeds that grow into false memories. One of my students, a professional counselor, informed me that she was taught to ask overweight clients if there were former sexual abuses whenever there was a complaint about a feeling of heaviness. If the client complaining of such a "heavy" feeling does so while experiencing a spontaneous trance state, a question about sexual abuse phrased in a leading way could actually create a false memory. It is my opinion that all professionals should be especially careful to avoid asking leading questions if they suspect any possibility of the client being in a trance!

Remember that a person in hypnotic rapport wants to please the hypnotist, and therefore becomes more vulnerable to any suggested fantasy--even if the "hypnotist" does not know he/she is acting in that capacity. Even during the pre-induction interview, a trained hypnotherapist should watch for signs of early trance--and avoid leading questions if this occurs. (There is more written about spontaneous trance in the last section of Chapter 9.)

Understanding the difference between guiding and leading questions is so important that I wish to include a portion of a recent session with a client who said that he had hidden some money while sleepwalking:

Finding lost money

(After induction and deepening, I lead the client back to the specific event that he described to me during the preinduction interview...)

RH: Now go back to when you are sitting on the bed holding the money in your hand... Which hand are you holding the money in? *[This leading question was appropriate here, because my objective was to lead him back to his last conscious memory of holding the money in his hand.]*

CLIENT: Right hand.

RH: What are you doing with it?

CLIENT: I'm counting it.

RH: What happens when you finish counting it?

CLIENT: I put it in a bag.

Client goes on to describe putting money under pillow and going to sleep.

RH: Move forward in time to when you first awaken... What happens?

CLIENT: The phone rings. It's Johnnie, and I want him to call me later... *[client pauses]* I'm half asleep. I have to go to the bathroom... *[client pauses again]* But I need to do something with the money.

RH: What do you do now?

CLIENT: I take the money with me...

Client describes holding money while going to the bathroom, and is now standing at the door.

RH: You're at the door now. What happens next?

CLIENT: I step outside the back door and hide the money under the siding of the house.

NOTE: If I had ended the session here, it would have been a mistake! What would you have done at this point? After a long pause, I break the silence...

RH: You just put the money under the siding. NOW what are you doing?

CLIENT: I'm standing back a few feet, looking to see whether or not it's visible.

RH: What do you think?

CLIENT: Someone could find it here. I'd better hide it

somewhere else... I know! I'll look for a place near the garbage can... *[pause]* The money's in my hand again, and I'm
looking at the garbage can... I look under the lid. I'll move
the can. Hmmm... *[long pause]* Perhaps this isn't a good
hiding place. I just want to <u>forget</u> about this and go to bed
with my girlfriend.

> *He was probably in a hypnotic trance state at the time he*
> *wanted to "forget" and go to bed, so his subconscious accepted*
> *the autosuggestion--and made him forget!*

RH: Where is the money now?

CLIENT: I'm still holding it in my hand. I need a better
place to hide it. There are some rafters in the basement--I
think I'll go into the basement... *[long pause]*

RH: What do you decide to do?

CLIENT: I'm going down the stairs now... *[another pause]*
I'll open the basement door, and... *[client opens his eyes and*
shouts excitedly] I KNOW WHERE IT IS!!!

Can you see where there were some traps that could have
prevented this from being a successful session? My client had
absolutely no memory (prior to hypnosis) of any of the
events described after his last conscious memory of holding
the money while sitting on the bed--not even the ringing
phone. What if I had asked him if he hid it in the bathroom?
How easy would it have been to assume that he left the
money under the siding? What if I had concluded that he hid
the money near the trash can? What if I'd asked him if the
money was thrown away? Worse yet, what if I had simply
asked him if he had put it back under his pillow when he got
in bed with his girlfriend? Might he have falsely accused her
of stealing it? Would you have avoided all these pitfalls?

Whether the regression objective is simply to remember
details of a forgotten event, or whether it is for emotional
clearing, we must remember to ask non-leading questions

that enable clients to tell us what happened according to *their own perceptions*--not ours! If we try to fill in the details, memories might easily become distorted from the truth--as should be evident to the reader by now.

Now what about the fact that clients may even respond to *guiding* questions with distorted memories of painful events? If the client's goal is *release* rather than laying blame, it may not be necessary to distinguish false memories from the real ones. If forgiveness and relearning can take place, the client can still become empowered.

Abreactions and Emotional Clearing

Since the goal of most regressions is to provoke the memories and/or perceptions of the *cause* of a problem so that the associated emotional feelings may be released, let's discuss emotional clearing now.

When the memories of the past event(s) are re-lived in the imagination, the emotions are remembered as well--and the client will usually discharge some of those feelings. This emotional discharge is called an *abreaction*. These emotions may surface from either real or perceived perceptions of an actual event remembered, or of an imagined event that could be either partial or total fantasy. Intense abreactions may even result from distorted perceptions of real events.

Some therapists are afraid of abreactions during hypnosis; but if handled properly, the appropriate release of emotions long suppressed in the subconscious can have a very therapeutic effect--and lead to release and relearning, the valuable third and fourth therapeutic steps to change.

If handled improperly, *or* if the client would rather blame others in order to justify keeping his or her problems, more hypnotherapy and/or counseling or psychological help may be needed to help the person resolve past issues--so *read this section very carefully*. I recommend that anyone facilitating hypnotic regressions make the following guidelines a way of practice...

Creating the opportunity for abreaction

Some clients will start abreacting immediately--before the hypnotherapist even knows what the event is. Others may resist going into the feelings by bouncing back into responses given by the intellectual mind. We can take our clients into their emotions with a question such as:

How does that make you FEEL?

Emphasize the word *feel.* Remember to keep the client in the present tense (as previously explained); however, the objective is to *create an opportunity* for abreaction in a client-centered manner--*not* to *force* emotional responses.

What do I mean by a client-centered manner? Read on...

Allowing rather than forcing

It is important to allow clients to discharge emotions in *their own ways* rather than in ways we might wish to project onto them. We should also allow each client to regress to those events which he or she believes are significant.

Some therapists seem so caught up with the "inner child" concept that they try to force clients into remembering childhood traumas. A client *forced* to abreact pains from childhood could feel emotionally violated--or, worse yet, could require additional hypnotherapy or psychotherapy as a result of such mishandling. A professional speaker told me that a psycotherapist used hypnotic regression to forcefully make her remember past sexual abuse--which she did not believe was relevant to her problem. She felt that her problem was directly related to a traumatic event that happened as an adult; but the therapist believed otherwise. In her own words, she said: "I felt *emotionally violated* and remained negative of hypnosis until I met you" (emphasis hers).

A similar thing happened to me personally in the mid-1980's when a hypnotherapist using "inner child" techniques insisted that my problem was due to a series of childhood molestations that I had long-ago cleared. Even though I told her during the trance state itself that I had already forgiven the offending relative, she still forced me to call back the hurt and anger and *feel* it all over again--with even greater intensity than before. I left the office feeling angry for having been forced into a non-essential abreaction. The therapist projected her own opinions into my regression, teaching me first-hand why a therapist-centered technique can be non-productive! I later went to another hypnotherapist (trained in the Tebbetts techniques) who took me back to the appropriate and recent relevant event, and finally released it.

Even when the the client remembers the correct event, we should not force anger; rather, let's allow him/her to express in whatever manner seems most appropriate to help facilitate release and create personal empowerment. One client might be very vocal. Another might only shed one lone tear, or simply express a sense of sadness. Whether the client shouts, cries, or sighs, let it be. If there is no emotion whatsoever, we may always repeat the question: "How does that make you feel?"

Allowing rather than stopping

How much time should we allow for the abreaction? According to Charles Tebbetts, anywhere from a half-minute to a full minute is usually sufficient. More than one emotion may surface. Also, just as forcing excessive emotion is unwise, it is equally unwise to stop the regression during an abreaction. It is very unwise to suddenly jerk a person out of hypnosis during emotional discharges. There must be at least either a partial resolution, or an agreement to resolve the situation later at the appropriate time and place.

The late Arthur Winkler, Ph.D., personally told me about one of his hypnotherapy students who went against his advice and facilitated a hypnotic regression too early in her training. When her hypnotized person started abreacting, she immediately terminated the trance state--leaving the person confused and in a state of anxiety. Dr. Winkler worked with the person for several weeks to undo the damage.

Some time back I learned of a self-appointed hypnosis teacher teaching others to *physically shake* a client out of an abreaction! Frequently, therapists who make serious mistakes with hypnotic regressions learned hypnosis from a "weekend certification" course, or from an inexperienced instructor of hypnosis.

Non-interference

We must not interfere during abreactions. This is NOT the time to offer advice or share our own experiences. Clients must be allowed to release their own emotional baggage--and the hypnotherapist must be a *good listener!*

It is very appropriate to ask questions that guide the client into release and re-learning. We can allow a client to come to his or her own conclusions by asking the right questions; but we must NEVER interfere with the abreaction by trying to "convert" a client to our spiritual, religious, or philosophical viewpoints. Furthermore, we must do our best to be non-judgmental in what we say. Criticism--particularly during an abreaction--could break rapport and leave a client quite upset emotionally. Someone who saw me several years ago told me that a Ph.D. criticized her for being rebellious while she was in the trance state! This hypnotic criticism greatly inhibited her ability to trust his professional help, and she stopped going to him.

I myself made a very unwise and costly statement in 1985

with a Jewish woman whom I mistakenly believed was a Christian. Even though she was deep in trance, she was resisting letting go of a grudge--so I asked her to imagine releasing it into the light of Christ. My error was costly! She immediately broke trance saying, *"I'm Jewish, and I resent your using the name of Christ in this session!"* She explained with emphasis that she was Jewish both by race and religion, and I felt like crawling under the rug. Even though she accepted my apology, she never returned--nor did she refer any of her employees to me for sales motivation as previously promised.

Reduction of intensity of abreaction

If a client is abreacting so much that it is difficult to work with him/her, a partial desensitization can make it easier for both therapist and client alike. Charles Tebbetts accomplished this with wording such as:

> **Let the scene fade away now. Clear your mind, and go deeper into relaxation, and enjoy this pleasant, relaxed feeling... deeper and deeper...**

> **Now come forward or backward in time to a scene in which you are HAPPY and ENJOYING yourself thoroughly! I am going to count to three and snap my fingers. At the snap of my fingers you are there--a happy scene. One, two, three *[snap]* you're THERE!**

> **Now feel how wonderful life is at this moment.**

> *You can also use the peaceful place. After a minute or two, go back to the traumatic scene once again with words such as:*

> **It is important to your future happiness that you go back to the scene you just experienced--but this time the feelings will be much less intense. For the sake of your happiness, are you willing to go back to that scene for just a short moment?**

Mr. Tebbetts sometimes took a client back and forth several times from a happy scene to the trauma until it was much easier for a client to deal with the feelings. It is also very acceptable to take a client to his/her safe place instead of (or in addition to) a happy place. My mentor also called this *implosive desensitization* (discussed in a section of Chapter 9).

When the client is ready, another technique should be used for further desensitization and release.

Desensitizing ("informed child" technique)

When the discharge slows down, we may desensitize with the "informed child" technique and take a client back through the experience again (in present tense) at the age it occurred, but with all of the present adult knowledge, wisdom, and understanding. This provides an opportunity for the client to reframe the event as he/she wishes--thus perceiving it with a new understanding as well as paving the way for release and relearning.

Some therapists create a trigger for the client's safe place through the anchoring of a brief touch on the back of the hand instead of a key word, etc., before ever starting the regression. I usually anchor the second statement below as my client's trigger for peace (refer to the last section of Chapter 5).

Come back to the present just for a moment...

Take a deep breath, and RELAX.

Take client to his/her safe place for a minute or two.

Now go back to that scene with all your present adult knowledge, wisdom, understanding, intelligence and experience, and RE-LIVE it knowing what you NOW KNOW.

Be the child, but with an ADULT MIND... What new perception do you have of this event?

Wait for the response, and allow the client to tell you while you LISTEN.

This becomes a good lead-in for the use of a technique that is very powerful when used during the hypnotic state.

Gestalt (role playing)

Mr. Tebbetts frequently combined Gestalt therapy with hypnosis with some profoundly beneficial results. This helps accomplish release and relearning by facilitating adult understanding at a subconscious level, where it gets results. My mentor frequently used this in conjunction with the *informed child* technique described on the previous page.

First: make it safe for the client to tell the other person(s) exactly how he/she feels about what has happened (as the informed child). *Second:* have the client role-play being the other party (or parties) in the experience. This may provide even greater insight to help facilitate release and clearing. This dialogue can be initiated with suggestions such as:

Your mother *[or father, or the person or animal who caused the hurt]* **must now listen to you talk. Remember, you have all your present adult knowledge, wisdom, understanding, intelligence and experience. Tell her** *[him or them]* **EXACTLY how you FEEL about what has happened...**

Wait for response, and allow the client to express. He/she may talk for several minutes!

Now, BE YOUR MOTHER *[or father, or the person or animal who caused the hurt]* **and RESPOND!**

If there is no immediate response, you may repeat the phrase and then summarize what the client expressed as though you are talking to that person rather than the client. For example, assuming a client's mother spanked too hard, say:

Now, BE YOUR MOTHER. Your daughter says you spanked her too hard *[or whatever was done]*. She doesn't know how you can love her and spank her so hard *[or do whatever was done]*. RESPOND TO YOUR DAUGHTER!

Taking the role of the other person leads to understanding, which leads to forgiveness and/or release. Depending on the individual client, you may facilitate this part of the regression in either a paternal or maternal manner. Do what you believe you would want if the roles were reversed.

WARNING: Do NOT suggest that the client imagine doing physical violence to the person(s) who caused the problem, as there is a danger of the subconscious accepting the idea that physical violence is an acceptable way of resolving problems. If the *client* fantasizes striking the person at the start of the Gestalt therapy (without you suggesting it), you may deal with what emerges accordingly--but the dialogue should lead to the next important step...

Forgiveness and/or release

Forgiveness heals, but it is even more important that the client can forgive himself/herself as well as the person or situation involved in order to clear the event. If forgiveness of the other person seems impossible, the next best objective is to reach understanding and release, so that we may still find a way of helping the client attain self-forgiveness.

One of my clients who saw me for professional confidence regressed back to a time during childhood when her father said that he wished she had been a boy. This imprinted her subconscious with the idea that *being a girl was not good enough!* When regression therapy helped her to remember the event, Gestalt helped her put herself in her father's shoes, and she created understanding in her father's role with the statement: "I wanted a boy so badly that it never occurred to me that my statement would hurt you. I love you and wouldn't do anything to hurt you. Please forgive me." She forgave her father, and then forgave herself for carrying the hurt all those years. Her confidence increased greatly.

Though forgiving is *not* condoning, I often tell students that there is no magic in hypnosis, but the power of forgiveness can almost be like magic! A crisis counselor stood up in my class several years ago and disputed this, however. She said that she had been molested as a child, and could *never* forgive the person who hurt her. She went on to say that she had been in therapy herself for five years just learning to live with the pain. When I told her that *she* was the one in bondage to her grudge, she exclaimed loudly: "You CAN'T KNOW what it's like to be raped as a child and have to live with it. There is NO WAY you can know what it's like!"

She never bothered to ask me about my past, and stormed out of the class before I had the opportunity to inform her that I had been raped repeatedly by a relative for several months when I was a child. But as a young adult I refused to believe those who said the scars would last for life. How do I know this event is released rather than suppressed? I can comfortably look the same relative in the eye and not even think of what happened so many years ago. In my mind, I gave him his problem back and forgave myself for any real or imagined participation in his former crime. If I had any reason to suspect he was molesting children today, however, I would go to the authorities--not out of spite, but out of a desire to protect others. I healed totally from that former pain before I ever knew whether he had successfully dealt with his issues, and I did *not* have to get angry to get my power back.

The woman who left my class in disgust never came back. Another student who witnessed the event--and also had professional counseling experience--expressed concern that someone choosing to stay stuck in her own bias against men is supposedly helping rape victims...?

Even when the client knows that the other person is still living and unwilling to change, he/she can still "give the problem back" to the other person to deal with at another time and place. If forgiveness of the perpetrator is not an option to the client, then at least seek to help the client obtain a greater understanding--as this is often essential to release. Then, whether the perpetrator is forgiven, or simply given understanding, measures to empower and protect the client from further hurt are strongly recommended. Competent family counseling and/or psychological help will most likely be necessary if the perpetrator is still a part of the client's life--and in some cases, legal help may be considered. *Refer where appropriate!* Also be aware that if your client is a minor who is the victim of abuse, you may be required by law to contact child protective services.

We also need to remember--as discussed before--that even client-centered techniques do not guarantee total truth. A family counselor trained in the art of hypnosis recently told me that a child said he was severely punished by his mother after unintentionally killing an animal. The mother's story was that she tried to comfort her son, who became so overwhelmed with guilt that he went into total hysterics and locked himself in his room. *Whose story was true?* If forgiveness and relearning are desired, it doesn't matter. Don't get sidetracked from the goal of release by spending time and energy trying to search for truth--unless there is an extremely important reason to determine which details are true.

In short, the emotion cannot be completely cleared as long as a client is holding onto a grudge. That anger is still a potential obstacle to change. But forgiving does *not* mean that the client has to forget. Just as I would not knowingly go into partnership with a dishonest person, I would not stay in partnership with a dishonest person even though I might choose to forgive. This is for my own protection. Yet how many victims of abusive relationships think that forgiving or understanding means they have to expose themselves to more abuse? Entire books have been written on abuse and dysfunctional families, so let's move on for now...

Confirming resolution and relearning

Once the client seems to be released, it might be wise to *confirm* simply by asking if the problem is now released and resolved. If I am not yet sure that my client has resolution, I may simply ask an affirmative question and wait for an ideomotor response:

> **Are you NOW RELEASED from that problem and its former causes? Please indicate by moving your YES finger...**

If the "yes" finger moves, I take my client's word for it unless subsequent backsliding indicates otherwise. If the "NO" or "I don't know" finger moves instead, then we may ask a question such as the following:

> **What else will it take for you to obtain TOTAL RELEASE from that problem?**

Depending on the response, we may proceed accordingly, whether during the same session or during a future session.

Once we have obtained as much release as the subconscious seems to allow, we may confirm new understanding and relearning. This may be done after each event regressed to, and/or at the latter part of the hypnotic session.

We may ask the client to express how he/she NOW feels about the event(s) with the new awareness. One such self-empowering type of suggestion might be:

> **Now that you have this NEW AWARENESS about the**

situation, how do you NOW feel?

There are different ways this question can be expressed. See the chapter section entitled "Verbalizing" in Chapter 9. You will find there several examples of how you may ask a question to facilitate relearning. It's also possible to facilitate relearning simply by leading the client back to the safe place, and suggesting that *new understanding and awareness* be revealed to the conscious mind. An ideo-motor response may confirm when this new understanding and awareness is realized.

Remember that it's entirely possible that more than one hypnotic regression could be necessary for complete clearing. If there is a negative response to the last question, more therapy is needed--even if it is in a later session. When this happens during one of my sessions, I do my best to follow the advice of Charles Tebbetts, who so frequently said: *"Deal with what emerges!"*

Additional Hypnotic Advice

We must also remember that a hypnotic regression should be the *client's* experience. Avoid projecting your own opinions into the outcome. Facilitate *diversified client-centered hypnosis.* If you are using regression therapy to uncover and release the cause of a problem, it pays to confirm with the subconscious that you released the real cause!

In a session I had with a middle-aged man lacking confidence, he indicated to me during the intake that his problem probably started when the "inner child" was hurt at age 4. (He was familiar with John Bradshaw's work.) His father scolded him, breaking a glass in his face. My starting point with this particular man was regression to that specific event, but his subconscious resisted. Instead of forcing him there, I changed to age regression. When he failed to stop me at any age all the way back to infancy, I again changed techniques and used the *feeling connection*. As a result, his subconscious took him to a time during his twenties when he paid dearly for the greed of another right after his greatest success. His boss underbid a contracting job, went on extended vacation (leaving the country), and left him to make up the difference. This almost ruined him financially, and came close to breaking up his marriage. Again, this case serves as further evidence that not all confidence problems stem from childhood. Furthermore, if age regression was the only method I ever used to initiate hypnotic regression, this man's problem would not have been released. (That's why several techniques were presented in this chapter!)

Also be aware that regression will not work for all the people all the time, no matter which regression technique you use. Charles Tebbetts frequently changed techniques in mid-trance.

Do both yourself and your clients a favor and be willing to learn and use a variety of techniques so that you may fit the technique to the client rather than the other way around. This diversified client-centered approach will serve both you and your clients far better than using one primary modality.

The information shared in the chapters that follow will give you additional width and depth, presenting techniques that you may choose to use when appropriate--to help you deal with what emerges.

Chapter 8

Parts Therapy

Now it's time to explore the legendary *parts therapy* that Charles Tebbetts so actively promoted.

Parts Therapy--WHAT and WHEN?

The best way for me to begin my discussion of parts therapy is to quote the actual words of Charles Tebbetts, taken from *Miracles on Demand* (page 31):

> *In 1952, Federn described Freud's ego states--id, ego and superego--as resembling separate personalities much like the multiple personalities illustrated in the celebrated case of "The Three Faces of Eve," but differing in that no one of them exists without the awareness of the others. I find, however, that in many cases different parts take complete control while the total individual is in a trance state of which she is unaware. A bulemic will experience time distortion while binging, eating for over an hour and believing that only five minutes have elapsed... Both personalities know that the other exists, but the first is unaware of the other's existence during the period of the deviant behavior.*

My mentor believed that we all have various aspects of our personalities, which he called *ego parts*. In some cases these parts may be physical as well as mental; and in the hypnotic state, one may actually call out these various parts and facilitate dialogue.

Mr. Tebbetts continues...

Surely, at some time you have thought, "Sometimes I feel that I want to do something. But at other times I think I would like to do the opposite." The well-adjusted person is one in whom the personality parts are well integrated. The maladjusted person is one in whom they are fragmented, and internal conflict exists.

Although my former instructor borrowed aspects of this technique from others, he refined it in an effective and artistic way. He taught his students how to use parts therapy to help clients easily and quickly find causes of problems, to release them, and to facilitate relearning. In so doing, he made what I believe to be one of the most profoundly beneficial contributions to hypnotherapy in the 20th Century.

Variations

Charles Tebbetts was not alone in his beliefs. Other therapists acknowledge the fact that we all have various personality parts; and many professionals today often refer to our parts as ego states.

John Bradshaw considers ego states to be developmental stages which remain intact, as evidenced on page 217 of his book, *The Family: A Revolutionary Way of Self-Discovery*:

Hypnotic age regression work clearly suggests that each of these developmental stages remains intact. There are an infant, a toddler, a pre-school and a school-age child in each of us, who feel and experience just as we did when we were children. There is an adolescent in us who feels and thinks just like we did in adolescence.

Mr. Bradshaw facilitates a group exercise where he has a person close his/her eyes while others in the room give positive affirmations--with gentle music playing in the background. Does this sound like hypnosis? It *is!!!* He encourages his clients to meditate with inner imagery, and to love the inner child. He then takes his clients through all the "developmental stages" to find out whether the needs were met in each stage. Suggestions for positive change are given to each stage (or part of the inner child)--and he gets results. You decide whether or not this is a variation of parts therapy.

Nancy J. Napier, a nationally known marriage and family therapist, also works with a variation of parts therapy. Her book, *Recreating Your SELF: Help for Adult Children of Dysfunctional Families,* actually gives examples of the origins of various personality parts. She calls them "protector" parts and "resource" parts, and actually provides some self-hypnosis scripts for identifying, cleansing and healing our various parts. She has researched through extensive written resources to back up her work, including *Unity and Multiplicity* (John Beahrs) and *The Theory and Practice of Ego State Therapy* (Watkins and Watkins).

Some variations involve *physical parts.* I have personally met and talked to a hypnotherapist who uses a variation of parts therapy by facilitating dialogue with various physical parts of the body. His clients role-play (like Gestalt therapy) being the heart, the brain, the liver, the foot, the ear, etc.; and he gets results.

Other therapists use a technique called voice dialogue, which is based on the same concept of parts therapy--except only a light trance state is used. Apparently two clinical psychologists, Sidra Winkelman and Hal Stone, have developed and refined this technique--and have promoted it and helped numerous clients benefit from it. They wrote about their work with voice dialogue in two books: *Embracing Ourselves,* and *Embracing Each Other.* The client, in a manner that could compare with Gestalt therapy, plays the role of each part by changing chairs or positions (although changing chairs is optional). The therapist facilitates the dialogue and proceeds accordingly. Having experienced this technique myself as a client, however, I found my own conscious mind interfering greatly in the process--thus watering down its effectiveness for me when compared with parts therapy a la Tebbetts. This same observation has come from some of my students who have experienced both voice dialogue and parts therapy.

Although other variations of parts therapy may be effective for some people, I prefer this valuable hypnotherapeutic technique the way Charles Tebbetts taught it--so lets explore it now. However, unless you are already an experienced hypnotherapist, I suggest you re-read and understand all the chapters preceding this one before proceeding any further.

When to use parts therapy

A good candidate for parts therapy would be someone experiencing internal conflict, as might be evidenced by a client who says, "A *part* of me wants to get rid of this weight while *another part* wants to keep on eating!" The ego part desiring to be attractive is in conflict with the inner child (or some other part) wanting the pleasure of sweets, etc., or possibly creating punishment for some past behavior. Appropriate use of parts therapy can help the two parts in conflict achieve resolution.

There are other times when parts therapy might also be appropriate (refer to the section in Chapter 6 entitled *Seven Psychodynamics of a Symptom*); but it is extremely important that such dialogue between the parts be client-centered rather than therapist-centered!

Charles Tebbetts sometimes used parts therapy as an uncovering technique, as he greatly preferred this technique above all others. In so doing, however, he frequently found clients unresponsive initially until after other techniques were employed first. There is no right or wrong here, only a matter of choice. Just be aware that a client experiencing internal conflict is far more apt to respond to parts therapy than one who is suffering from an imprint or the hurt of a past experience. Furthermore, we need to provide an explanation of parts therapy to the client *prior* the the use of the technique! The reason is explained in the next chapter section. Also, because spontaneous regressions often occur during parts therapy, *training in regression therapy is an important prerequisite!*

Before You Begin...

If we are considering the use of parts therapy, we should explain the process to the client before hypnosis begins. Keep the explanation as simple as possible in order to avoid confusion.

I make my explanation personal--discussing my own actual personality parts--to help alleviate fear. For example, I can take my wife to a Friday night movie and think to myself, "We could see this at a bargain matinee price on Saturday afternoon." That's the *"C.P.A."* inside my mind reminding me to get the best price. At the same time, my own *inner child* feels that I've worked hard and deserve to have fun when the time is convenient. Under hypnosis, I could easily get into the emotional energy of each part and present conflicting arguments to the hypnotherapist. In an actual past therapy, my *inner child* had to make a bargain with my *professional self* in order to reach a personal goal.

If you have never experienced parts therapy for yourself, you will do both yourself and your clients a service by seeking out a hypnotherapist properly trained with the technique so that you appreciate it from first-hand experience. Not only will this help you speak more convincingly to your clients about its benefits, but you will most likely find your actual confidence in the use of the technique increasing as a result.

If you ever have reason to facilitate parts therapy without having given a pre-induction explanation, I strongly recommend that you leave some time at the end of the session for discussion so that your client does not leave your office thinking there are multiple personalities present! Although I've never facilitated parts therapy without advance explanation, I'll concede there could be a rare exception under an unusual circumstance.

Also, I very rarely use parts therapy on a client's first visit, as I believe the first hypnotic encounter should be enjoyable from start to finish as well as free of abreactions. The exceptions are with other hypnotherapists, or with clients who have enjoyed previous success with hypnotherapy.

Let's assume the client accepts the explanation, and is willing to accept his/her role in the parts therapy process. What is the role of the therapist?

The Therapist's Role: *Arbitrator*

In an article about parts therapy written by Mr. Tebbetts (for his workshops), he stated:

> *Once the parts concept is accepted by the subconscious, other parts often speak up, and the therapist takes the role of arbitrator.*

Remaining neutral and objective can sometimes be a real challenge, especially when a client is spending money to reach a goal and the "part" that is blocking success vents vehemently. But it's vital that we resist the temptation to take sides! Why? Read on...

If an unresolved dispute with your friend or work associate resulted in a request for me to mediate, how would you feel if I sided in with the other party before you ever got an opportunity to be heard? Most likely there would be little or no rapport left between you and me in such a scenario.

The same is true in a parts therapy dialogue. If you break rapport with one of the parts, you risk breaking rapport with the subconscious. You may lose the ability to reach resolution; and there is a possibility the client could pop right up out of trance.

Let me comment briefly about doing parts therapy on yourself in self-hypnosis. Since the dialogue must be facilitated objectively, it is very difficult to stay objective without a facilitator. Even though I *literally* wrote the book on self-hypnosis (*Master the Power of Self-Hypnosis*), another therapist must facilitate my own parts therapy for me--as it's too easy to get emotionally drawn towards the desired outcome. We may often resolve some of our inner conflicts with the conscious mind; but the major ones that trouble us are usually more easily resolved with objective outside help. By expressing this to my client, I help him or her to feel good about seeking assistance when necessary. This also reveals to others in a personal way that I believe enough in the technique to have experienced its benefits. In addition, the client expects me to remain objective--and will likely be more comfortable with the entire process.

O.K., we are ready to proceed with an objective attitude--now what?

How to Get Results

It has been said millions of times that fools rush in where wise men fear to tread. The same can be said for anyone foolish enough to attempt parts therapy without knowing and using ALL of the vital steps!

If you intend to utilize the valuable techniques presented in this chapter, please do both yourself and your clients a favor and memorize the steps so completely that they just become automatic whenever you use them. Furthermore, before beginning the parts therapy process, we must be sure that the client is hypnotized to a sufficient depth to minimize the risk of interference from the analytical mind. My recommendation is to take the client at least to a medium depth.

1. Identifying the part

Usually I begin by identifying and calling out the part that is blocking success first. This is done with words such as, "There is a part of you that is causing you to snack frequently..." But before that part is asked to speak, it must be made to feel comfortable communicating with the therapist as well as with the client's other parts. (Note: At your option, you may first wish to call out the part that desires to change, as described in Step 6.)

2. Gaining rapport

Just as rapport must be built with a client before hypnosis, it must also be gained with a *part* in order to make it feel safe and accepted. This is done by complimenting it in some manner--even if the client criticizes it!

3. Calling out the part

When the part is identified and complimented, it can be called out and asked to speak. Remember to make it feel safe speaking.

Let's look at a sample script which combines the first three steps:

> **There is a part of you that makes you snack frequently between meals** *[or whatever the client concern is]*, **and it is doing a very good job. I'm sure that you are doing what you think is right for [*client name*], and there is a reason why you are doing such a good job. However, another part of [*client name*] is unhappy, and feels that better communication can enlighten both of you with a few ideas that could make [*client name*] much happier. If you would**

like to gain more information and communicate, [*client name*] is willing to listen to whatever you have to say. Would you please let us know you are willing to communicate by either saying the words, "I am here" or by moving the YES finger....

Wait for response. If there is no response within about a minute, continue with suggestions such as:

I am only a mediator, and am telling you what [*client name*] told me to say. We are willing to listen to whatever you have to say. Will you please enlighten us, and let me know when you are ready to speak by saying, "I am here" or by moving the YES finger....

Wait for response.

If there is still no response after two attempts, you may either ask only for an ideo-motor response, or call out the part that is motivated to change instead. If there is still no response, try going through another part that is less involved. Also, there may be *conscious interference*. At your option, you may deepen and try again, or switch to another hypnotherapy technique altogether. I have a videotape (which I show in my classroom) of Charles Tebbetts working with a woman who would not allow her parts to emerge--yet when my teacher changed techniques, she responded--and her session was very successful. This was an excellent example of client-centered hypnotherapy!

4. Thanking it for emerging

Thanking the part for emerging maintains rapport--which is essential to good communications. If you were a mediator at a bargaining table, you would probably begin by thanking all in attendance for their willingness to come and discuss their differences.

In a sense, the therapist is taking on the same role--and

we need to realize this throughout the entire parts therapy process.

5. Asking about its purpose

Now the objective is to *uncover the cause* of the problem (the second hypnotherapeutic step to facilitate change). The best advice for us to remember from Charles Tebbetts about this step is simply to ask the five "W" questions: *who, what, when, where, why?*

By asking "who" first, we may find a part disclosing its purpose in its name. Also, even if the part takes a proper name, we may be facilitating frequent dialogue back and forth between two parts, or among three or more parts--and it's wise to ask a part which name or title it wants us to call it by. Then if we can obtain an answer to one or more of the other four "W" questions, it should help uncover the cause of the client's problem and pave the way for resolution.

A sample script for steps 4 and 5 is as follows:

> **Good. You are a very important part of [***client name***].**
> **Thank you for communicating. Do you have a job, a title or**
> **name you wish me to call you by?**
>
> *Wait for response. Make a note of the name or title so you*
> *may address the part appropriately.*
>
> **[***client name***] wants to know <u>what</u> your purpose is and**
> **<u>why</u> you are doing <u>what</u> you are doing. He [she] is willing to**
> **listen. Would you please enlighten us?**
>
> *Wait for response.*

If there is no response to the last question, then ask the *when* and *where* questions--and then be ready to facilitate a *possible regression therapy* with that part. (This is why training in regression therapy is an important prerequisite to parts therapy!) Once the regression therapy is complete, remember to complete the other steps of the parts therapy as necessary and integrate before awakening.

Once the part has expressed itself, encourage that part to listen to the other part(s) express. Say something like:

> **Thank you for sharing this important information with us. There is another part of [*client name*] that may have something to say. Are you willing to listen for a moment?**
>
> *Wait for a "yes" response. If this part wants to express further first, allow it to do so--then suggest that it listen to what the other part(s) might have to say.*

6. Calling out other parts as necessary

The next step is to call out the part that desires change (unless you did so in Step 1), which in some cases might be role-played by the client's conscious mind. Very often the part motivated to change will provide the client's given name when asked how it wishes to be called. Even when this happens, we may still effectively proceed with parts therapy in the normal way.

Here is a sample script to get you started:

> **[*client name*], there is a part of you that desires to change, and that part is most certainly interested in your happiness. And when that part of you is happy, [*client name*] will be happier. If the part of you desiring change is willing to talk, please say the words, "I am here."**

Wait for response. Ask how it wishes to be addressed--making a note of it--and continue with:

> **Did you hear what [*part #1 name or title*] said? How do you respond?**
>
> *Wait for response. If the part does not start expressing itself immediately, facilitate communication with words such as:*

[*part #1*] said that... *[summarize argument of the first part]*. **That part of you appreciates that you were willing to listen, and is now willing to listen to you in return. What do you have to say in response?**

Allow both parts to express--and now the fun begins! It would be almost impossible to write a script for what to say next, as the best advice I can give is to again repeat what Charles Tebbetts said so many dozens of times in his class at Edmonds: *deal with what emerges!*

Also be aware that we may sometimes find it necessary to go back and forth between this step and the next one--as sometimes more than two parts are needed for resolution. Be prepared to call out other parts whenever necessary, with words such as:

Is there another part that can provide some helpful suggestions or information?

7. Negotiations and mediation

In a way, we could compare parts therapy to Gestalt, except that the client is role-playing different parts of his/her personality rather than role-playing other people. Yet the goal is to facilitate release, followed by relearning. Often the best way to accomplish this is to find compromise, acceptance and resolution through negotiations and mediation.

It is vitally important that we remain non-judgmental throughout the process even when a part says something that seems ridiculous. Often clients will show a variety of emotions during the process, laughing at themselves, swearing at themselves, and/or expressing surprise at what they say about themselves.

We need to stay calm, maintaining rapport with all parts. Usually before a resolution can even be reached, each participating part must feel like it was able to present its case and be heard! Once this is done, we may then proceed to the next step.

8. Seeking terms of agreement

Often the parts themselves will come to terms of agreement; but frequently it's necessary for conflicting parts to compromise and bend a little (with our assistance). Our job as hypnotherapists is to ask the right questions, and remain as objective as possible while looking out for the best interests of the client.

My former teacher taught that good therapy is a matter of trial and error, changing, adapting to the client, and always dealing with what emerges. Often a part agrees to take on a *new job*. In some cases of internal conflict, we may have to go for *temporary* terms of agreement--and seek a permanent resolution later. Sometimes we may have to accept only a partial resolution, along with agreement to continue negotiations later.

Some of the questions we may ask are as follows:

What would it take for you to honor [*client name*]'s request?

If you do what [*client name*] asks, what do you want in return?

If [*client name*] loves and accepts you, are you willing to take on a new job?

Is there another job you can do for [*client name*] that will make you happy?

You are a part of [*client name*], and you can only reach your full potential of happiness [*peace, achievement, security, or other goal*] if [*client name*] is happy and content too. Are you willing to do something that will make [*client name*] happier?

Can you make a compromise until we can continue negotiations at the next session?

Are you willing to do this on a trial basis for one month, or would a one week trial period be easier?

If you are running out of time:

We only have a little time left. Are you satisfied with today's progress, and are you willing to continue negotiations next week?

If a part is totally uncooperative, we may call out whatever part has the highest wisdom and ask its assistance. If *(and only IF!)* we know in advance that our client has Christian beliefs, we may call out "the Holy Spirit inside" as a "part" to assist in the negotiations if needed. If the client believes in a "higher self" concept, we may ask to speak to the "higher self" in the same manner.

I witnessed a therapist at a convention workshop trying to dismiss an uncooperative part. We should only consider dismissing a part when _both_ of two circumstances occur: (1) the request is initiated by the client or a part; AND (2) all the other parts *unanimously* request that the uncooperative part leave, including the client's conscious mind. Otherwise we should make every attempt to seek its cooperation with the other parts, and/or encourage it to take on a new job. (Be sure to read the section on unwise choices!)

9. Confirming terms of agreement

At a bargaining table, it's the better course of wisdom for the mediator to confirm that all parties are in agreement of the terms before adjourning the meeting. The same is true for parts therapy.

When we believe that all participating parts have reached terms of agreement, then we may confirm with words such as the following:

> **[*Part #1*], are you satisfied with the agreement reached here today?**
>
> *Wait for response. Proceed with all other participating parts in the same manner.*
>
> **Is there any other part that wishes to express itself?**
>
> *If so, deal with what emerges accordingly. If there is silence after this question, wait ten to fifteen seconds and then proceed to the next step.*

10. Giving direct suggestions as appropriate

Once the terms of agreement are confirmed, direct suggestions may be given either before and/or after integration of the parts. Any suggestions given *before* step 11 should conform strictly to the terms of agreement reached, along with confidence to do so and direct suggestions for the parts to cooperate together. Additional suggestions (both direct and indirect) may be added after the integration step.

11. Integration of parts

Charles Tebbetts usually asked the parts to shake hands, or to embrace, or to hold hands, etc., for mutual love and acceptance. Then he would ask the client to allow all the parts to merge into an integrated or complete whole, and to *confirm* when the integration was complete by raising a hand. One of my clients visualized his parts dancing on the deck of a boat just before integrating. He still raised his hand when the integration was complete.

I have heard of some therapists who use words other than "integration." For example, some refer to it as "harmony" rather than integration of parts, asking their clients to *see a green light* when all parts are in harmony, and a yellow or red light if more work needs to be done. This could be appropriate for a visual person--or even a non-visual person in some cases, provided he/she is deep enough to accept visualization suggestions. However, I would recommend that you find a *non-visual* way of working with clients who don't visualize well--because they may or may not be telling the truth when indicating that they can "see" whatever you ask them to see, etc. (Be sure to read the subsection in Chapter 9: *Cautions about imagery.*)

The bottom line is: when facilitating parts therapy, *it is very important to integrate before awakening*--regardless of your choice of words. Also, whether you ask your clients to imagine seeing, hearing, or simply feeling when this inner harmony or integration is complete, make it easy for them to give you confirmation when it is done. I now use an Ericksonian double-bind statement, suggesting that the client may either raise a hand or move the "yes" finger when all parts attain inner harmony or integration.

12. Additional suggestions

Sometimes, after integration, additional techniques (described in Chapter 9) are helpful. In any event, it's usually a good idea to give at least one or two therapeutic post-hypnotic suggestions before awakening to reinforce the progress made during the parts therapy. In some cases it may be appropriate to combine both direct and indirect suggestion with guided imagery, and/or use a script. If time permits, I sometimes finish with an appropriate script from *Hypnotic Inductions and Prescriptions* by E. Arthur Winkler, PhD. For additional reinforcement at home, my mentor often gave the client a hypnosis tape with various suggestions and guided imagery. I do likewise.

Cautions...

Increasing numbers of hypnotherapists around the country are discovering the highly effective parts therapy techniques that Charles Tebbetts taught and wrote about in his book, *Miracles on Demand*, even though calling it "ego states" or using other names for the technique.

Although it is by no means the only effective hypnotherapy technique that Mr. Tebbetts taught, its high success rate made it his own favorite technique. But there are reasons why my former mentor felt that one should be adequately trained before attempting to use parts therapy--so let me advise the reader of some cautions by discussing the results of a few unwise choices that have been brought to my attention or that I have personally known of...

Avoid taking sides

Pioneers may break new ground, but often learn from their own experience...and Charles Tebbetts was such a pioneer. In his earlier years, he often took sides and started a debate with the offending part, as evidenced in his writings. Even though he often enjoyed getting into this "Great Debate," he eventually changed his opinion and maintained that it was best to *mediate objectively.*

If you break rapport with a "part" by failing to be a good listener while it presents its case, your role as a facilitator becomes difficult if not impossible. One of my own former students went against this advice by taking sides when he thought it was appropriate to do so. His client's stubborn part refused to talk further with him that day--and he spent one entire session just trying to get his client back into hypnosis in order to apologize to the offended part. He learned the hard way that it is much easier to maintain rapport than it is to regain it after losing it. (I believe he gave her two more free sessions to compensate for his mistake.)

What might a part do if criticized?

One of my students in training tried criticism once and got into a shouting match with the student who was in hypnosis. While the part that was criticized during trance told the student therapist to go take a hike (plus unrepeatable words), another part of her apologized for her behavior. No real damage was done, but the hypnotherapy session was not successful because rapport was broken. This situation provided a learning experience for others present.

Results of improper explanation

A client seeing me for motivation several years ago had what she considered to be a negative past experience with hypnosis. She said it took her two years to muster the courage to seek hypnotherapy again, because parts therapy had been done on a first visit without advance explanation from the therapist. She got scared that she might have "multiple personalities" and did not go back. After adequate explanation of the therapy technique, she felt much more comfortable--and was successful with her sessions.

Avoid taking control in an authoritative way

Determining the best solution yourself and telling all the parts what to do would be like a mediator giving orders at a bargaining table. One part might feel vindicated while another feels slighted, making resolution more difficult. Client-centered parts therapy, where your client comes up with the solution (even if you help), is far more likely to be accepted by the subconscious than a series of post-hypnotic suggestions given as a result of you "taking charge" in an authoritative way. Remember, it only takes one rebellious part to prevent total resolution.

A professional woman told me that she got angry at another hypnotherapist for "trying to dominate" the session, so she failed to keep her next appointment and never told him why. If you have a need to control the parts, avoid the use of parts therapy.

What about creating a new part?

Charles Tebbetts believed that it was better to ask an existing part to take on a new job rather than to create a new part, and I totally concur.

I have heard of some therapists who actually "create" different personalities to do different jobs! Why would any therapist even want to consider fragmenting someone rather than helping the person become more whole? Don't we all have enough "parts" to contend with already? Also, is there a risk of someone becoming a multiple personality from having new parts intentionally created? These are *serious questions* that I strongly urge you to consider before you ever try to create multiple personalities in a client!

Although I am not qualified to give a psychological opinion on the risk of any emotional and/or psychological damage that might result from employing such a technique, I have serious concerns. Although some psychologists may appreciate the extra business generated from this risky practice, the client may find a way to make you pay. Let me state that I am opposed to creating new parts, because of my belief in a potential risk of fragmenting the mind. While some could argue that there might be an occasional exception, I personally do not want anyone trying to create new parts in *my* mind.

What about destroying a part?

Never take it upon your self to initiate the destruction of a part! When and why might you respond to a client's request to do so? Read on...

If a "part" seems to serve no valuable purpose to your client, and is totally unwilling to take on a new job, you may ask your client (or the other parts) to determine the fate of that uncooperative part. Then, only if the *client (or a part)* initiates the request that you expel a part or "send it into the light," you may do so--provided the client's conscious mind and the other parts agree *unanimously.*

Sending any parts you believe are "entities" into the light could be equally as unwise. What if the part that you believe is an "entity" is really only a subconscious part that is caught in a negative emotional energy? Given the opportunity, could the part take on a productive job for your client? What might be the results of doing a therapist-centered "exorcism" if it is a constructive but wayward part that is destroyed?

A woman I know personally had been abused by both her father and her first husband. She went to a Ph.D. who apparently had only minimal training in parts therapy. When a part got argumentive, he rebuked it authoritatively in the name of Christ and commanded it to be consumed with the spiritual flame of God. (This was witnessed by a mutual friend.) This left her feeling guilty and in a state of anxiety. She later realized that the part he tried to destroy was a necessary part of her own personality that was there to *protect her from male authority figures who might try to dominate* her. How do you feel the Ph.D. was perceived? Two years later she still refused to work with any male therapist--with or without academic credentials.

What about immobilizing a stubborn part?

If we get into a situation we cannot seem to resolve, let's first of all realize that people don't always resolve their differences in only one discussion--and the same is sometimes true with parts therapy.

A domineering hypnotist kept trying to make a client's uncooperative part submit--apparently not knowing how to complete a parts therapy session where more resolution was needed later--and then unwisely chose to "freeze" this part into a statue. The client told another hypnotherapist that she felt like a part of her mind had been amputated! Her condition got worse, and it took several hours of trance work for that other hypnotherapist to undo the damage and get the frozen part to take on a new job. Had this second hypnotherapist not known how to intervene appropriately, this woman might have had to spend many months in psychological counseling.

A mediator would be very unprofessional and inconsiderate if he or she locked all conflicting parties at a bargaining table and left them there until the next session. Paralyzing a part of the mind is a very inconsiderate and unwise way of dealing with an uncooperative part. We are there to facilitate resolution, not to bring punishment; and if you find yourself in doubt as to how to bring the parts to terms of agreement, then get them to agree to seek resolution at a later time and place. Then integrate, awaken, and either seek help, change techniques, or refer the client elsewhere.

Getting sidetracked

This almost seems too obvious to mention, but it's amazingly easy to get sidetracked and forget that parts were called out when something unexpected emerges in a session, such as a spontaneous regression. Often constructive parts therapy results in combining several different techniques, so it's important to remember which part(s) you are dealing with--or whether you are giving suggestions to the entire person (all the parts of the whole).

Once when I personally experienced parts therapy for a personal issue, the therapist got sidetracked into a regression of one of my parts. She awakened me after facilitating the regression properly, but she forgot to integrate my parts. After I spent the next day thinking about the regression almost every waking minute, I reflected back on the session and realized her mistake. That oversight resulted in my being greatly distracted at work until I corrected the situation. A simple autosuggestion and a brief self-hypnotic meditation was sufficient for me--I gave myself the idea that my finger would move when my parts were properly integrated. Even if I had not known what to do, I do not believe any permanent damage would have resulted; but most likely I might have experienced several days of strange thoughts before my mind would eventually integrate itself. (It turned out that the therapist had not received actual training in parts therapy; she had only read about it in *Miracles on Demand.*)

Also, a friend of mine was only in a light state of hypnosis when a counselor trained in "N.L.P." techniques used *voice dialogue,* a variation of parts therapy which is often done only in a light trance state. My friend felt his conscious mind analyzing so much that, after several minutes into the voice dialogue technique, he exclaimed, "This isn't working!" Since both he and the therapist falsely assumed that he was out of trance, there was no integration process. This left him disoriented, because his "parts" had actually emerged during a light trance state; and it took several days for his mind to integrate by itself.

If you believe that you could have made any of the above mistakes, then I urge you to seek "hands on" training before using parts therapy. In any event, be sure to follow all the steps that were explained in the chapter section called "How To Get Results."

Examples of Successful Parts Therapy

Now that we've discussed some potential pitfalls, let's talk about some successes. (Some of the techniques used in conjunction with parts therapy in these examples are discussed in Chapter 9.)

Charles Tebbetts wrote about numerous case histories involving the use of parts therapy in his book, *Miracles on Demand*--which I hope comes back into print again sometime. All of the case histories he wrote about were documented on videotape. Even though some of them may have become lost, I still have some videotapes in my possession-- which Charlie personally gave to me while he was still living. They are shown in my classroom at Tacoma Community College. There are so many more successes, however, that the ones he wrote about in *Miracles on Demand* represent only the top of the tip of the iceberg.

One of the most profound examples of a success is a man I know personally who experienced a session with Charles Tebbetts in the late 1980's. So dramatic are the results that I devoted the entirety of Chapter 12 to his story.

Another example is a session my teacher facilitated with a businesswoman who wanted more motivation for success. She had a part calling itself "Slave driver" who was in conflict with another part identifying itself as "Slow down." The *slave driver* felt that she was not able to reach her full potential, while the part slowing her down felt that she was always so busy that she never took enough time to enjoy her success and do the things she enjoyed doing. Both parts had to reach a mutually acceptable compromise, and it was a very dynamic session. Several years later I was informed that this woman became quite successful.

I also met a middle-aged hypnotherapist who was once diagnosed with *multiple personality disorder*. She had been to several psychologists and two psychiatrists over a period of many years, and informed me that hypnotic regressions had only kept her stuck in her problem. According to what she told me, a psychologist with competent hypnotherapy training had used parts therapy to successfully integrate her former personalities. Although I personally have never worked knowingly with someone who had multiple personalities, it makes sense to me that parts therapy might be the most logical way to help.

Now let's discuss some of my own client successes. (The names are changed to protect client confidentiality.)

Linda, a smoker, failed to respond to my usual benefits approach. One part of her wanted to "live long and prosper," while another part felt compelled to make a statement of rebellion against a society which is manipulating her into quitting. This same part really wanted choice--so when another part of her convinced her that she was actually being manipulated into remaining a smoker because of other people's prejudice, she realized that she was giving her power of choice away and burning up her spending money! When I used the verbalizing technique (for relearning--discussed in Chapter 9), she decided that it was time for her to make her own decisions instead of being ruled by the smoking habit.

Ron, an overweight client who was self-employed, had an inner child that felt he was working too hard--so excess junk food was his only pleasure. This inner child was not about to give up evening snacks until Ron agreed to balance his life by taking more time for personal fun and recreation. He was quite pleasantly surprised at having to make a bargain with himself to spend at least four hours a week playing fantasy role-playing games on his computer, going to at least two movies monthly, and agreeing to take his wife out to dinner more often. After integration, I used open screen imagery to have him imagine his success.

Betty, an overweight counselor/therapist, had a part (like Ron did) making her stay heavy by overeating in order to punish her for working too many hours and not taking time for herself. She also had to make a bargain with herself to find more time for recreation in her life.

Ted, an insurance salesman afraid of rejection, was in conflict with his desire to reach sales quota--because a part of him believed that others perceive all salespeople as dishonest. His father imprinted him with this opinion while he was a child; so adult understanding had to be facilitated at a subconscious level where it could get results. Parts therapy digressed into regression therapy with the informed child technique, adding Gestalt therapy for "Teddy" to role play with his deceased father, verbalizing the new understanding, and returning to the parts therapy for further negotiations lasting for several sessions. His commission income rose significantly.

Joan was a professional woman, and also a work-a-holic who lacked confidence. She felt compelled to "prove her worth in a man's world" simply because a part of her was angry at her father for wishing she had been a boy. A more spiritual part of her reminded her to forgive her father for his prejudice, and to get on with her own life. Once the part verbalized this, there were no negotiations left to do, as that part decided to do all the changing.

Bill was a realtor who kept getting bogged down with too much paperwork even in prospecting habits, because a part of him wanted to be perfect. As a child he had been told repeatedly, "Don't do a job unless you do it right!" This resulted in his subconscious making him work twice as hard as necessary until his parts came to terms of agreement. This client took several sessions because one of his parts--the one causing him to work too hard--wanted to hide out of fear of criticism and punishment. Initially I could only speak to this part through another part, which acted as a messenger.

Jane was a career woman who spent years--and thousands of dollars--trying every weight program under the sun. The part of her eating incessantly said, "This weight stays until she resolves another issue she has been putting off dealing with, and I'm not budging until then!" The conscious part of Jane said she realized what it was, and would consider her options later. She told me after the session that she wished she had used hypnotherapy several thousand dollars earlier to discover that her weight was a symptom of something else. I was not trained to help her in her unresolved marital issues, so she had to decide whether to live with the weight or consider other professional help. Although I never saw her again, she telephoned me several months later to thank me for helping her gain valuable insight about herself.

Randy was a hypnotherapist who felt unworthy to be in this profession. His perfectionist part felt nothing was good enough unless it was done perfectly. He needed to learn how to forgive himself for not being perfect, and to simply be the *best he could be*. This part learned to be professional instead of trying to be perfect; and that our best on one day might be better than our best on another day.

There are many more successes....

Parting Thoughts

Remember to do for the client what you would want done in a role reversal. Effectively facilitated, parts therapy is one of the most profound techniques available for facilitating change--but it cannot be done in part. Either understand and use *all the steps properly*, or don't use this technique at all. Hopefully this chapter has shown that the up-side of parts therapy has a *client down-side* if facilitated by a hypnotist or any other professional who short-cuts this type of therapy.

If possible, seek actual training in this technique before using it.

IMPORTANT! Please do both yourself and others an important service... Even if you are a hypnotism instructor, do

NOT attempt to teach this technique to other hypnotherapists or counselors until you have personally used it with clients for at least a year or two! Students frequently ask teachers questions that can only be adequately answered from the experience of having facilitated many such therapies themselves.

Allow me to share a letter written by a very reputable hypnotherapist two weeks after my workshop at the 1993 Annual Convention of the National Guild of Hypnotists:

> *As a participant in your recent NGH class "Parts Therapy" I would like to thank you for both your teaching ability, and your skill at clarification. Having read "Miracles on Demand," a few years ago I had been using parts therapy on many clients, and in most cases had been successful. However, I always felt that there was something that I was not doing correctly or skipping. Through your detailed presentation I discovered and now have learned what I always felt was missing. I am now much more confident in returning to using parts therapy as a therapeutic modality. Again, thank you.*

I respect the professionalism and integrity of the well-known hypnotherapist who had the courage to write this letter, and I hope his clients realize how fortunate they are. With his years of experience in the field, this man could easily teach me things I don't know about hypnosis; yet his actions demonstrate what all of us need to realize--we can all be each other's teachers and students in the game of life. But when it comes to parts therapy the way Charles Tebbetts taught it, I believe that both my own professional training and experience provide me with something worth sharing.

As my schedule permits, I will make myself available to those who wish "hands-on" training. If you are interested, contact one of the professional hypnotherapy associations listed on page 14, or contact me directly if you wish to be a sponsor of such training for a group of professionals. Note that I'm also available to facilitate training on the other major areas of this book. My address, phone and e-mail are as follows:

Roy Hunter, M.S., CHI
Alliance Self-Empowerment Inc.
30640 Pacific Hwy. S. -- Suite E
*Federal Way, WA 98003 * (253) 927-8888*

e-mail: *rhunter@halcyon.com*

www.royhunter.com

Chapter 9

Other Rapid Change Techniques

Quality hypnotherapy involves more than simply using only one technique and hoping it works. There are many hypnotherapy techniques used today with varying degrees of success--and perhaps some highly effective ones that have yet to be discovered. Charles Tebbetts taught primarily the ones he believed to be the most effective, so those are the ones primarily presented in this book.

My teacher, however, believed that any technique which gave benefits to the client without risking the client's welfare was appropriate--but he encouraged his students to use the ones that got the best results. Mr. Tebbetts admitted in his class that NO technique will work for all of the people all of the time--but if the therapist knows enough different techniques to change easily from one to another when the first one is unsuccessful, his or her success with clients will be greatly enhanced. He also believed that it was not necessary for a competent hypnotherapist to know every technique that has ever been used--so he chose to teach the ones that he believed to work the best.

My mentor also believed strongly, as I've previously stated, that the *technique should fit the client* rather than vice versa. In his opinion, any therapist who advocated his/her own pet technique as a panacea for everyone was not serving the profession as well as possible. This is another way of saying that Charles Tebbetts taught and used client-centered hypnotherapy! (Since I believe some people just might read this chapter before any others in this book, I felt these opening comments were appropriate.)

Now let's look at what he called the *rapid change techniques of hypnotherapy.*

Imagery

Many people, including speakers, ministers and therapists, facilitate various forms of guided imagery and/or meditations with visualization. Whether or not they realize it, or whether or not they admit it, they are using a form of hypnosis.

Imagery works quite well some of the time even with groups, especially for relaxation, or for a person who primarily needs only the first of the four hypnotherapeutic steps (covered in Chapter 2). Imagery has additional applications in the therapeutic setting when used in conjunction with the other three therapy steps.

There are three basic types of imagery that we may use advantageously during hypnotherapy. The first, called *open screen imagery,* is totally client-directed. At the opposite end is *programmed imagery,* which is totally therapist-directed. Everything inbetween has elements of both of the others, and I call it *indirect guided imagery.*

Open screen imagery

Some therapists use a technique where the client is asked to imagine watching a movie screen or television screen and see a better future--or to imagine seeing a play with characters in the play. The client can imagine it exactly as desired. The client has total power to write his or her own script.

When I am facilitating the benefits approach and ask my clients to imagine their most important benefits in ways that are satisfying--while doing something they totally enjoy doing--they are experiencing *open screen imagery.* However, since some people are not visual, I project them right into the future with as many of their five senses as possible. This seems more effective than simply having them watch a screen--which may not work at all for someone who does not visualize well.

As a side note, if my client is a Star Trekie, I give the suggestion to "Go to the *holodeck of your mind* and create the desired program." In this way, he/she can add in all of the five senses--but someone who is not familiar with *Star Trek* would need some other method to facilitate open screen imagery. Use your *own* creative ideas to come up with something if you wish. If your *client* can *imagine* it--and it feels safe to him or her--there is a good probability of a successful fantasy, even if the client is primarily auditory.

As mentioned in Chapter 3, I add in the suggestions that my clients imagine how they feel *emotionally* at the fulfillment of their desires so that their own positive emotions may help empower them towards success. Since emotion is the motivating power of the mind, this helps clients create more positive energy attracting success into the subconscious.

My former teacher believed that open screen imagery was beneficial when the client needed help from the creative part of the subconscious to help reach a goal. Some therapists also use open screen imagery instead of regressions for uncovering the cause of a problem and *reframing* it. This is explained later in this chapter under the section, "Silent Abreaction."

Indirect guided imagery (Ericksonian metaphors)

The use of metaphors or stories and indirect suggestion is what Charles Tebbetts used to call *guided imagery* (Dr. Milton Erickson made this famous). Since others often use "guided imagery" to refer to almost all types of imagery (including the third type discussed next), I believe it is more accurate to call this *indirect guided imagery*.

While the story is directed by the therapist, the *applica-*

tions are client directed.

My mentor taught that this can be quite effective when used with other therapies, but he also felt that it could be "band aid therapy" if used alone. Let me quote some of his words, taken from *Miracles on Demand* (page 37):

> *Milton Erickson became famous for his metaphors in which he used mental imagery as a method of indirect suggestion. A therapist who is creative can come up with numerous stories the client can identify with, or he can borrow from Shakespeare or even the Bible. I once worked with a very religious man and a psychopathic liar. I used a quote from the Bible but changed it to fit the case.*

My teacher went on to use the parable of a man whose house was built on sand and fell, while another whose house was built on rock stood firmly because it had a solid foundation in truth. Although the story was directed by Mr. Tebbetts, the client could then add in his own visualizations about truth, weaving in some of his own open screen imagery by identifying with the metaphor. And since the story came from the Bible, it appealed to his religious beliefs.

One successful case that I witnessed during my training was with a man who lacked the courage to keep his father from constantly meddling in his life. After other techniques had already been used, Mr. Tebbetts talked about how an eagle is kicked out of the nest when it becomes old enough to fly. Although the ground comes up fast, when the young eagle spreads its wings something wonderful happens! The young bird soars freely over trees, lakes and streams--and can see for miles in all directions! The feeling of freedom is wonderful. The student in trance directed his own applications of that metaphor and imagined himself flying through life freely, finally having left the nest of his parents' home.

There are **two cautions** here, however. Mr. Tebbetts addressed the first one with additional words of wisdom starting on the same page of the previous quote:

> *An eager beginner gives great reverence to such methods, and they have validity. However, because a method sounds creative, different or profound does not mean it is better than a simpler, tried and true method. Many of these exotic methods work, at times. But a good, experienced therapist should know that they can also be an ego trip for the hypnotist. It is pleasant to think you have done something profound, but your initial purpose is to help your client, so such flights of fancy as these must be used only in conjunction with the basics. In the case of the psychopathic liar, I had to deal first with his lack of self-esteem.* (*ibid* p. 37-38, emphasis mine)

A **second caution** is that we should only draw stories from the Bible if we know in advance of facilitating hypnosis that the client is Christian. I already disclosed a costly mistake I made back in 1985 after assuming a religious person was Christian rather than Jewish. (A story from the *Old Testament* might have been acceptable for my Jewish client.)

In addition to the above cautions, we are well-advised to realize that what might be comfortable to most people could actually cause discomfort to some people--such as going up or down an elevator or going in a boat, etc. If the main character of your story is whom you wish your client to identify with, and he/she does something in the metaphor that your client absolutely would not do, this could lessen the benefit-- or even neutralize it altogether.

In short, metaphors will work for some of the people some of the time, but not for all of the people all of the time; and Mr. Tebbetts believed that they were more effective when used along with other techniques rather than when used alone.

Programmed imagery(direct guided imagery)

Programmed imagery (or direct guided imagery) is the use of direct suggestion for the client imgagine suggested things, such as details about goal achievement and/or a peaceful place. It is *therapist directed.*

I use programmed imagery in conjunction with my benefits approach by having clients vividly imagine their specific benefits in detail (refer to Chapters 3 & 4). Even though my client supplies me with personal benefits in advance, I actually use direct suggestion and "program" the imagery before switching to open screen imagery later in the session.

Another application of programmed imagery is discussed in conjunction with systematic desensitization, described in the next chapter section. It can also be helpful with patients of major disease--but should not be done as a substitute to appropriate medical treatment. Refer to the subsection on page 140: *Disease or illness.*

Cautions about imagery

Charles Tebbetts taught that all forms of imagery are powerful methods of change when used with hypnosis, because they reach the subconscious; but he also taught that we should know whether a person is visual, auditory or kinaesthetic before we use imagery. Please remember that some people don't visualize well, but find it much easier to imagine sounds and feelings. A suggested visualization may not reach the subconscious nearly as deeply as a suggested auditory or kinesthetic exercise of imagination for the non-visual person.

The most common mistake made by beginners and veterans alike involving imagery is the *erroneous assumption* that every deeply hypnotized person must be able to visualize when the suggestion is given. Speaking from my own experience, however, I have often found my subconscious lying to therapists about visualizing just to avoid a trance-terminating debate about whether or not I am actually visualizing. Why?

On more than one occasion I have informed a therapist while I was in deep trance that I could not "see" a waterfall, etc., and was criticized for not allowing myself to visualize. I've had to reject critical suggestions such as, "Anyone can visualize by going deep enough," or "You're not going to release this unless you visualize what I ask you to see!" Statements like these break rapport or lower self-esteem--or both. One therapist actually went so far as to tell me that she could not help me until I was able to visualize a lake. It wasn't until I had been in the hypnotherapy profession for several years that I realized such statements are therapist-centered rather than client-centered! One therapist, as recently as 1990, actually tried to make me feel inadequate for being a hypnotherapist who couldn't visualize well! I told him that such criticism was simply his own bias; but how might his bias impact some of his clients?

Having been on the receiving end of both successful and unsuccessful hypnotherapy sessions since 1978, the *common denominator* in all of my own *non-productive* sessions was the incorporation of *visualization* with guided imagery. While it's true that I sometimes visualize vividly during a regression, more than one very competent hypnotherapist has erroneously believed that I have successfully released a problem just because a suggested ideo-motor response came after some sort of releasing technique involving visualization. The response was given by my own subconscious just to please the therapist, so the problem was not really released...

That part of me who has been the frustrated client must

ask an important question: when are you visualizers going to learn that some of us *do not visualize very well?* Quit trying to make us fit your pet techniques. They simply do not work for everyone.

Systematic Desensitization

Systematic desensitization is a form of programmed imagery. Though the technique is primarily applicable for an anxiety or simple phobia (discussed in the next chapter), the description of the technique itself belongs here.

The client lists several anxiety-provoking scenes in order of severity, then the therapist may use programmed imagery until the anxiety is gone. This technique is called *systematic desensitization.* On occasion it might be effective even if done in a therapist directed way, although my mentor suggested that the client should make the list of scenes used during the session. (Please note that he rarely used this technique unless there was resistance to regression therapy!)

The example Charles Tebbetts uses in *Miracles on Demand* is for a woman to imagine a spider web ten feet away, and to raise her hand when she feels anxiety. Then the process is repeated until she is free of anxiety. The next scene might be seeing an actual spider several feet away, then a foot away, etc. Here are his words about this technique, taken from page 39:

> *Viewing these scenes while enjoying the extremely relaxed feeling of hypnosis is similar to Wolpes idea that a response contrary to anxiety occurring in the presence of a fear-evoking event will suppress the anxiety response. This is even more effective while the subject is in a trance state.*

Again, *scenes* would not be as effective for a non-visual person. Another drawback can be stated simply: this may not work for an intense phobia. (Chapter 10 is devoted exclusively to phobias.)

Implosive Desensitization

When a client has an abreaction during a hypnotic regression back to a traumatic event, and is then taken to a happy or peaceful place before being returned to the trauma with less emotion, this is called *implosive desensitization.*(This is also discussed in Chapters 6 & 7.)

Any valid regression technique may be used to guide the client back to the event (if known); but Charles Tebbetts felt that the feeling connection was usually the most reliable technique when the event was not known.

He taught that we should allow the client to regress to the past trauma with an abreaction lasting from 30 to 60 seconds. Then we may fade the scene away and come forward to happy time--or take the client to his/her safe place. Then we may take the client back to same scene again with the informed child technique, adding Gestalt (or other techniques) until only normal discomfort is felt. Then verbalizing (discussed later in this chapter) can lead to relearning.

Desensitization by Object Projection

As with many other imagery techniques, object projection may be either indirect guided imagery or programmed imagery. Numerous therapists ask a client to project a problem or a pain outside of themselves and imagine that it's a brown ball (or some other specified shape and color).

Charles Tebbetts preferred to allow the client to choose the shape, size and color; then he would ask for a description from the client. Next he would ask him/her to make it bigger, and then shrink it down to its normal size. Then he would suggest that it shrink to the smallest size possible. If the problem were pain, he would suggest that the client could do the same thing again with the same pain whenever desired. If the problem were emotional, it could be disposed of or released in one of many different ways through open screen imagery, programmed imagery, or indirect guided imagery. (N.L.P. therapists note: Mr. Tebbetts had already been using this technique for many years when I saw him use it in 1983!)

Releasing techniques I've witnessed range from shrinking a problem to nothingness, burning the problem, throwing it into the sea, burying it, sealing it in a space capsule and sending it into the sun, and more. I have an Ericksonian script about a hiker with a backpack that is lightened, and another about a bird that is set free to fly. Personally, on those occasions I choose to use object projection, I normally *ask the client* what he/she wishes to do with the problem--and proceed accordingly. So you could say that I use *client-centered* object projection. Whatever releasing imagery you use, be certain to ask the client to confirm when it is done.

Once again, this technique is likely to be ineffective for the non-visual person (you might try touch or sound). Also remember to avoid using this for pain control without an appropriate medical referral. (Read the chapter subsection on *pain control and symptom removal* in this chapter.)

Silent Abreaction (Reframing)

This technique may be very useful if the client resists regression therapy (and is visual). Charles Tebbetts normally used regression therapy as the first choice (when called for), but he did present this technique as an alternative second choice. It combines imagery with passive regression, as the following sample script indicates (also taught in 1983):

> **And now just allow yourself to be in your own private meditation room, which ONLY YOU can enter. Everything that happens in this room can only be seen and heard by you. Imagine the room is decorated exactly as you wish, and**

you are sitting in a chair that is as comfortable as you wish. You may imagine the color of the walls, the carpeting, and the furnishings. When you are there, let me know verbally or by moving your finger.

Wait for response. If there is no response within a minute, rephrase the suggestions and ask for a response. Once the client indicates he/she is in the safe room, continue...

Imagine there is a movie screen, or a T.V. with a very large screen. Let me know when you can see it.

Wait for response.

As I count from one to three, the screen will light up and the sound will be turned on, and there is a movie of your life...

If the event is known, say the following:

The movie is now replaying that part of your life which seemed very emotional. Back up the movie to what happened JUST BEFORE this event, and tell me what you see and hear. You can see and hear passively, as you are only watching a movie...

If the event is not known, say the following:

The movie is now at a very important part of your life, relevant to your present concern. Let the events unfold on the screen, as your subconscious knows how to replay them. You can view this impassively, because you are only watching a movie...

After saying whichever applies, continue with:

You may now edit the movie and rewrite the script any way you wish. With all of your present adult understanding, knowledge, wisdom and experience, rewrite the script. In your imagination you have total power to do anything you wish, so you may reframe it frame by frame, or CHANGE THE MOVIE ANY WAY YOU WISH. Let me know when

this is done...

Wait for response--it may take several minutes.

According to my mentor, this can help the client face new situations with different feelings and/or a better emotional state of mind.

While Mr. Tebbetts referred to this as *silent abreaction,* most therapists call it *reframing.* It could also be called a variation of *rewriting history.* Since I don't choose to get hung up on labels, you may call it whatever you wish--it will still be just as powerful when used appropriately.

Inner Guide

Some therapists use a client-centered imagery technique that combines aspects of several techniques. The client is asked to enter a room or go to a meadow (or some other place) and imagine meeting a wise guide who can provide insight and answers. This technique can be expanded upon greatly, depending on the client. This inner guide can be perceived as a spiritual guide, an angel, a wise mentor, or a wise personality part, etc. As such, the inner guide technique may help with discovering the cause as well as release and relearning. Furthermore, the guide might also provide some suggestions that greatly benefit the client; thus this one technique alone may help some clients accomplish all four hypnotherapeutic steps to facilitate change.

Verbalizing

Verbalizing is a powerful method of facilitating adult understanding at a subconscious level, where it gets results--and can be effective for both the visual and non-visual person alike. Let's examine the words of Mr. Tebbetts himself, taken from *Miracles on Demand* (page 41):

After sensing the feelings that accompanied the original sensitizing event, the client is encouraged to dis-

cuss them at length. The more she talks about them, the more she understands them and the less power she gives them. As she discusses the feelings she experienced during the trauma and the relief she feels after having faced it, you may give her positive suggestions both in and out of trance.

Verbalizing helps accomplish the fourth hypnotherapeutic step: *relearning.*

To facilitate verbalizing, a question such as one (or more) of the following may be asked when appropriate:

What is your NEW PERCEPTION of that problem now?

What is your NEW UNDERSTANDING of that situation?

Now that you've forgiven and released that person or yourself, how can you best accomplish your goal?

How do you feel NOW about what happened?

How can this new understanding best benefit you in the present?

What words of wisdom does your inner mind have for you now?

What is your best resolution to that problem?

What is the most important awareness you've gained from this session?

How can you best achieve your goal?

What is the most important thing you can do to achieve and maintain success?

You may formulate your own questions using these examples as guidelines. Verbalizing can become very productive with many situations. At times clients may actually give themselves post-hypnotic suggestions during this process--which we may repeat to them for emphasis just prior to awakening.

If the client verbalizes something that you believe to be a very unwise choice, you may wish to suggest that the proposed resolution be discussed at a conscious level first. If necessary, seek a second opinion--or refer your client to other professional help as appropriate. Bear in mind, however, that unwise statements are often verbalized during a Gestalt therapy *prior* to forgiveness and release. As long as forgiveness of both the client and the other person involved still takes place, name-calling may sometimes lead to understanding--which may then lead to forgiveness and/or release.

Once the Gestalt is completed (if used), and the cause is supposedly released, we must listen very carefully to what our clients verbalize. It's important that what our clients relearn is beneficial without being negative. If in doubt, ask the client to state his or her desired result in a positive way. Verbalizing is one of my favorite techniques, because it frequently helps the client to both feel and become more self-empowered.

Direct Suggestion

Charles Tebbetts almost always gave direct suggestion at the conclusion of any hypnotherapy session, even after he employed the use of uncovering techniques and/or parts therapy, etc. Even when he used indirect suggestions and/or Ericksonian metaphors, he still generally ended with some direct post-hypnotic suggestions.

As should be obvious to the reader by now, I discourage relying totally on the use of direct suggestion alone during a session unless the client's motivating desire is strong. Refer to Chapter 8 of *The Art of Hypnosis* (my first volume of this work) for more details on direct suggestion, as well as for indirect suggestion--which is briefly discussed next.

Indirect Suggestion

Although Mr. Tebbetts sometimes used indirect suggestion and metaphores, he usually did so in conjunction with other techniques; but he discouraged his students from relying *exclusively* on indirect suggestion. Refer to the second subsection of "Imagery" earlier in this chapter. I believe we should blend both types of suggestion in most sessions.

Important Advice from Charles Tebbetts

My former mentor believed that anyone with average intelligence and a sincere desire to help people could be trained in enough techniques to make a difference in the lives of many clients. He proved this over a period of many years at his Hypnotism Training Institute in Edmonds, Washington.

Even though he taught that hypnosis was not of and by itself harmful, he strongly believed that some techniques should only rarely be used, or not be used at all without written consent from an examining physician. He also felt somewhat critical of certain techniques that are popular with some therapists. Let's briefly discuss a few of them now.

What about aversion therapy?

Mr. Tebbetts almost never used aversion therapy (promoted in some books about hypnosis). He generally wanted people to imagine *results* rather than problems. Nonetheless, exceptions can occur.

On very rare occasions, if *all else fails,* a smoker could be given a suggestion to imagine the smell of a skunk when lighting up a cigarette--but there still is a risk that the "rebel button" could be pushed unless there is a strong motivating desire to quit smoking. I will always opt for the more considerate method first, using an aversion suggestion only if my client insists, or if all else fails. Then, in my opinion, the only discomfort should be in the *temporary* act of lighting up--with said discomfort leaving immediately upon putting out the cigarette.

Suggesting serious aversion is unwise. A stage hypnotist in Great Britain gave an aversion suggestion of 10,000 volts of electricity going through a woman--and she died several hours later. As of the first writing of this book, the courts were trying to determine whether the suggestion directly caused her death, because the family went after the hypnotist for a rather tidy sum.

Also, suggesting long term aversion as a consequence of failure is very unwise. In my opinion, those who ask smokers to imagine disease are making some potentially unwise choices! The mind is very powerful. What might happen to the person who indulges in imagining cancer and/or heart problems if he/she keeps on smoking??? I am most certainly not willing to take that risk.

There are many hypnotherapists who ask clients to imagine worms and maggots emerging from sweets, etc. In my opinion this is a very insensitive and inconsiderate method of breaking a sugar addiction. Such a suggestion tends to disempower the client, depriving him/her of free choice. I used to be addicted to ice cream--and I would resent anyone trying to make me sick when eating ice cream. (I've gone from a quart a night to a quart a month.) Let's get real, and realize that it is totally unrealistic for us to live the rest of our lives without ever having anything sweet to eat! What ever happened to balance and moderation? Even with smokers, there are some who simply do not choose to quit--and yet with determination and the help of hypnosis, it is possible for them to reduce greatly the amount they smoke. Why should we insist that they have only two choices--to quit totally or remain out of control? *Occasional smoking is an option* for some people!

On those rare instances where Charles Tebbetts used aversion therapy, it was only a small part of a lengthy session where he still found the cause. He still endeavored to obtain release and relearning, and to focus on the desired results. Let's accentuate the positive and eliminate the negative.

Pain control, headaches and symptom removal

Since stress often magnifies pain, the simple act of relaxing into hypnosis will often reduce one's pain without any suggestions other than relaxation. However, pain is a warning that something is wrong with the body--and it should not be removed or reduced by suggestion unless you have a written consent from the client's examining physician, or unless you are working under the direct supervision of the patient's physician. An exception is if you are a licensed physician working with your own patient.

For example, suppose you took it upon yourself to remove a client's headache--but the pain had actually been caused by a brain tumor or internal bleeding rather than stress. To say you were choosing unwisely would be putting it mildly! In the above scenario, if you had been asked to simply help your client deal with stress--and you had done so without discussing the headaches--the client might actually be *more* inclined to check out the source of the pain if the headaches still continued after dealing with the stress.

Charles Tebbetts discussed symptom removal with no uncertain words on page 43 of *Miracles on Demand:*

> *If a client comes to your office and asks you to cure his headache, unless you are a medical doctor, tell him you require a doctor's referral before you can help him...*
> *You are legally restricted from treating or diagnosing (in*

*most states), and with good reason. If the client happens
to have a brain tumor, the pain would be serving a
necessary purpose as a warning signal. If you relieve his
pain, or teach him to do so with self-hypnosis over a
period of weeks, the tumor might grow to a point where
it would become inoperable.*

Even when the physician has prescribed hypnosis for pain
removal, we still might want to proceed with more than just
direct suggestion alone. Read the words of Charles Tebbetts,
written on page 57 of *Miracles on Demand:*

*There are times that the client may have a subcon-
scious need for his pain. He may be punishing himself,
protecting himself or enjoying a secondary gain. In cases
such as this, removing the pain may cause the client to
become depressed, so uncovering is indicated. The hypnotherapist must convince the client's emotional mind
that the pain is no longer needed or deserved. Only after
he has agreed to give up the pain should it be removed....*

If in doubt as to how to begin (assuming the client has
the written referral), we may start with ideo-motor responses
and go through the seven psychodynamics of a symptom (see
Chapter 6). Once the cause has been uncovered and
released, appropriate suggestion can then be used to reduce
or remove the pain. Charles Tebbetts frequently accomplished this with the use of object projection or "White
Light Healing"--both of which are discussed in this chapter.

Disease or illness

The same cautions for pain control and/or symptom
removal apply here.

Once the cause has been uncovered and released (if
psychosomatic), indirect guided imagery and/or programmed
imagery may be used to help the client or patient. A hypnosis

tape might also be beneficial. Many different types of visualizations may be suggested, even if somewhat humorous or silly--as we are dealing with the subconscious rather than the conscious mind. For example, little pac-men in the blood stream may be imagined to consume invaders carrying illness, etc.; or a Star Trek teleporter could be transforming cancer cells into healthy cells. Whatever the patient finds emotionally appealing could be effective.

Dr. Bernie Siegel, M.D., has done some profound work in this area, and is an advocate of meditation and hypnosis for cancer patients. Any hypnotherapist interested in this field should read his book, *Love, Medicine & Miracles.*

Mr. Tebbetts also praised the work of Dr. Carl Simonton for his use of imagery to successfully work with cancer patients. Let me quote from *Miracles on Demand,* p. 38-39:

> *He asks the patient to picture and imagine millions of microscopic creatures in her blood stream, and to visualize the creatures attacking and destroying the cancer. To help him visualize creatures more clearly, he asks them to sketch a picture of one of them. The patient may choose tiny white knights cutting the cancer with swords, white sharks biting chunks out of it, or an attack by any other predator they choose. Here is a case of a medical doctor thinking beyond the scope of his training and realizing that mental processes can both cause and cure disease. This is one of the principles of hypnotherapy, and visualization is one of the techniques of hypnotherapy.*

In addition to the above, one of my former students has used hypnotherapy with an AIDS patient to help him improve his life style. I met him in 1993, and he looked as healthy as any of us. (There is more about this in Chapter 17 under the chapter section on medical applications of hypnosis.) Hypnotherapy techniques apparently gave this man several additional years of life.

Thank God that increasing numbers of physicians and psychologists are accepting the artistic hypnotherapy community. It is my hope that many more profound benefits of hypnosis will yet be discovered through an increasing cooperation between the scientific community and the artistic hypnosis professionals. There are too many diseases with too little hope for too many people. Let's find a way to work together and create a multiple win for a society that is in desperate need of healing! But let the healers be trained adequately, and experientially qualified. Those of us utilizing the art of hypnotherapy must do our best to increase our competency--especially when working with people who have disease or illness.

White Light Healing Technique

When Charles Tebbetts facilitated a medical application of hypnosis for pain control or disease, he often used what he called the *white light technique.* Let him describe it in his own words (*Miracles on Demand,* p. 59):

> *I follow pain relief with the white light technique. I had used this method before, but I have Paul Stevens to thank for liquefying it. He calls it the brilliant, healing, liquid white light. An example of my use of this method to accelerate the cure of a lung cancer patient follows: I first obtained a medical doctor's permission to use hypnotism in conjunction with his chemotherapy. I asked the hypnotized patient to open her eyes and to stare into mine, and then proceeded with, "Keep staring, deeply and intently into my eyes. I am now transferring my energy into your body. It is entering your head rapidly now. It is combining with your energy and growing more powerful with every second that passes. It is beginning to*

GLOW. Now close your eyes and feel it. Your head is glowing in a brilliant white light. Now allow the energy field that surrounds your body to move up into your head. This forceful combination of my energy, your energy and the force field from around your body melts into a brilliant, glowing, liquid white light. It is now surrounding and bathing every tiny cell in your head, every molecule and every atom. FEEL it as its powerful energy moves down into your neck now. Your entire head and neck are glowing brightly as they are being bathed in this brilliant, liquid white light... Your normal cells are now HAPPY CELLS, and any cells that come in to replace those the white light eliminates are also happy cells."

He goes on to move this white light down throughout the body, wherever required or desired, ending with suggestions that the client feel wonderful and be the normal person that nature intended.

If--and ONLY if--you know that the client believes in God, you may add words such as: *"This liquid white light comes from the river of living waters. Take all the healing energy desired or required. The supply comes from God and is limitless."*

Past Life Therapy

Although Charles Tebbetts neither encouraged nor discouraged the use of past life regressions, nor admitted publicly whether or not he believed in them, he felt that a client's request and belief system should be respected by the therapist. With that in mind, he sometimes facilitated past life regressions when asked to do so. He also dealt with the occasional spontaneous regression into a real or imagined past life (which can sometimes be triggered by use of the feeling connection). Because of the increasing interest, Chapter 13 is devoted entirely to this topic--with various theories to explain what may or may not be taking place.

Other Cautions

Some students have the impression that Mr. Tebbetts discouraged the use of any techniques other than those he taught. Even though he taught enough of a variety to help most of the people most of the time, he was willing to consider the validity of any technique that provided benefit without risk. I proved this myself by developing and teaching the benefits approach, which he later praised.

There are some techniques that he expressed concerns about--such as those discussed earlier in this chapter. Let me discuss a few more.

Exclusive use of one technique

Charles Tebbetts frequently expressed concern about those who felt that one particular technique or style of therapy was the only appropriate one to use--as was evidenced by his criticism of those whom he believed to be locked into the use of only indirect suggestion, reframing and/or N.L.P. techniques. Trying to fit the client to the therapy technique could easily result in lack of success, as has been evidenced in some of my own past sessions when hypnotherapists have tried to fit me to their techniques.

No matter how effective a technique might be to some people (or even to most people), there will always be a few who resist. It's unfortunate that some therapists perceive this resistance as a lack of willingness to change rather than recognizing it as the result of therapist-centered hypnosis. Some therapists, however, seem to have the opinion that they can manipulate any client into responding to the therapist's own pet technique. A hypnotherapist who studied hypnosis under the guidance of a Ph.D. informed me that her instructor said (and I quote): *"I believe that given enough time I can make you do anything I want you to do."* Can you believe this was actually said by a Ph.D. to a hypnotherapy class?

Guru consciousness

Mr. Tebbetts also discouraged getting locked into only those techniques taught by one person. (Perhaps this is one reason why he encouraged me to be open to learning new techniques after finishing his training course!)

The flip side is that some people good at marketing are often promoting a new or unique technique that is represented as so profound that it will work with almost anyone. Some hypnotherapists are tempted to look up to a teacher of these "profound" methods as a guru--and could make the mistake of discarding other proven techniques.

Charlie believed that we should grow beyond the *guru* consciousness, and I agree totally. So allow me to grow beyond what he taught me by saying: *if a technique benefits the client without harm--and you would be comfortable in a role reversal--use it, even if it is your own creation.* Just make certain you have the client's welfare at heart, and that you are not taking any unnecessary risks to your client's physical, emotional or financial health.

Be willing to use common sense and choose those techniques that are best suited to your clients rather than trying to lock them into one or two techniques that you've mastered. In other words, let's fit the technique to the client instead of vice versa, and do *client-centered hypnotherapy*. Also, if you want your former instructor's opinion on a new or unique technique that someone is promoting, accept it as just that-- an *opinion*. If he/she discourages the technique without giving you an obvious valid reason, seek another professional opinion. Once you've determined a technique to be beneficial to a client, feel free to use it...but not exclusively. This advice also applies to my own students who are reading this book. I'm still learning.

Exclusive use of cognitive therapy

Charles Tebbetts was very critical (perhaps overly so) of those who were locked into psychological techniques used only on the cognitive level. For example, though he frequently used Gestalt therapy along with other techniques, he frowned on its use outside the trance state. (I do not share this last opinion, as I believe that people could easily enter a spontaneous trance state while participating in Gestalt therapy.)

My former teacher believed that incorporating hypnotherapy into the practice of traditional counseling could greatly accelerate the benefits to the client; thus, he held a very low opinion of any professional who opposed the use of hypnotherapy. Being competently trained in hypnotherapy expands the counselor's ability to help clients.

An even greater risk of exclusive cognitive therapy is the unintentional misuse of spontaneous trance by a therapist who is not trained in the art of hypnosis. Even when the therapist has no intention of using hypnosis, there still is the potential of a client entering spontaneous hypnotic trance. What happens then? If the therapist is trained in the art of hypnotherapy, this could be very beneficial. Even with only training in basic hypnosis, the therapist could effectively give a few calming suggestions and awaken the client before continuing cognitive counseling. But if the trance state is not recognized, there could be a real problem...

Danger of unrecognized trance

I must conclude this chapter with a warning to ministers, counselors and psychologists who have not been adequately trained in the art of hypnosis: *learn how to recognize and facilitate the trance state.*

Just because formal "hypnotherapy" is not agreed upon by therapist and client does not mean that a person is immune to entering a hypnotic trance during a session. Remember that all hypnosis is self-hypnosis, whether or not it is recognized. Anyone seeking help may easily slip into the state of hypnosis while talking to a minister, psychotherapist, or other professional. Once this happens, the cognitive mind takes a back seat while the subconscious, the seat of imagination and emotions, opens up. When this occurs, it becomes very important *what* is said as well as *how* it is said!

For example, discussing problems from childhood--or even a troubled marriage--could trigger a spontaneous trance. If a person starts having an emotional discharge, there is a very high likelihood of spontaneous trance. At such times, the client is very vulnerable to what is spoken, and the words of the therapist may go right into the subconscious. Also, a client with guilt or shame could verbalize some very negative statements about himself or herself, subconsciously reinforcing the problem! If this happens, the therapist needs to know more than just cognitive counseling; because if desensitization, release and/or relearning is not facilitated while the person is still in the state of hypnosis, it actually may become much more difficult for the person to change.

Even *trained hypnotherapists* should realize that a client may actually enter the state of hypnosis before a formal induction begins--especially if it is not the first session. One of my hypnotherapy students, a family counselor with a masters degree, voiced the opinion to other students in the classroom that learning to recognize the hypnotic state has helped her tremendously in sessions with her clients, because she chooses her words more wisely when she recognizes a probable spontaneous trance.

Another one of my hypnotherapy students was abused by

her former husband. While in a psychotherapist's office (trying to rebuild her life), she tripped out into a spontaneous trance state and was criticized during trance. She was told by the therapist that she was *caught in the victim trap* and obviously must have attracted an abuser into her life because of her low self-esteem. All this did was compound the guilt which she already had, making it more difficult for her to heal. She informed the class that before her marriage, she had been a successful salesperson with a good self-esteem; and that her husband, a wealthy man in the business world, slowly tore down her self-esteem through both verbal and physical abuse over a period of years. She had no idea what she was getting into until after it was too late, as her husband had gradually turned up the intensity of manipulation and abuse over a period of several years. Negative comments from another professional made this woman's path even more difficult.

Therapists who work exclusively at a cognitive level would do both themselves and their clients a service by seeking enough training in hypnosis at least to learn how to detect the spontaneous hypnotic trance. With adequate training, release and/or relearning can be more easily facilitated. Even with minimal training, a few positive suggestions followed by appropriate awakening could help the client be more receptive to help presented at a cognitive level.

There is also the danger of false memories being planted because of the therapist asking leading questions rather than guiding ones if the client enters a spontaneous hypnotic trance. Be sure to read the chapter section entitled "Guiding vs. Leading" in Chapter 7 if you've not yet done so.

In my opinion there is a far greater risk in the unrecognized trance state than in any real or imagined risk of experiencing hypnotic trance with a trained hypnotherapist who is well aware of the state of mind the client is experiencing. Also, I believe the hypnotized person is safer in the office of a love-centered (and *competently trained*) certified hypnotherapist with only a bachelor's degree or less, where both parties know hypnosis is taking place, than the person tranced out in the office of a highly educated traditional therapist who fails to recognize the state of hypnosis.

Unfortunately, most professionals who should read this chapter subsection probably will never even see this book. Perhaps you might recommend it to other professionals. Meanwhile, let's move into the next chapter.

Chapter 10

Phobias

According to *Webster's New World Dictionary*, the definition of a phobia is an *irrational, excessive and persistent fear of some particular thing or situation.* Some people, for example, are afraid of elevators even though they may tell themselves with the logical mind that they are safe. Others are afraid of flying, etc., etc., and the fear persists in spite of whatever logical reasoning is used.

As with so many other problems that are seated in the subconscious, hypnosis can help release phobias more easily since it deals with the subconscious. But before you read any further, be aware that many psychologists consider treating phobias to be part of the practice of psychology. Some states may restrict you from working with phobias unless you are either already licensed in another health profession to do so, or unless you have a professional referral from someone so licensed. But suppose you can legally work with phobias, or have a client with a written referral--now what?

Charles Tebbetts taught that most phobias generally can be traced back to an original *sensitizing event* and one *activating event*--which activates the phobia. These may be either two separate occurrences or one single event. The therapist's objective is to uncover the cause(s) and desensitize the client from the phobia through use of appropriate techniques. This sounds simple enough--and indeed it is in many cases--however, some phobias are more complex. Let me explain.

Just as no two people are identical, the same is also true for phobias. There are two basic types: *simple* and *complex*.

Simple Phobias

Simple phobias are those which seem to be isolated to themselves, such as a fear of cats but not dogs or other animals--or fear of elevators, flying, bridges, etc. Often one session is sufficient for total release from a simple phobia. In 1984 I saw a woman only *once* for fear of flying, and used the techniques taught by my mentor. In December of 1993 I bumped into her at a public place, and she told me that her success was permanent, and that she had flown over a third of a million miles since!

A simple phobia usually has only one basic sensitivity that is easy to identify, even though there may be several events that have compounded that sensitivity. It is the problem itself rather than the symptom of other unresolved problems. Some people may prefer to call a simple phobia an *anxiety*.

Complex Phobias

Complex phobias are those which are multi-faceted, such as fear of going out in public, fear of the opposite sex, etc. These may have been *activated* by a single event; however, the phobia itself is usually not the real problem--but, rather, a symptom of one or more other unresolved issues. There may be emotional energy tied to different circumstances not directly related to the phobia--such as low self-esteem being linked to fear of going out in public, which could have been further compounded by an abusive parent or abusive relationship, etc., etc. In order to completely clear a complex phobia, the intertwined emotional issues usually must also be resolved--whether through hypnotherapy, psychotherapy, psychological help, marriage counseling, pastoral counseling, legal counseling, etc., or a combination of the above.

A woman who saw me several years ago for agoraphobia had her first public panic attack several months earlier at the Tacoma Mall (a shopping center about 30 miles south of

Seattle). From that time on, she experienced an increasing fear of going out in public. Although three sessions helped her achieve partial relief, her own subconscious revealed that unresolved marital issues had caused the anxiety which triggered the phobia. She needed other professional help. She still appreciated the partial relief as well as the awareness of what had actually caused the phobia. Another woman who was afraid of going out in public was a woman living with an abusive alcoholic. Although I gave her a free consultation, I did not feel that I was qualified to work with her issues, so I referred her elsewhere. I rarely work with complex phobias; and when there is an exception, the client is advised of the potential need for additional professional help.

The information presented in this chapter is written primarily for the hypnotherapist working with simple phobias; but it may also be useful for the professional working with clients or patients who have complex phobias.

Sensitizing Event(s)

An occurrence making one sensitive to certain situations is a *sensitizing event.* One such event may not necessarily cause a phobia of and by itself--but could be one of a series of similar situations that make a person more sensitive to whatever is disliked. For example, a bad fall might make a child sensitive to falling, but not necessarily leave a permanent phobia of heights even though the sensitivity remains. The relationship to the actual phobia might not appear logical (as in the example described on page 162). Furthermore, there may have been additional sensitizing events before and/or after the event that activates the phobia.

In regression therapy, a client may need to go back to the first sensitizing event and/or the most traumatic. (Some hypnotherapists use other terminology, such as the primary cause, or the primal cause, the original anchor, etc.) Usually the feeling connection provides the best likelihood of uncovering the original or most relevant sensitizing event--although age regression can also be used, especially if we already know which event(s) to explore. Charles Tebbetts recommended implosive desensitization (or *circle therapy*) as the technique with the best probability of success, followed by the informed child technique and Gestalt to facilitate release and/or verbalizing for subconscious relearning. (See the chapter section: "Potential Therapy Techniques.")

More than one session might be required in some instances, depending on the particular phobia and its relevant causes. Furthermore, remember to ask the client's subconscious which event activated the phobia if it is not obvious.

Activating Event

The *activating event* is the occurrence which activated the phobia. This may be the original sensitizing event, or a situation that happened several years after the first sensitizing event (*Miracles on Demand*, p24).

One case that took place in my teacher's classroom at Edmonds involved a hypnotherapy student who had an abnormal fear of heights. The sensitivity to heights began during pre-school age when he fell off the edge of a flight of stairs; yet the phobia was not activated until several years later when he was looking off the edge of a skyscraper while his mother got him scared about what would happen if there was an earthquake at that moment in time. The student had remembered one of the events consciously, but not both of them--however, his *subconscious* knew!

Now let's discuss how Mr. Tebbetts handled phobias...

Handling the Pre-induction Interview

Besides the normal procedures and information-gathering, we may ask the client to describe when the fear or anxiety first developed. In this manner, we just might discover the main sensitizing event(s) and/or the activating event before beginning hypnotherapy. When sufficient information is gathered, we should determine which therapy techniques to use--and then be ready to change techniques if necessary.

If planning any programmed imagery during the session, it would be very wise to discover whether the client is visual or non-visual, auditory and/or kinesthetic. Furthermore, we might wish to ask the *client* to describe his or her ideal peaceful place; as it would be very wise to anchor the safe place into the subconscious before beginning the regression. In addition to the above, it would be an excellent idea to ask whether there are any *other* phobias or strong dislikes. For example, we would NOT want to incorporate imagery of a forest if someone were afraid of the woods!

Although I normally do not use hypnotic regressions on a client's first session, a phobia is an exception since the simple ones can often be cleared with regression therapy in only one or two sessions. Before proceeding, however, I believe it is appropriate to provide my client with a brief explanation of hypnotic regressions (refer to Chapter 7 under the chapter section, "Client Preparation").

When the relevant information is gathered, and the client is informed and prepared for hypnosis (as well as the planned hypnotherapeutic technique), the next step is to spend enough time inducing and deepening the hypnotic trance <u>to at least a medium level</u> before proceeding with therapy. Deeper levels reduce risk of conscious interference.

Potential Therapy Techniques for Phobias

These techniques taught by Charles Tebbetts should be sufficient for most simple phobias, and may also be helpful even for some of the more complex ones. The numbered techniques are shown in the order he usually employed them. If you have not read Chapter 7, please do so before reading further--as a thorough understanding of regression therapy is essential for competent use of most of these techniques.

1. Hypnotic regression

This was my mentor's first choice for phobias.

We may use whatever regression techniques are appropriate to discover the activating event and the main sensitizing event(s) if not already determined during the pre-induction interview. Often the *feeling connection* will take the client to the appropriate event if one of the other techniques fails to do so--and this will often work even in light trance. (The feeling connection is described in Chapter 6.) It is not necessary to use the same technique for uncovering both the original sensitizing event and the activating event. Besides, the client can often move forward or backward in time to different events during the same regression.

2. Implosive desensitization

This technique (described in Chapter 7) virtually always follows the feeling connection, and has a high success rate. Even a regression to a specific event could lead to the use of implosive desensitization unless there is no abreaction. If the subconscious resists regressing to the appropriate event(s), use another technique.

After the initial abreaction begins to subside, remember to take the client to a happy or safe place. This may be done several times if desired. (Some professionals call this *circle therapy*.) The therapist may now utilize the next technique.

3. The informed child technique

Taking the client back through the scene a second time with all his/her present adult awareness, knowledge, wisdom, understanding and experience facilitates desensitization during regression therapy. Additional information about this technique can be found in Chapter 7 in the subsection: *Desensitizing ("informed child" technique)*.

4. Rewriting history (reframing)

The first part of this technique has already taken place when the informed child technique is used. Even though the conscious mind knows that something happened one way, imagining that it happened a different way makes it possible to facilitate both release and relearning.

The second part of this technique can be accomplished with Gestalt therapy or role-playing to allow the client to say what he/she would like to have said to the person who caused the hurt in the first place. Some hypnotherapists have even had a client role-play being the *dog* or the *bridge,* etc.

Sometimes the Gestalt may be skipped. After a client "rewrites history" with the informed child technique, the event may simply be reframed by the client in his/her imagination easily while regressing as the "informed child." Verbalizing should follow afterwards.

One way of facilitating this process is to ask a question such as:

Tell me how the ADULT in you would like this situation handled... ?

Although this technique incorporates creating a false memory at a subconscious level, the purpose is for release and relearning--*not for laying blame!* (Any hypnotherapist, psychotherapist, or professional who "rewrites history" in a way that makes a client fantasize physical or sexual abuse that never took place could end up facing the consequences in a court of law if said client blames his or her family for something that never happened.) Remember that the client is seeking hypnotherapy to *release* a problem--not to compound it. Too many people justify hanging onto their problems by constantly blaming others instead of forgiving and releasing--and getting on with life. Let's use the *rewriting history* technique wisely!

When appropriate, we may also use one or more of the additional techniques described in this chapter section, such as open screen imagery...

5. Open screen imagery

An optional substitute for the first four techniques described in this chapter section is the use of open screen imagery with silent abreaction for reframing (refer to pages 124-125, and 132-134).

Once the client has seen the movie of his/her relevant event(s), then suggest that the script be rewritten (or reframed), and then continue with verbalizing. If the client does not wish to verbalize, then we also have the option of indirect guided imagery (also discussed in Chapter 9).

6. Verbalizing

Whether or not Gestalt therapy is used, *verbalizing* is a very client-centered way of getting the mind to work out its own resolutions (see pages 134-136).

Why is this better than simply giving post-hypnotic suggestion alone? Perhaps any trained salesperson can verify that a person is far more apt to buy a product or service if the customer tells the sales clerk what he/she wants rather than the other way around! When a person tells himself or herself during the trance state what the new understanding should be, this provides an excellent opportunity for *relearning*-- which further opens the door of receptivity for appropriate post-hypnotic suggestions.

Again, listen carefully to what the client verbalizes. Frequently the client's own verbalized advice will likely have good results. If you have serious cause to doubt the wisdom of what is verbalized (other than during the Gestalt portion of therapy), then suggest that it be discussed at a conscious level first. Also, as stated in Chapter 9, get a second opinion or refer the client to other professional help if appropriate.

What kind of verbalizing might be unwise? If a client said he/she would commit an act of violence as a solution, any hypnotherapist would be foolish to allow that idea to remain. In all my years of hypnotherapy, not one of my clients has ever made such a foolish statement other than during the Gestalt portion of therapy--and with the right questions on my part, the client has always been able to verbalize a better solution. Do NOT allow the fantasy of violence to persist.

7. Use direct suggestion as applicable

Repeating and/or rephrasing what the client verbalizes adds more power in many cases.

If the client tends to respond well to direct suggestion, then whatever affirmations and/or new understandings were verbalized may be repeated back to the client as spoken, but in the second-person format. If the client tends to respond better to more permissive techniques, then whatever was verbalized can be paraphrased and spoken by the therapist, mixing both direct and indirect suggestions.

Once the appropriate suggestions are given, we may wish to confirm subconscious acceptance with an ideo-motor response--and also to confirm release of the phobia itself.

8. Indirect guided imagery

If metaphors are to be used, it might be a good idea to have a script or story prepared in advance that would be applicable--unless you are an excellent story teller. Indirect guided imagery alone with scripting may work in some instances--provided you are using a well-written script and your client is responsive.

Dr. Arthur Winkler has written some scripts blending both direct and indirect suggestion together for a variety of problems, including phobias. They are contained in a book entitled *Hypnotic Inductions and Prescriptions* (by Arthur E. Winkler, Ph.D.), and can be purchased from St. John's University in Louisiana. The book of scripts will only be sold to certified hypnotherapists, or hypnotherapy students who have completed half of their training. It is well worth the investment. The telephone number is (225) 294-2129.

9. Systematic desensitization

Although a more gentle approach, Charles Tebbetts felt that systematic desensitization may not be as quick or effective as implosive desensitization; however it is an acceptable alternative if there is a reason to avoid regression therapy. (This is described in Chapter 9.) It may be more helpful with anxieties than with phobias.

One of my students (who does professional counseling) contacted a hypnotherapist several years ago about a phobia. She told the class that when systematic desensitization was described on the telephone, she imagined her fear, started crying, and hung up immediately. This is an emphatic example showing that systematic desensitization will not work for everyone; and in her case, I had to use age regression and implosive desensitization to facilitate release.

About the only time I use systematic desensitization as a first choice is with people who have a fear of speaking in public (usually this would be considered an anxiety rather than a phobia). Since I have professional speaking experience, and have been a member of National Speakers Association for several years, I feel qualified to add the element of some cognitive counseling on certain techniques to improve public speaking skills. It is my opinion, however, that a hypnotherapist who is also afraid to speak in public might have a more difficult time working with a client wishing to overcome this problem.

10. Positive programmed imagery

Positive programmed imagery can be used prior to awakening to have a client imagine himself/herself comfortable in a situation where there might once have been a phobia--and to move a hand or finger when this is done.

Used alone, this technique might be wasting the client's time and money; but after the use of other appropriate techniques, programmed imagery can be intertwined with post-hypnotic suggestion and verbalizing. For example, once the cause of a fear of flying has been removed, the client can be asked to imagine getting on an airplane and being seated. Then he/she can be given a post-hypnotic suggestion to take a deep breath and feel comfortable as the plane takes off, etc., and indicate by ideo-motor response when the subconscious accepts this. Programmed imagery is also a *must* when using systematic desensitization--as it *makes the process work.*

Now What?

Even though many simple phobias can be cleared in only one or two sessions, we should put ourselves in the client's shoes by leaving the door open for additional assistance if desired or required. One of my clients felt guilty because another hypnotherapist said he could "fix" his problem in only one session--and he felt like he had failed because the hypnotic "quick fix" didn't work. We should be careful to avoid the other extreme as well, as it would be inconsiderate to make a client come back repeatedly when not necessary.

Remember that a person emerging from trance is still very responsive to suggestions for the first few minutes--so we need to choose our words carefully and plant seeds of confidence. A seemingly innocent statement such as, "Now don't get scared spitless next time you fly!" could initiate the wrong image in a subconscious mind that is still very open to suggestions. Remember that many clients, even after emerging from hypnosis, will still be very susceptible to suggestions spoken by the therapist. Keep the words positive. Again, let's say what we would want said if the roles were reversed.

Also remember that the original sensitizing event may not appear to have a logical relationship to the phobia. A woman I saw only once had a fear of birds, which several psychologists and other hypnotherapists had failed to clear. Those who used regression therapy kept looking for past encounters with birds; but the *original sensitizing event* involved an emotional encounter with her parents, who would not allow her to cry when she was scared of moving to the big city. The activating event took place over a year later when her mother yelled at her for stepping on a dead bird, at which time there was transference. The bird now became a symbol for her fears. Through the feeling connection, her subconscious finally made the connection that others had failed to obtain. After forgiving her parents, she changed the symbol for birds from fear to confidence and freedom!

Glossary

Charles Tebbetts usually gave his students a glossary of common phobias; and that's a good place to end this chapter. Even today I still provide my students a piece of hypnosis history by photocopying that 1983 handout from the Charles Tebbetts Hypnotism Training Institute with my former teacher's letterhead at the top. If it were reproduced in this book, the print would be too small to read--however, in order to preserve some additional Tebbetts training history, I've plugged the definitions into my computer exactly as he wrote them. I've added asterisks, however, by those phobias which I believe are more likely to be complex rather than simple--but remember, there could be exceptions either way.

Here is a partial *Glossary of Phobias* as distributed by Charles Tebbetts at his hypnotism training institute in Edmonds, Washington:

Phobia	Fear of:
acrophobia	heights
*agoraphobia	open places
aichmophobia	sharp objects
ailurophobia	cats
*algophobia	pain
*androphobia	men
bacteriophobia	germs
ballistophobia	missiles
belonephobia	needles, pins
claustrophobia	confined spaces
cynophobia	dogs
dipsophobia	drink
erythrophobia	blushing
*genophobia	sex
*gymnophobia	nakedness
hemophobia	blood
hypnophobia	falling asleep
*lalophobia	talking
*lyssophobia	becoming insane
melissophobia	bees
mysophobia	dirt, contamination
*ochlophobia	crowds
osmophobia	odors
*pedophobia	children
photophobia	light
pyrophobia	fire
siderodromophobia	railroads
*sitophobia	eating
tocophobia	childbirth
triskaidekaphobia.	number 13
*xenophobia	strangers

* Asterisk = probable complex phobia

Chapter 11

Putting It Together

How did Charles Tebbetts use the tools he taught?

He frequently changed from one technique to another when the client failed to respond to the first one--and he combined several in the same session masterfully. Once again, this is because he believed that we should fit the technique to the client rather than the other way around. (And since he also believed that repetition is an excellent form of emphasis, that last statement has been intentionally threaded throughout this book.)

This chapter will overview some actual case histories that were videotaped by my mentor and made available for student learning. Except where noted, the names have been changed. Some (but not all) were written about in *Miracles on Demand*--which is why detailed scripts are omitted. (Chapter 12 is devoted exclusively to the case of Scott, who has given permission for details to be printed in this book.) To simplify reading the case history reviews, every reference to Charles Tebbetts in his chapter section will be with the italicized letters, *CT* (except for the first paragraph).

Also included in separate chapter sections are a few examples of therapies done by my own students, as well as samples of some of my own successes.

Successes Facilitated by Charles Tebbetts

Let's begin with some of my mentor's successes...

Harry--a multi-faceted approach

Harry was a retired law-enforcement officer changing careers who wanted hypnotherapy from Mr. Tebbetts for anxiety, violent headaches, insomnia and claustrophobia.

Shortly into the session, *CT* uncovered the cause of the headaches--a form of self-punishment. Through parts therapy, a part of Harry called "Power Plant" revealed that it was producing the headaches to get Harry to stop working too hard and quit worrying. This part of his mind complained that Harry even spent time in bed at night thinking about more ways to earn more money.

The part of Harry that wanted more money agreed to slow down. He made an agreement with himself to set aside only certain times daily for planning and devote *only the designated time* to the concern about increasing his financial earnings rather than worrying about it in bed. When this agreement was made, "Power Plant" agreed to stop causing the headaches and feelings of anxiety. And by not spending time in bed worrying about money, he would be able to sleep better.

After completing a successful parts therapy, *CT* integrated the parts and dealt with Harry's claustrophobia with age regression back to a specific event that had been revealed during the pre-induction interview. Harry re-lived having his brother lock him in the closet--first as it happened, and then with the informed child technique to desensitize and rewrite history. Another event involving his sister was also relived in regression therapy. *CT* concluded with both programmed imagery and appropriate post-hypnotic suggestions, telling Harry that he would integrate into a happy, wonderful individual.

Over a year later, Harry mailed a letter thanking Charles Tebbetts for the successful hypnotherapy. I'll quote just two sentences of his letter--which was printed on page 303 of *Miracles on Demand:*

> *After years of suffering, numerous medications and doctor-recommended prescriptions which failed, I am now virtually headache-free with hypnosis. I practice self-hypnosis daily and find that I cannot only control headaches but improve many other facets of my life.*

Grief therapy

Ruth felt guilty for loving her grandfather more than her perfectionist father. Her guilt and loneliness for the loss of her grandfather caused her to partly blame herself when her husband had been arrested for molesting children, causing her to be depressed.

CT began with Gestalt just moments into Ruth's trance state, having her dialogue with her father. This helped her accept her father while telling him that she was living her own life now. She told him she would continue to listen, yet she emphasized that she has the right to make mistakes--because we learn from them. She thanked him for the love, and said she was now taking responsibility for her own life.

With this resolution, *CT* used age regression to the last time Ruth saw her grandfather. He had died without her being there. *CT* used the re-writing history technique to let her say goodbye to her grandfather, and allowed her to abreact at his parting. *CT* concluded this portion of the therapy with the suggestion that her grandfather's memory would make her even more capable of living, because a wonderful person can have a great influence on a life. (This is a powerful way to help a client release grief from the loss of a loved one.)

Finally *CT* utilized parts therapy to resolve Ruth's other issues, calling out "Happy" and "Ugly" for facilitated self-dialogue. "Ugly" said that Ruth had always blamed herself whenever something went wrong around her. Those two parts could function in harmony if Ruth would let go of her guilt and dump most of her negative emotions.

Changing techniques in mid-trance

CT attempted to use parts therapy to help Mary resolve an apparent inner conflict about being overweight; but the subconscious resisted and tried to keep the cause hidden. He changed techniques, using age regression to uncover past traumatic events--including past sexual abuse. In another session, Mary was regressed again with the *informed child* technique, incorporating Gestalt therapy to facilitate release. She was allowed to rewrite the script at a subconscious level, and *CT* finished hypnotherapy with the use of direct suggestion.

Past life digression

When *CT* used simple age regression to help Carol go back to the origin of her health problem, she digressed from the present life--and unexpectedly tripped out into a real or imagined *past* life. Her mother in that apparent lifetime was crippled; and to make matters worse, Carol abreacted through fear as her uncle supposedly killed her while she was only three.

CT moved Carol forward into being three years old during her present life. During trance, she stated that her health problem originated at that age rather than years later when diagnosed. Her subconscious, however, would neither reveal why she went back into another lifetime, nor what the connection was between that life and the present one. Somewhat perplexed, *CT* deepened and used ideo-motor responding to try to uncover the cause. When this also failed, he asked if her subconscious would reveal how she could be released from the cause--and got a positive finger response.

Through verbalizing, Carol expressed a need to visualize both the problem and the solution while hypnotized--which *CT* allowed her to do. After imagery for perfect health, she verbalized her relearning process, including some steps that she had to take to restore her health. The session concluded with *CT* giving her post-hypnotic suggestions for confidence to make wise decisions about her health and life. Thus, here was a session that was successful even though the subconscious did not directly reveal the cause of the problem. This also demonstrates that sometimes a session can still succeed even if one of the four hypnotherapeutic steps is missing; however, my mentor usually attempted all four steps.

Increased learning ability

Brent kept postponing taking an exam because of test anxiety, and asked Mr. Tebbetts to help him through hypnotherapy. Regression therapy was my mentor's starting technique in this particular case.

CT regressed Brent back to the first time he had the feeling of being a "dumb" person, and he went back to a time in school with his 2nd grade teacher. He was scared of being scolded for having difficulty with the alphabet. When it became apparent that there was more to this event, *CT* took him back to the first time he was ever scolded--and he went back to the day of his birth! His arm was twisted in the birth canal, and the doctor wanted to break his arm to get him out. He abreacted as he relived having his head pinched, and this rude introduction into the world had apparently left him scarred at a subconscious level for many years.

Brent was allowed to re-experience both these events with the informed child technique in order to facilitate new understanding at a subconscious level. Verbalizing helped with this process, as he now realized that the doctor was doing what needed to be done. Finally, guided imagery and post-hypnotic suggestions capped what proved to be a successful therapy session.

Stuttering

Bill had gone to several psychologists over a period of several years, but still stuttered. Consciously he knew what had caused the problem, yet his subconscious was still stuck in old patterns. *CT* regressed Bill back to childhood encounters with strict parenting. Use of the *informed child* technique coupled with *Gestalt* and *verbalizing* helped him with both release and relearning, and I have a videotape showing this man speaking without stuttering!

It's interesting to note that stutterers speak clearly while experiencing the trance state.

A Few of My Successes

Nothing speaks louder than results; and though many clients leave my office and never see or call me again, some have written or called with some encouraging feedback. Chapter 8 includes a few involving the use of parts therapy. Here is a sampling of some of the others (with names changed):

Biting fingernails

Laura wanted to stop biting her nails. In her first session I wanted her to enjoy hypnosis, so I helped her with stress management. For this, I simply used both open screen imagery and indirect guided imagery to help her create a safe place, and employed the use of both indirect and direct suggestion. Regression therapy was the primary technique for another session, with age regression back to when and why she first began biting her nails. The informed child technique helped her rewrite her subconscious script, along with release and relearning through Gestalt and verbalizing. (She had to forgive her parents for being strict--and the informed child technique, followed with Gestalt therapy, had helped her understand that they did the best they could.)

Some additional work was done with self-esteem, including open screen imagery and programmed imagery for attractive fingernails--followed by direct suggestions for touching her thumb and finger together briefly as a replacement for nailbiting (remember anchoring and triggers). A year later she saw me personally to show me her long, natural nails!

Claustrophobia

Andy was a hypnotherapy student who asked me to work with him during my class discussion of phobias. He felt panic attacks whenever he got enclosed in tight spaces, and was going to have a medical test that he knew would activate his claustrophobia. He could not consciously remember the sensitizing event, so I used the *feeling connection* to uncover it. He went right back to a time as a small child being bullied by an older brother who kept him trapped inside a box. After implosive desensitization, I guided him back into the event as the informed child, allowing him to dialogue with his older brother through Gestalt therapy to facilitate release and relearning. It turned out that this one event was both the sensitizing and activating event--and the phobia was cleared. The following month he reported to the class that he had simply used self-hypnosis to go to his safe place during the medical test, and got through it just fine.

Enjoying the benefits of quitting smoking

Carol had tried for years to quit smoking; yet while other programs failed, she found the benefits approach sufficient to help her go the distance. She really wanted to get her energy back again. Eighteen months later she mailed me a postcard from Hawaii, where she was enjoying the tropical beaches of Paradise (inviting me to show the card to clients). This was her reward to herself for finally enjoying success as a non-smoker. Guess how she financed her trip!

Resistance to smoking cessation

Donna saw me for smoking cessation, yet failed to respond to the benefits approach. She said she had an inner conflict about smoking--a part of her wanted to smoke continuously while another part of her wanted to stop totally. When she failed to respond to parts therapy, I used ideomotor responding, only to discover that she smoked because she enjoyed it. Upon changing to verbalizing, she stated that she really did not want to quit totally, and was only being manipulated into quitting. She added that her subconscious would cooperate as a controlled smoker lighting up only occasionally. After bringing her out of hypnosis and discussing this at length, I gave her some guidelines on how to maintain conscious control to keep smoking at a minimum--including always keeping cigarettes out of arm's reach so that she would have to make a conscious choice before lighting up. Her subconscious confirmed acceptance of this when I re-hypnotized her, so I concluded the session with programmed imagery and direct suggestion to take one deep breath at the times she used to light up automatically. She was happy with this outcome, reducing to less than a dozen daily, and said she might quit totally in a year or two. (Other smokers have been able to cut down to only six to ten cigarettes daily as well when they were not ready to quit completely.)

Record sales after hypnotic motivation

Tami (her real name) saw me only three times for sales motivation via the benefits approach, motivation mapping, and stress management. Here is what she wrote to me six months later:

I broke the all-time company record for highest sales volume in a single month in November, ending up at 245% of Quota. I also am top sales representative for the first 7 months of our fiscal year.

She went on to become a sales manager, and eventually became a district manager. Several years later she became product manager for the entire company.

Additional business motivation

Another sales motivation program for a business owner in 1990 involved the benefits approach, motivation mapping, and stress management. Less than two months later he mailed me a letter describing his success:

Not only do I feel less tension, but my self-confidence is greatly improved after just three sessions of hypnosis... The business techniques and assertiveness I have learned in your office have been very profitable for my businesses. I only wish I had found out about your service at the beginning of my being self-employed. We have made what would have been six months worth of sales in just the last month. I hope others benefit as much from your counsel.

In addition to the above, I've received news from more than one realtor enjoying a six-digit increase in annual income after going through my sales motivation program.

Quitting pot

One example I'll share with you took place during the summer of 1987. A businessman who successfully quit smoking asked me to help his teenager quit smoking pot. He came with his son, signed the disclosure form, and left the angry boy in my office. Within minutes it became apparent to me that there was no way this boy wanted me to hypnotize him into quitting, so I simply asked, "Why are you here?" He responded by saying it was a dumb question to ask, because I already knew the answer.

After I repeated the question, he said, "You *made* my father quit smoking, and my father wants you to *make* me stop pot."

When I told him that I could not *make* him do *anything,* he asked me why he was in my office. I responded by saying, "Let's assume this is 1997, and ten years ago your father dragged you to a hypnotist to try to get you to quit smoking pot. Let's suppose you decided to go along with it."

At this point in time, he interrupted me because I implied that he had some choice in the matter. He told me that absolutely *NO ONE* had ever told him he had a choice before. My response was that even something illegal involved a choice, because one could choose to be a law-abiding citizen, or choose to break the law and pay the consequences. So I told him that he could *choose* to keep on smoking pot and *pay the consequences,* or he could choose to quit and enjoy the benefits. A Navy recruiter had already told him that he could not enlist if he was still smoking pot after his 16th birthday (which was a few days away).

At this point I went into the benefits approach, and he listed three: Navy career, money for sports car, and clearer thinking. During hypnosis I used programmed imagery to have him driving down the Oregon coast in a red sports car-- wearing his Navy uniform, and having an attractive woman in the passenger seat. I suggested that he fall in love with his personal benefits.

His father contacted me two years later and informed me that his son had not smoked once since his first session with me, and that he had also been accepted into the Navy.

Requested past life regression = grief therapy

June simply told me she wanted a past life regression to satisfy her curiosity. She said that her life was fairly happy, but her session became a good example of *dealing with what emerges!* When I used open screen imagery to help her create her peaceful place before attempting the regression, she told me her father was there. She started crying immediately, because she had not been with him when he passed away. When I used Gestalt therapy to have her play the role of her deceased father, some powerful words of love and encouragement were verbalized. This proved to be a very emotional session, even causing me to wipe my eyes! She also forgave the nurse who had kept her from entering the hospital room during her father's passing. A month later she called me to thank me for changing her life, and then came back to experience the past life regression that her subconscious would not allow her to experience during her first session.

Another grief therapy

Michael (his real name) was a perfectionist who had feelings of guilt. The feeling connection took him back to a time during childhood when his brother was killed on a bike, and he had wished that he could have died in his brother's place. Gestalt therapy helped him say goodbye to his brother and heal from many years of grieving. Since I knew of this man's Christian beliefs, I enabled him to verbalize his own therapy by asking him what Jesus would want him to do now. I summarized his verbalizing in the form of direct suggestion and concluded the session. He came to see me two weeks later for some additional issues, and informed me that the session was profoundly beneficial to him. He mailed a letter to me some weeks later, which he said I could quote in this book:

Thank you so very much for the recent work you've done for me in the grief session. I feel I have been able to set at rest my sorrow for not being able to have said goodbye to my younger brother and my father at the time of their deaths. I especially appreciate your sensitivity concerning my religious, or spiritual, preferences--I really felt a burden lifted from my mind. I now feel completely at peace with my brother and my father.

There are many more, too numerous to mention.

Student Therapy Successes

Charles Tebbetts believed that these techniques could be used by anyone with average intelligence if done properly; so he insisted that his students actually participate in twelve therapy sessions as a part of the learning experience. Remember: these therapies take place during the second and third parts of a hypnotherapy course lasting for *nine months.*

The student must be the client in at least four of the twelve therapies. Let me share just a few, as done in class and/or reported in writing by my own hypnotherapy students. Again, the names are changed to protect confidentiality--and the examples range from 1988-1994.

Confidence and self-esteem

Mindy had a confidence problem and low self-esteem even though she was an excellent student of hypnotherapy. For one of the therapy assignments, Bill hypnotized her in front of the class, and used the *feeling connection* to uncover the source of her problem.

Mindy regressed back to a time during childhood when her mother lost her temper and slapped her in the face. She abreacted greatly for a couple minutes, feeling that her mother did not love her because she was unacceptable. Bill took her to her safe place for a minute or so, and then regressed her back into the scene with much less feeling, using the *informed child* technique. Through *verbalizing* her new adult understanding of the incident, she was able to rewrite her own subconscious perception of her mother's actions. Further subconscious "rewriting history" was facilitated through Gestalt therapy, as the *informed child* was able to express her feelings openly to her mother. Taking her mother's role AFTER regressing with the informed child technique gave her both empathy and a new understanding of her mother's frustration of working two jobs while trying to raise a family. This paved the way for forgiveness and release. Whether or not she ever chooses to confront her mother is totally at her own discretion, as her session objectives were accomplished--and she now had new empathy and an attitude of forgiveness for her mother's former strictness.

Abuse from childhood

Betty writes about herself as the client working with another student: "This therapy helped me to get rid of some old baggage I was carrying around connected to childhood abuse. Rewriting history after going in with my adult perspective *[informed child technique]* made such a difference for me. Checking the results really made me feel that we accomplished our goal. I have felt like a million pounds have been lifted from my shoulders ever since."

Weight management and confidence

Jane writes about working with another student for professional confidence and weight: "Linda dropped to a medium state. I worked with her to improve confidence in her ability to access anything, anytime, that's stored in her mind, which I likened to calling up a file on her Mac computer. Frustrated by inability to recall a sequence of events that could unfavorably impact her on the job, she was able after two sessions to recall it with clarity *[to provide needed information for her boss]*. This same therapist experienced several sessions with direct suggestion to reinforce ability to enter self-hypnosis easily, after which she was able to experience parts therapy successfully *[to deal with her weight]*."

Author's note: seven years later, she is still slim!

Smoking cessation, benefits approach

Bob, an excellent student who was already a certified NLP practitioner, volunteered to experience just one session of the *benefits approach* in front of my enitire hypnotherapy class in order to quit smoking. (He had already learned to manage stress through self-hypnosis, and also knew what his smoking motivators were.) Both programmed imagery and open screen imagery were used. He discussed his success openly with other students in the classroom, and was still a non-smoker last time I saw him.

Example of object projection & verbalizing

Jeff, only four months into his training, didn't know where to proceed when a female client (another student) indicated authority imprint from past religious training as the cause of her problem, so he used the *verbalizing* technique. She said she wanted to get rid of old ideas, so he decided to use *object projection* to facilitate the process. (Note that he had already established that she was visual.) He allowed *her* to decide the shape of the object, as well as how to release it. This experience helped Jeff appreciate the value of *client-centered* hypnotherapy!

Self-esteem

Alice worked with Charlotte for low self-esteem. She also felt impatient working with elderly dependent family members, and was apparently self-critical of her impatience. Three sessions were done, employing regression therapy through the feeling connection, parts therapy, various types of imagery, and direct suggestion to establish an anchor to calmness. Alice reported: "Client is feeling calmer and appreciating her ego strengths."

Smoking cessation permanent

Richard writes of his experience as a client: "We went through some preliminary stuff, looked at the benefits... better health, more money (and some suggestions on using it), greater social acceptance, clear throat and lungs, professional image... I had a last smoke, then the induction. I was in a medium to deep trance. Several times I was so deep in my thoughts I forgot what was happening. I remembered another loose cigarette in my car (months old). And then it was over. I destroyed all my cigarettes..." *[Second session: motivation mapping]* "We went over the 5 methods of subconscious motivation... Three days after, I deliberately took one hit off a cig. The aftertaste was unpleasant. I haven't had a cig. since. As time goes by, I think of them less and less."

He was still a non-smoker after the end of the course, replacing each old smoking trigger with a deep breath.

Anxiety

Mark writes: "Jill is not a typical client, in that she has been involved with hypnosis both as a student and a teacher for many years... I used the feeling connection to reach her first trauma. The scene was a serious complication of her own birth. She experienced a mild abreaction but overcame it without much difficulty. We reframed the incident... I then took her a year into the future to anchor a positive outcome of her therapy. I gave her a word which would call up the positive feeling that she experienced in trance. I am pleased to report that because of the good feelings she had with the therapy, the planned future sessions became unnecessary. This session took place two months ago and the anxiety has not returned."

"My God, I have parts!"

Mark also writes about when he was client: "My God, I have parts! This session may be the most incredible hypnotic experience that I will ever have. It was the first time that my parts became known to me. My left brain just sat there with its metaphorical jaw open in total amazement. Sue, very skillfully, brought forth five parts of my personality...."

The confidence gained from this session motivated Mark to make a major career decision. Today, he is a successful hypnotherapist.

Now let's talk about Scott.

Chapter 12

A "Miracle on Demand"

One of the most profound therapies ever facilitated by Charles Tebbetts involved a man from the Pacific Northwest who is in business for himself.

Scott Lamb came from a broken home, and had been plagued with epileptic seizures since childhood. As a student of hypnotherapy training under Mr. Tebbetts, he wanted to find out whether hypnosis could help uncover a subconscious cause of his epilepsy and create a cure. Since the Charles Tebbetts I knew was always ready to go adventuring into the field of hypnotherapy, he accepted the challenge and preserved it on videotape. With Scott's written permission, that remarkable session is reproduced in this book.

Let's find out what happened after the induction...

Charles Tebbetts (hereafter called CT): Be aware that your body is relaxed...and now just relax your mind... Allow your mind to go any place it wishes to some scene that you'd like to be at... It might be at the beach, it might be out in the woods, it might be any place where you'd enjoy being. Choose your scene, and go to that scene, and BE there. I'm going to talk to your subconscious mind; and your conscious mind can listen if it wishes, but it's too involved with the scene you're in to care... because your subconscious mind has something to tell you and me--if you allow it to tell it. You'll understand more about yourself, understand yourself much better, and enjoy life much more. So just go deeper now... Relax your mind, and go deeper.

CT pauses.

CT: Scott, at a very young age you did a lot of sleeping, and when you did sleep, you were out of this world and didn't have to participate in it at all. When you were awake, you also had some method of getting out of this world. I want to ask your subconscious mind why you wanted to get out of this world? Why didn't you want to participate at that young age? There must be some reason. The part of you that did it--the part of you that wanted to let the world go by and just sleep it out--would that part come forward and answer the question? *[pause]* Now that part's here; and if it's available and wishes to talk, say I am here!

Another pause...

Scott: I am here.

CT: Good. Why--for Scott's benefit, not mine--I'd like you to let his conscious mind know why you didn't want to be alive and live a normal life. There is some reason, obviously, and it's a good reason, and every part of you is doing something to make you feel better, to make a better person out of you. Was this part doing this for some particular reason?

Scott: Dad's an ass hole.

CT: Oh, I see.

Scott: He... I have the seizures to keep my mom and him together, maybe. Dad has to pay the bills, and he has another lady that he's with right now.

CT: But he still has to pay the bills?

Scott: Uh huh, he does with this one.

CT: Are you punishing him then to some extent?

Scott: Well, more bills--then maybe he can't afford it.

CT: Oh yea. Then he will come back?

Scott: Mom, she's crying. He's a son of a gun. I'll get to him, 'cause I get to his pocket book, and that gets to him more than anything.

CT: Good... How old are you when you found this out?

Scott: *[Ignores question.]* I'm having problems with him. My ears feel warm.

CT: Would you like to tell him off? At that age you couldn't do it. And now it would be a good idea to rewrite history. Tell him what you really think of him.

Scott: Well, when I was sixteen I did that.

CT: You did?

Scott: I hit him so hard that I knocked his teeth out.

CT: Oh, you did?

Scott: It felt good, though. I had a beer afterwards.

CT: *[Laughs]* Would you like to tell him again right now? Anything you want to say to him? Picture him right now across the table from you. You're not where you can hit him, you're just across the table from him sitting in a chair. Picture him right there close to you, and tell him what you think of him.

No response.

CT: Tell him anything you want to say to him.

Scott: You don't know how to pick your women. One out of three isn't too good, Buddy! The wife you've got now is about as worthless as... NOT MUCH!

CT: Hmmm.

Scott: You don't see your kids or your grand kids. You're treating them like you did your kids. You want 'em to be there but YOU'RE not there. The world goes both ways, Buddy! My sister, she--uh, she's like you, too bullheaded to come see ya. And you're too ignorant to go see her because of your wife. You're doin' what she wants. Old Girtie, she's your boss, Buddy!

He talks to Charles Tebbetts now...

Scott: Ha! I see him with a dog chain. Right in there she's

got him on his hands and knees. She's walking him down the street.

Both Scott and Mr. Tebbetts laugh.

Scott: Oh, God. That's it, Buddy! That's how you look. That's it, too. She gotchya around a chain.

CT: *[Laughing]* That's good.

Scott: Back on the bottom end there, he's got a dollar bill sign on, and she's petting it! He's making good money. *[More laughter]* That's it, Buddy! Ohhhhhh.

CT: Be your father! Put yourself in your father's place now. Be him. Answer your son. He's told you just what he thinks of you, and illustrated real well. Answer him... *[pause]* Have you anything to say to him?

Scott (as his father): We could get along a lot more now if we would have stuck it out. It's my fault, though, I goofed up. But we were young when we got married, and we just--I was thinking between my legs instead of between my ears... She just wouldn't stop nagging, and I had to talk to someone who was on my side.

CT: Yea.

Scott (as his father): You know, Granny and your mom built up against me, and I just couldn't take it anymore.

CT: Granny too, huh?

Scott (as his father): She just... PEGGY'S ALWAYS RIGHT! *[Sighs and breathes heavily several times.]*

CT: Now, be Scott again! Scott understands now. He's heard his father's answer, and he understands him to some degree. Just tell him what you think of him now... Do you forgive him or understand him?

Scott (as himself): Dad, you just got to, uh--you did the right thing at the right time, or so you thought. But yet you had two kids at the time; and if you make 'em, you got to pay for 'em! And it's not just a dollar bill.

CT: That's right. It's more than a dollar bill.

Scott (as himself): Hey, I gotchya pretty good, didn't I, Bud?

He laughs, causing Mr. Tebbetts to laugh also. Note how Scott now jumps back and forth between past and present...

Scott: *[Speaking to CT in the present]* He told me I was Number One a long time ago, and I am.

[Speaking again to his father...] That's O.K., I like ya.

CT: He did stick by you enough to support you and pay the bills, didn't he?

Scott: *[Again speaking to CT in the present]* You know, he did--all except for when I was thirteen years old... because he was going through his second divorce at the time. And for six months I had to pay the bills.

CT: Oh!? *[in surprise]*

Scott: That's true.

CT: Did you have as many seizures?

Scott: I didn't have any! I had to be the dad. I had to be the boss. My mom couldn't afford us, and I made the house payments, and I made the payments on the car, 'cause she just couldn't afford it.

CT: And he couldn't afford it either, because he didn't have any money, right?

Scott: *[Regressing back to childhood once again]* Oh, he can afford it! He's just too busy fooling around--out getting ready for Number Three.

CT: Oh, yes.

Scott: He doesn't see us. He doesn't even wanta talk to us.

CT: He's quite selfish?

Scott: Extremely!

CT: Well, I guess everybody is selfish to some degree. He was probably excessively selfish in rejecting his own family.

Scott: He's just like his dad.

CT: He's just like his dad, huh?

Scott: *[Jumping back to the present again]* I never met my real grampa. He was always too busy doing his own thing, and fooling around, and I never met him.

CT: You probably understand your father better because you know he was raised that way, don't you?

Scott: Uh huh, and I know why my granny liked my mom so much. She loved my mom, because she went through the same thing that my mom went through.

CT: Oh, yes.

Scott: That's why my dad didn't have a fighting chance. Two against one just don't work.

CT: Oh, that's right. So you understand him pretty well?

Scott: Uh huh.

CT: It's surprising you do understand him, but you're a very reasonable person. Even in your subconscious mind you figured it out pretty well, haven't you? You know your dad pretty well, and you know why he was like he was.

Scott: We're closer now than we've ever been.

CT: Because you understand him. You are a very lucky person, and you're a very intelligent person to realize that he was a victim of his raising. And he couldn't help it. Your mother couldn't help it. Nobody could really help it. Do you think they could help it?

Scott: No. I understand that now. But I didn't understand it before.

CT: That's right, and you understand it subconsciously now, and that's the important part. You could understand it intellectually, and it wouldn't mean a thing. But you understand it emotionally now. And that's the whole key to happiness really, is understanding things emotionally.

Scott: Yea, he....

He stops talking abruptly. CT decides to continue...

CT: You're lucky you're smart enough to do it.

Scott: He put us through a lot. I understand why.

CT: You're a very lucky person to be so understanding; and also, he's lucky you understand him. You're a very tolerant person. He couldn't help it.

Scott: No. I just wish he wouldn't be so bullheaded though with my sister. He's missing out on her kids.

CT: He's still that way, huh?

Scott: He would do it, but his wife doesn't want him to.

CT: Well, he's...

Scott: *[Interrupting, but remaining in the present]* He's a dog on a chain with a dollar bill on his bottom.

CT: He's stuck with her...

Scott: "Too old to start again!" he says.

CT: That's wonderful to understand. Do you forgive him?

Scott: I understand why he did it. But to forgive him, he... Yea, I forgive him.

CT: Good. It's good to forgive him because you understand him.

Scott: Uh huh.

CT: *[Returning to parts therapy]* I'd like to call out the part of you now that is giving you the seizures once in a while... that part was doing it for a good reason, but now I think you've decided it's not necessary any more... Could you let that part come out and talk?

Part causing seizures: Ah HA! *[emphatically]* I'm HERE!

CT: Good. What do you think now about this situation. Do you think it's necessary anymore? *[pause]* It's an awful handicap, you know...

No response...

CT: You don't need to punish your father any more, and you don't need to get your mother to do things for you any more. You're capable of having a good life of your own. You're doing a good business, and you're a good hypnotherapist. I'll say that! I'm your teacher, and I know who's good and who isn't. And you're good. You're creative, you have a creative mind, and you have a lot on the ball. Do you need this any more?

Part causing seizures: It keeps Scott on his toes.

CT: It keeps him on his toes?

Part causing seizures: Yea, 'cause he knows I'm around. And if he doesn't do it right, he knows that I'll be there and I'll give him the old BUZAROO! *[Last word spoken with emphasis!]*

CT: Well, that's a good idea. That's your job, really. And you'll keep your job if you know he's doing wrong to hurt himself--but you don't want to hurt him, do you?

Part causing seizures: I want to keep him in line.

CT: That's fair enough, to keep him in line. And he's decided to stay in line pretty well, hasn't he?

Part causing seizures: He could do better.

CT: He could do better?

Part causing seizures: Uh huh.

CT: Now let's talk to the part that wants to get rid of the seizures. Is he here? Please say, "I am here."

Part wanting release: Yea, I'm here.

CT: You want to get rid of the seizures; but on the other hand, there's a part of you that thinks you're not doing well enough. And he threatens that if you don't do better, he's going to give them to you. What do you have to say to him?

Part wanting release: What do I need to do, Bud? What do I need to do?

CT: Yea, ask him. Now be the part that gives the seizures. What does he have to do?

Part causing seizures: Quit drinking TOTALLY, you dummy!

CT: Oh! *[showing surprise]* That's good. Now that's a smart idea. You're a smart man, and you're a smart part.

Part causing seizures: You just got to quit drinking, you idiot! If you don't, then you're going to get the BUZAROO.

CT: That's a smart answer. Be the part that wants to get rid of the buzzing. Be the part now and answer.

No response.

CT: Before I do this, what's the name of the part that's giving him the seizures?

Part causing seizures: Ass hole.

CT: Huh??? *[very surprised]*

Part causing seizures: Ass hole... *[groaning]* I'm an ass hole.

CT: How do you spell it? *[trying hard not to laugh--but laughs anyway]* I didn't get it.

Part causing seizures: ASS hole.

He laughs, causing Mr. Tebbetts to laugh again as well. CT regains his composure and continues...

CT: I get it. That's your name. Well, ass hole... *[laughs again]* I like you. You're not really an ass hole. You're doing what's right, but you were mistaken, probably, in doing so much of it when he was younger. But it served a good purpose. You thought you were doing the right thing. Every part of you is doing the right thing in its opinion, so you're not remiss in doing it. However, I'd like to have you listen to the part that wants to get rid of the seizures. Now, the part that wants to get rid of the seizures, would you talk to ass hole? What's your name, by the way?

Part wanting release: I'm Mr. Lovely.

CT: Mr. Lovely? You're not lovely when you're drunk.

Part wanting release: Ahhhhhhh...

CT: Oh, you're Mr. Lovely anyway. So talk to him. Answer him. He says you've got to quit drinking or he'll give you the BUZZ once in a while. What do you think of that?

Part wanting release: I'm trying, and I'm doing other things so that I don't get bored. The only reason I go in there is so I'll have something to do.

CT: Yea.

Part wanting release: I'll have a few beers with somebody, and then the next thing you know... but I'm doing something else now, so I'm getting out of that routine.

CT: Good.

Part wanting release: It's stupid, and that's why I'm an idiot for doing it.

CT: He says it is, too, and that's why he wants you to quit. He says it's stupid. Answer him and tell him what you'll do... *[pauses]* Are you willing to quit drinking?

Part wanting release: I'm going to do it. I'm doing it. I'm done with it.

CT: Good. Are you done with it right now?

Part wanting release: Yep--done with it. I've had enough. NADA MAS! *[Spanish for "NO MORE!"]*

CT: Now that's your subconscious mind talking to you. It knows that if you say this subconsciously and emotionally, you won't do it. That's a good deal.

Part wanting release: There are better things to do.

CT: Yea, that's right. Tell him. Tell ass hole--I don't think that's a fitting name any more, but he's the enforcer. Call him the controller.

Part wanting release: We'll call him "C.A."--controlling ass hole.

CT: *[laughing]* That's good! Tell him, "Hey, C.A.!" Tell him what you're going to do now.

Part wanting release: Hey, C.A., I'll stop drinking if you don't give me any more buzzes, Buddy!

CT: That's a good deal.

Part wanting release: How's that sound? I like that.

CT: Now be C.A.

Part causing seizures (as C.A.): I'll believe it when I see it. And if you do it, you get it.

CT: If you do it?

Part causing seizures (as C.A.): ...you get it!

CT: If Scott does it, then you'll agree not to give him any more seizures?

Part causing seizures (as C.A.): Yep! He's done it. He did what we've had to do, and we've definitely been through it. I'm getting tired of doing it, but I'm going to keep doing it until he shapes up.

CT: Good! Now, do you have an answer for that one?

Part wanting release: Well, if I don't have to go through the seizures, then if that's what it takes, I'm done! *[done drinking]*

CT: Good.

Part wanting release: No more Miller time! I'm done with it.

CT: That's terrific! You're going to be a much happier person. You are now a much happier person, because you've decided something that's in your favor. This will make you a better person, really, and help you enjoy life more.

Part wanting release: That's it. I'm done.

CT: Yea, you're enjoying life much more right now. You built in a habit that was binding you, and you're no longer a slave. Isn't that the way you feel?

Part wanting release: It feels nice to, uh... I don't know how the whole body feels. I just had a smile on it.

CT: Yea, that's right, 'cause you conquered it.

Part wanting release: It's been a long time.

CT: You've broken the yoke that bound you, really. Just cast that yoke off your shoulders. And you're lucky you're smart enough to do it. And you're lucky enough to have a C.A. enforcer that will keep you doing it, because you know he's doing what's best for you, don't you?

Part wanting release: Uh huh. He gives me the warnings, and that's all he will do. If I even think about drinking, he'll give me the warnings.

CT: Good. So any time you get a warning, you'll get your mind off drinking, right?

Part wanting release: That's it.

CT: That's good.

Part wanting release: I'll do something else. I'm done.

CT: C.A., will you agree to give him the warnings? If he starts drinking, will you give him the warnings?

Part causing seizures (as C.A.): *[Loudly]* No doubt about it!

CT: Good. He won't drink. He's agreed not to.

Part causing seizures (as C.A.): As I say, I'm still here.

CT: You're serving a good purpose. You're a good part, really; you've done well by him all the time. But now, it's inappropriate to do what you used to do. Do you realize that? ...unless he gets out of line.

Part causing seizures (as C.A.): That's it. The old body, you know, is getting in better shape--and gonna do it. But if he gets out of line, boy, he's HAD it: the old BUZAROO!

CT: Well, he won't do it. I'm sure, because this is his emo-tional mind talking now, and he has agreed emotionally not to do it. That's the key to everything. If he agreed consciously with his intellectual mind, you wouldn't have anything. The agreement wouldn't be worth a darn. But now, emotionally, the part of him that makes him drink has decided NOT TO. You're secure!

Part causing seizures (as C.A.): I'll enjoy it.

CT: Both parts will enjoy it.

Part wanting release: I see old C.A. with horns, and he's shaking my hand. He has a smile; but with the other hand, he's pointing at me.

CT: Put your arms around him. C.A., put your arms around him. Hug him... *[pause]* Good... He's trying to help you. Rather than hindering you in life, he's trying to help you.

Part causing seizures (as C.A.): This is what I wanted to do all along. The idiot didn't figure it out, and now he has.

CT: Well, that's a wonderful breakthrough! You made a good breakthrough tonight. I'm proud to have been here listening to it. You did this yourself, I didn't do it. I just helped the two parts talk to each other, and that's all that happened. And they agreed.

Mr. Tebbetts pauses and speaks more slowly...

CT: All right, just go deeper now, and enjoy this wonderful, relaxed feeling. As you go deeper, I want to talk to the class. You can listen if you want to...

Mr. Tebbetts explains to the class that Scott's own mind came up with drinking as the current cause of seizures. He also explained that Scott's key to recovery was the fact that Scott's emotional mind made the agreement to quit drinking. My mentor then speaks very slowly, giving some additional suggestions to his client:

CT: Any time you feel yourself thinking about liquor, you'll get the buzz. On the other hand, because you might get the buzz, you can take a long deep breath, and hold it in for a minute. And do a job of self-hypnosis, and relax all over, and feel good. And now you've taken care of C.A.'s wishes. Relax, and go about your business without thoughts of what might have occurred to you. Any time you have this feeling of possibly wanting to do something that would cause the buzz, just take a long deep breath. C.A. will be proud of you, and you'll be happy with him. Go deeper now. And as you go deeper, you know that when you come out of hypnosis, you feel terrific...

Mr. Tebbetts integrates the parts, gives some additional suggestions about feeling good, and then awakens.

Scott's first comment upon awakening was: "That was interesting!" After a few minutes of discussion, Scott expressed his confidence about the benefit of the session. In a taped testimonial interview made many months later, he told Mr. Tebbetts that he had not had a seizure in months. Scott said that his motto was: "A new decade, a new year, a new life!"

During a guest lecture to my hypnotherapy class, he informed my students that he was almost as surprised as Mr. Tebbetts was when "C.A." brought up the drinking problem as a cause of seizures. Neither he nor Mr. Tebbetts had any conscious intention of dealing with that issue until it emerged during the session.

As of the original writing of this chapter (4/26/94), Scott's record continued without a drink and without a seizure for over four years. By honoring the agreement he made with himself to quit drinking, he has been released from his former epilepsy. As of its first revision (January 1996), Scott's record was *still perfect.*

For Scott Lamb, Charles Tebbetts truly facilitated a *Miracle on Demand!*

Chapter 13

Past Life Regressions

Even as the new millenium dawns, people both inside and outside of the hypnotherapy profession still hotly debate the topic of past life regressions.

While it's a proven fact that clients in hypnosis may be intentionally guided into what seems to be memories of a former lifetime, stranger yet is that it can happen spontaneously. Even clients who do not believe in former lives may, on rare occasions, trip out unexpectedly into real or imagined memories of a "past" life during what was intended to be a present life regression. Regardless of whether a hypnotherapist chooses to facilitate past life regressions, they will occur--and therefore simply cannot be ignored. Why? This chapter will attempt to answer that question to your partial satisfaction, regardless of your personal, professional, philosophical or spiritual beliefs.

Sadly, yet true to human nature, most available information on the subject either attempts to promote the theory of reincarnation or attempts to discredit the idea altogether. Some highly educated people believe that the concept of living more than once is totally unscientific; yet others with medical degrees and other advanced degrees do believe that we live more than once. Likewise, while most Christians argue vehemently against the concept on theological grounds, there are a few ordained Christian ministers who believe in reincarnation.

Charles Tebbetts sometimes facilitated a past life regression (called a "PLR"); however, he avoided saying whether or not he believed in them. He did feel that ANY technique that helped a client without risk of harm should be used. He did not feel that a PLR would harm a client who requested it; but when asked by students about his own belief, my mentor kept us guessing.

One chapter in a book cannot even begin to address all the questions regarding this controversial topic, nor should it. The most professional thing I can do is attempt to present past life therapy in both a useful and an objective manner. Regardless of your opinions of the PLR controversy, I believe that it will be worthwhile to both you and your clients for you to read this entire chapter.

Let's begin by considering some possible explanations of the phenomenon.

Possible Explanations

There are several popular theories to explain what may be taking place during a past life regression. You are free to choose the theory (or theories) which will fit comfortably into the framework of your personal or professional beliefs.

Fantasy or metaphor

Any competent hypnotherapist knows that hypnosis enhances one's own ability to imagine or fantasize; and this most certainly provides a logical explanation for many PLR's. Such fantasy could spring from curiosity, fascination for a particular time period in history, and/or identifying with a certain historical person--or might simply be the result of a subconscious metaphor which may facilitate change in your client. There could be other reasons for the fantasy--such as a story, movie, TV program, dream or event that made a subconscious impact during one's present life even if forgotten consciously.

I will admit that I believe some past life regressions fall

into the category of fantasy or metaphor; but there has been enough documentation over the years to indicate that at least some people have tapped into actual documented lives that others have lived in the past. In light of this, it may be worthwhile to consider one or more alternative explanations for at least some of the PLR's.

Actual soul memories (reincarnation)

Many believe that past life regressions prove reincarnation, as is evidenced by the many books written on the subject. Even some Christians have accepted the belief that the family of Jesus was among the Essenes--who believed in reincarnation.

A late Methodist minister of many years, Arthur Winkler, Ph.D., facilitated thousands of PLR's during his life. He studied numerous results, and eventually formed the opinion that many of them were valid. (Of course, there are millions of Christians who believe that reincarnation is in total conflict with Christianity; and this is not the place to debate it.)

The National Guild of Hypnotists has a publication called "Past Lives of Alan Lee" which can amaze even the skeptic by providing some astounding documented evidence that real lives were tapped into during PLR experiments. These regressions were carefully monitored scientifically; however, this does not necessarily prove that the individual in hypnosis was the same soul who actually lived those lives. There are other possible explanations...

Soul-tapping

The person in hypnosis may "tap into" the actual memories of another soul who lived in the past, finding those memories from the Universal Book of Life or from the Akashic records--or by telepathically reading (or channeling) actual thought patterns from the soul of another who is in spirit form.

The subconscious and/or super conscious finds something relevant for the client at the time for the person's soul growth, and we "play" the memories much like a VCR playing a videocassette. Some who object to the idea of reincarnation on religious grounds may find this a very acceptable explanation for past life regressions.

Universal consciousness

This theory is similar to the one above. The belief is that we are all interconnected through the spirit of God, and therefore all memories of all lives ever lived--both past and present--are instantly available through hypnosis if needed for one's own personal or spiritual growth.

Genetic memory

Some believe that memories may be passed on through heredity. This theory does not hold water with regressions where one remembers his/her death. It would not explain why memories for a particular life would continue after one's last child was conceived; and neither would it explain a Japanese client of mine regressing into an apparent American Indian lifetime in the late 19th century. Nonetheless I've discussed this theory with at least one scientist who firmly believes it. He can offer explanations for the two concerns mentioned in this subsection.

You are free to consider still other possible explanations besides these; but perhaps this gives you a starting point for opening your mind to possible explanations for those PLR's which seem to be more than just fantasy. But even if you don't wish to choose an explanation, there still remains the mystery of the occasional spontaneous past life regression.

Spontaneous Past Life Regression

Whether or not you believe in past lives, on rare occasions a client might--as mentioned before--spontaneously "trip out" into a real or imagined past life. For example, using the *feeling connection* technique can sometimes trigger such a regression--even when that was not the intention of the therapist! This can happen even when the client does not believe in past lives.

If a client experiences a spontaneous PLR, stay calm. Take a deep breath and say "relax" to yourself (and to your client) if you need to calm any of your own anxiety, since this can be picked up by the client's subconscious. If you are comfortable dealing with what emerges, guide the client through the experience. Handle it much the same as you might handle a present life regression--making sure to suggest a total return to the present day before awakening. Remember to *allow* (but not force) abreactions, and make certain that you understand how to deal with them.

If you are not comfortable handling the spontaneous PLR, bring your client back to the present life quickly but gently--and do NOT awaken from hypnosis just yet. You might take him/her to a safe place and use the verbalizing technique to discover possible relevancy to the present life, etc.; or you could just give some soothing post-hypnotic suggestions for peace and well-being, along with suggestions that any relevant information be dealt with at another appropriate time and place. Then, after awakening, ask the client to tell you how he/she feels about what happened during hypnosis. If the client wishes to explore the real or imagined past life, you have an important decision staring you in the face.

Under no circumstances should you criticize any client for regressing back too far in time. If he or she believes in former lives, then you would serve him/her better with a referral to an ethical hypnotherapist who is comfortable working with past life therapy; otherwise, learn to become more comfortable with past life regression techniques yourself so that you may easily facilitate the rare spontaneous past life regression. You have no obligation to accommodate a request for past life therapy; however, with a little experience and sensitivity, you just might find yourself able to facilitate this upon request! (Some of the techniques mentioned later in this chapter might also help you and your client.)

A devout Lutheran who saw me to deal with the fear of flying regressed back to a real or imagined death experience. She did not believe in past lives, yet she vividly described suffocating to death. With the verbalizing technique, she said that it was not being in the sky that she feared while flying, it was the fear of running out of oxygen and dying again like before. When I awakened her, she exclaimed, "That seemed pretty real! Did I really live before this life?"

My response was that it wasn't my place to say whether or not her experience was real. She could have seen a movie or heard a story as a small child, or her subconscious could simply have produced this story as a metaphor to help her. I finished by saying, "Whether or not you really lived that life isn't nearly as important as your release from the phobia, is it?"

To invalidate her experience might have neutralized the therapy. To validate it might have caused anxiety over her religious convictions. The most considerate and professional response was to give her an answer that allowed her to explore her own conclusions. Let me add that her release from the phobia was permanent.

It is my hope that you agree with the next chapter section on ethics...

ETHICS

Work within the comfort zone of your client! Remember to do for the client what you would want done if the roles (and beliefs) were reversed. Let's explore the ethics of three possible situations...

If you believe in past life therapy:

It is unethical to intentionally initiate a past life regression unless your client requests it. Even if you believe the problem originated in a former lifetime, you risk the credibility of hypnotherapy by taking it upon yourself to force the person into a PLR unless that is what the client, of his or her own free will, desires.

Furthermore, some people may feel it is an infringement on their own beliefs even if you solicit their consent prior to the hypnotic session--so the client should initiate the request unless you already know for a fact that your client can accept the possibility of past lives. Several people have complained to me after going to another hypnotherapist who tried to convince them that their problems originated in past lives. Besides, presuming that the cause of someone's problem was past life karma is not client-centered hypnotherapy--and borders on *diagnosing.*

Also, remember that even a spontaneous past life regression does not prove that your client actually lived that life. Do not attempt to use the experience to convert that person's belief system to match your own. Put yourself in your client's shoes!

If you believe we only live once:

The flip side of the coin is that you may appear as being cold and insensitive if you try to convince a client that it is stupid or unscientific to believe in past lives just because your opinions differ.

All of us are certainly entitled to our own belief systems, and that includes our clients. In my professional opinion, we as hypnotherapists have a responsibility to do our best to work with our clients as much as possible *within the framework of their own spiritual beliefs.* Yet I've heard complaints from several clients who experienced criticism from a psychologist or a hypnotherapist for believing in reincarnation. Worse yet, more than one client has complained to me about another hypnotherapist who said it was *unethical* for any hypnotherapist to do past life regressions. This is easy to believe, because I personally heard a well-known figure in the field of hypnotherapy *publicly* criticize past life therapy in 1990! This type of criticism hurts our profession and creates more division.

The ethical thing for the past life skeptic to do is to give the clients who request past life regressions the courtesy of tactfully referring them elsewhere *without criticizing either them or their beliefs.*

Remember that we are here to serve the client, *not* to convert clients to our own spiritual, mental, medical, philosophical or other beliefs. The client's need is more important than our own religious beliefs or ego.

We certainly do not appreciate it when prospective clients are convinced by outside prejudice to avoid hypnosis. Since we want the general public to be open-minded about hypnotherapy, we owe it to our clients, ourselves, and our entire profession to keep an open mind about ideas we might not use in our own practice, including past life regressions! Asking others to be open-minded about hypnotherapy while remaining closed-minded about the potential benefits of past life therapy has a rather strange ring in the ears of many of us.

If you are undecided:

If you are in this group, it is easy and relatively safe to be totally honest about your undecided opinions. It would be totally acceptable and professional to admit to a client that you do not know whether or not the experience was real or metaphoric--and the client will most likely respect your honesty.

I have personally told my clients, "I am not a scientist, so is it *not* my job to research the validity of past lives. And my opinions may or may not be correct, so it is up to you to decide for yourself. As for me, I choose to keep an open mind." Very few people could criticize this type of response as unprofessional unless they cling to very biased opinions.

Now that we've considered possible explanations and some ethical issues, let's look at some actual techniques that can be used to facilitate the requested past life regression. Before you read any further, however, be certain that you understand how to facilitate regressions and handle abreactions.

Techniques to Initiate Regression

The somnambulistic state provides the best probability of a successful past life regression; however, clients will often respond even in a medium depth of trance. In a light level of hypnosis there is usually too much conscious interference to allow a successful regression, although I have seen a few exceptions.

As with hypnotic inductions, the ways of initiating a PLR are as limitless as the imagination. We'll consider some of the more commonly used methods of helping a client become an explorer of real or imagined past lives. Before we begin, however, we should consider giving the client (or explorer) a safeguard.

Building a link to the present (a safeguard)

Prior to starting hypnosis, I ask my clients to agree to be aware at all times of my voice and to return immediately to the present when asked to do so. I explain to them that these are the "conditions" of being an explorer--and that I will also ask them while hypnotized if they still agree to the "conditions." After the induction, I guide a client into his/her safe place, and ask for an ideomotor response to indicate acceptance of the conditions. Then I usually use one of the regression techniques described below, which has been chosen by the client before beginning hypnosis.

The time tunnel

The explorer enters a time tunnel of deep hypnosis, going deeper back through time, etc.... The tunnel may be lit softly with the explorer's favorite color. Also, one may walk or float through the tunnel, or sit on a vehicle such as a Disneyland-type boat, etc.

Once you have guided the client inside the tunnel, you may say words such as:

> **As you go deeper into the tunnel, you go deeper into hypnosis--always aware of my voice. Deeper and deeper, going back... to another time, another space... another life, another place... another body, another face... the choosing of your higher mind...** *[inner mind, higher self, etc.]*

> **Off in the distance now is the tunnel exit, where you will come out into another time, another space... another life, another place... another body, another face...**

> *Repeat the previous paragraph if desired.*

> **You are nearing the exit now... leaving the tunnel, and becoming more aware of where you are as I count from one to three. Number one: out of the tunnel now. Number two:**

becoming more aware of anything you see, hear or feel. Number three: BE THERE! Make a report...

At this point, the client may be guided through the regression. (See the comments at the end of this chapter section for the clients who don't respond.)

The cloud

The explorer can simply imagine becoming surrounded by a hypnotic mist of his or her favorite color. Then words such as the following can be used:

As you begin drifting deeper and deeper into hypnosis, you feel lighter and lighter as though you are floating within the mist of deep hypnotic sleep... In fact, you find it more and more enjoyable just to let yourself go, drifting into the cloud... and you are always aware of my voice as you keep on drifting way back through time, farther and farther into hypnosis.

Drifting way back... to another time, another space... another life, another place... another body, another face... the choosing of your higher mind...

Repeat the previous paragraph if desired.

The cloud is slowing down, now... slowing down and ever so gently descending down, down, down... gently setting you down... And as I count from one to three, the cloud will vanish, allowing you to become more and more aware of where you are. Number one: the cloud is beginning to disappear now. Number two: becoming more aware of anything you see, hear or feel. Number three: BE THERE! Make a report...

The crystal hall

The explorer enters a long hallway with walls and ceiling of crystals--and a floor of fine marble, glass, or gold. At the other end of the hall is a door with a huge, emerald doorknob. I usually have the client enter the hall from his or her safe place, saying words such as:

> **Now that you've agreed to the conditions, you may find the door to the crystal hall appearing. As the door opens, you may enter the hall. It may be rounded, or shaped in whatever manner you wish. It's walls are covered with glittering crystals or jewels of many colors. It's floor is fine marble, glass, or gold. Move your finger when you are in the hallway.**

> *Wait for response.*

> **This is a hallway back through time and space. At the end of the hall is a door opening up into another life, another place... another body, another face... the choosing of your higher mind. There is a huge emerald knob on the door, and when you are ready, you may touch the knob and the door opens...**

> **Touch the knob now, and step through the open door... As I count from one to three, you become more and more aware of where you are. Number one: the door closes behind you, and you become aware of where you are. Number two: becoming aware of anything you see, hear, or feel. Number three: BE THERE! Make a report...**

Note that the explorer MUST exit the hallway! If he/she fails to exit through the door on the first request, it is appropriate to make a second attempt in a somewhat more direct way. If the client is still stuck in the hall, then guide him/her back to the safe place and use another technique. I frequently have to change techniques in mid-trance because some visual clients want to stay in the hall after getting dazzled by the beauty they create in their minds.

Another variation on the above technique is to have numerous doors, with the client selecting that door which is most appropriate and beneficial to open.

The elevator through time

The explorer enters an elevator which descends down through the ages...

> **Imagine this elevator any way you wish it to be... and as you enter, you begin to feel it moving down, taking you down deeper into hypnosis, and deeper into the past...**

> **It's going way down now, down through the years, and you are going way down into a very deep, hypnotic sleep. The elevator is taking you way down through the ages, to another time, another space... another life, another place... another body, another face... the choosing of your higher mind...**

> **The elevator is slowing down now, coming to a stop. As I count from one to three, you become more and more aware of where you are. Number one: the door opens. Number two: step out of the elevator and be aware of anything you see, hear or feel. Number three: BE THERE! Make a report...**

It is very important to be sure the client is comfortable with elevators before using this technique! If you are changing to this technique after lack of response to another, then you may ask for an ideomotor response to determine whether the client is comfortable with elevators.

The bridge across forever

The explorer crosses a meadow, noticing a river with a footbridge. On the far side of the bridge is a strange mist, with a rainbow where the path enters the mist. After stepping under the rainbow into the mist, the mist clears--leaving the explorer in another time, another space, etc...

Age regression before birth

There are those who simply take a person back by age

regression (or calendar year regression) back to birth--and
before--and then deal with what emerges. This might seem
very appropriate at first glance to the novice, but there may
be more than meets the eye. I personally never use this technique unless a person asks to go back to what he/she believes
to be the most recent lifetime before the present one, because there is a possibility that the information produced by
the subconscious may not have any relevance on the person's
problem.

If there is no response...

If the explorer doesn't immediately answer, we may sometimes trigger responses with one or more of the following
questions:

Are you inside or outside?

Are you standing, seated, or lying down?

Is it dark or light?

Is it cool, warm, or comfortable?

If there is still no response, then we may take the client
back to his/her safe place for a moment. After additional
deepening, we may then try another technique.

If there is no response after two or three different regression techniques, there may be a reason for resistance. If this
happens, we may take the client back to his/her safe place,
and use open screen imagery and/or verbalizing (or simply
use ideo-motor responding) to help uncover the cause of the
problem. Perhaps this person is not ready for past life
therapy. Remember, we cannot force--we can only guide.

Guiding vs. Leading

Once the explorer starts responding, we must allow it to
be a *client-centered* experience! In other words, let's allow

the client to tell what is happening rather than the other way around. Why do I say this?

Inappropriate leading seems to be too common among therapists who facilitate PLR's. Metaphysical practitioners who consider themselves to be very intuitive (or psychic) are often tempted into leading rather than guiding. Asking leading questions can result in a client fantasizing what he/she is asked to fantasize, ending up in a therapist-centered experience that is projected onto the client. (Also refer to the chapter section, "Guiding vs. Leading" in Chapter 7.)

For example, let's say an explorer reports being on the beach. Ask, "What are you doing at the beach?" rather than asking if the client is swimming--which could be perceived by the subconscious as a suggestion to do so. Suggesting that the client swim could interfere greatly with what takes place in the mind, as there could be any number of reasons for being at the beach other than for a swim. Likewise, asking a client whether there is a boat or ship within view could also cause the subconscious to fabricate whatever is suggested.

When one experience is completed, we may guide the client forward or backward in time to a very important event, or to a happy experience, or to the most important day of that life, etc. As appropriate, we may also guide the explorer all the way through the death experience to "the first moment of total peace after the transition" and ask him/her to talk about it. But let's make certain that we avoid projecting our own opinions into the experience.

A close friend of mine saw a female "rebirthing" counselor who claimed competency with past life therapy. She told my friend that he was a mass murderer in another lifetime, and tried to make him abreact into feelings of guilt. When he brought himself out of trance and lectured her against leading, she tried to convince him that her intuition was very accurate, and that he should let her give him more therapy. He refused; and after some questioning, he finally got her to admit that she had received no formal training in hypnotherapy. The rebirthing counselor apparently refused to believe that she was actually practicing a form of hypnotherapy.

Past Life Abreactions

When facilitating past life therapy, we must be prepared to handle abreactions.

As discussed in Chapter 7 of this book, abreactions represent **emotional discharges** taking place because of real or perceived perceptions of either actual events remembered, or of imagined events that may be either partial or total fantasy. Remember, then, even an intense abreaction could be a *distorted perception* of a real memory. Since this is true whether one is experiencing either a present life regression or a past life regression, the guidelines for handling abreactions are basically the same for either present life or past life regressions.

Remember to allow but not force the emotional discharge! It is also possible to use a variation on the informed child technique as described next.

"Informed Soul" technique

This is similar to the "informed child technique" with a major modification. We may suggest that the client re-live the situation as it happened, but with all the spiritual awareness and wisdom possible for a mature and spiritual understanding of the situation. If he/she believes in a "higher spiritual self" concept, then we may suggest "higher self" awareness. If the client believes in God and/or Universal Intelligence, or in the Holy Spirit, we can suggest that such higher power grant spiritual awareness as he/she re-lives the situation. We may then use "rewriting history" or Gestalt, or any other appropriate technique, to help the person get past the abreaction enough to facilitate forgiveness and release.

Bypassing abreactions of the death experience

To help a client bypass abreactions at a re-lived death experience, suggest:

> **Now move forward in time all the way through the transition to the first moment of total peace AFTER the transition.... How old was that body when it died?... What was your main spiritual lesson in that lifetime?**

Another way some therapists remove clients from the death experience and/or abreactions is to have them imagine observing such as though watching it on a movie screen (the *silent abreaction* technique).

Forgiveness and release

Even in a past life regression, forgiveness and release should be included among the therapeutic objectives. If Gestalt is not used, we may still choose other desensitizing techniques which might be appropriate for present life regression therapy. And since clients who believe totally in reincarnation are still very distanced from that past life, we may often facilitate a *generic release* with suggestions such as:

> **If there is any other person or situation to release from the lifetime just glimpsed, just take a deep breath and think the word RELEASE as you exhale.**
>
> *Wait for response.*
>
> **Do you now forgive yourself for having carried that hurt as long as you did?**
>
> *Wait for response--verbal or ideo-motor.*
>
> **I wish to ask your spiritual self (or that part of you most**

closely connected to God, Holy Spirit, or Universal Consciousness) to indicate if you are released and clear from that life...

Wait for response.

You may now use the verbalizing technique by asking the client the following question:

How can the lessons learned in that past life benefit you in your present life?

Note the wording carefully! This suggestion allows the client to derive benefit whether or not he/she perceives the regression as fantasy, reality, or metaphor, etc.; because the "past life" is referred to as "that" past life while ownership is only suggested for the *present* life! This fine tuning of wording may help prevent one from staying "stuck" for days in a remembered real or imagined past life. Also, this last question creates the opportunity for the client to verbalize whatever new insight was gained from the session even if both you and the client believe the regression was fantasized.

Additional Remarks

There are numerous books written citing "case histories" as so-called proof of former lives; and conversely, there are religious writings condemning all who participate in past life regressions. (I would remind Christians that Jesus was accused of doing the devil's work during his life.) You are free to pursue your own research if you choose, and to form your own opinions. One interesting contribution from the scientific community is: *Through Time into Healing* by Brian Weiss, M.D. -- Simon & Schuster.

If you currently believe in past lives, please use caution in advertising past life therapy--as this invites criticism from skeptics. If you are totally against the concept, please remember to respect those who choose to maintain an open mind. If you are undecided, those who already have their opinions formed would be well advised to respect your open-mindedness.

Regardless of our own personal beliefs, let's all remember the bottom line: If a client who believes in past lives is relieved of a problem after regressing into a real or imagined former lifetime, a *valuable service has been rendered!*

Maybe it's time for us to change our paradigms.

Chapter 14

Peak Performance

Once in a while we hear a speaker who gives us something so profound that our lives are forever touched. This happened to me in New York City in 1989 at the annual convention of the National Guild of Hypnotists. I heard a dynamic speaker, Richard Zarro, give a presentation that I will remember for the rest of my life.

What he shared with his audience was so profound that my life was permanently changed for the better. The technique he taught is so powerful that it has improved the lives of many of my clients. It is so valuable that I have incorporated it into my hypnotherapy class. It is so beneficial that I must include it in this book.

What is it?

Power Points for Success

Richard defined it as a way of establishing power points for success. By using self-hypnosis to anchor past successes into a trigger for success, we can help both ourselves and our clients create triggers for peak performance.

First, this involves hypnotic regressions to remember former successes to anchor the trigger. Second, we may use imagery to imagine using the trigger for future successes. Third, we must choose to use the trigger for peak performance whenever we have a need to be at our best.

Now let's discuss how and why all this is done.

Why Use Regressions?

One of the amazing qualities of the subconscious is its ability to store emotions as well as feelings. In previous chapters we've explored the use of hypnotic regressions to uncover and release negative emotions stored in the subconscious; now let's flip the coin over and consider the benefits of regressing into *pleasant* experiences and tapping into the positive emotional energies stored in the mind along with those pleasant memories.

Somehow it seems as though we can suppress good emotions just as easily as we suppress the unpleasant feelings. This is especially true when our self-esteem is suffering. For example, there have been times I went out of my way to help someone; yet when that person praised me for my efforts, I responded by saying, "It was nothing."

Have you ever neutralized a compliment in this manner? Whenever we cancel compliments, we deny ourselves the warm fuzzies that make us feel good deep inside. And I have often done this at the very times in my life when my own self-esteem needed those compliments! Most likely, so have you--and *so have our clients!*

How often are people hindered from being their best because of low self-esteem and/or fear of failure? Sometimes people are so busy trying to be perfect that they focus all their awareness looking for what was wrong with a performance rather than appreciating what was good about it. If we put our awareness continually on weakness, molehills seem to grow into mountains. Yet when we put our awareness into strengths, those strengths seem to improve while the mountains turn into molehills.

Through the benefits of hypnotic regressions, I help my clients remember former successes and feel the warm fuzzies they might have denied themselves. Several different successes are explored: athletic, artistic, academic, social, romantic, professional or career, spiritual or self-awareness, overcoming an obstacle, and one additional success of each client's choice.

Choosing Power Points

During the pre-induction interview, I briefly discuss the concept of anchoring and triggers with my clients (see Chapter 5). In order to create a trigger for peak performance, confidence and success must be anchored into that trigger. Richard Zarro calls it a *power point,* and I do likewise.

I encourage each client to choose his or her own personal power point for peak performance prior to the start of hypnosis. It should be a gesture or movement that would appear to be natural to an observer; yet something that the client does not ordinarily do. My own power point, which I disclose and demonstrate, is to put my right thumb into the palm of my left hand. It is a trigger that looks normal, so I can activate my power point without others noticing while being introduced to speak in public. One client might choose to touch the thumb to the middle finger. Another might choose to pinch his/her earlobe, or touch the nose with the little finger, etc. One of my clients, a singer, chose to touch the roof of his mouth with the back side of his tongue.

Whatever power point the client chooses is not as relevant as the importance of it being comfortable to the client; but remember that your preference might not be comfortable to your client. Remember, in client-centered hypnotherapy, let's allow our clients to make as many choices as possible--including the selection of personal power points.

The Session: CELEBRATE YOUR SUCCESS!

Once the client is hypnotized and sufficiently deepened, the journey begins.

In group workshops, Richard Zarro uses only a very light state of meditation with audience participants; and he has them draw an imaginary winner's circle on the floor. With each remembered success, the winner literally steps inside his/her winner's circle to feel the triumph! In the privacy of my office, I deepen to medium depth and use open screen imagery to take the client to his or her safe place, and to create whatever type of winner's area is desired.

Here is my own script, which you may use with clients. It also contains some positive suggestions designed to help enhance self-esteem since we live in a world that makes it difficult for us to love ourselves. Please do not record this on tape, however, as it is *copyrighted material*. (You may purchase cassette tapes from me to give or sell to clients--see my note following the script.)

Notice that I omit the category for romance. Depending on your client, you may or may not wish to add this category as well as other categories. Also, pause briefly at the dots...

I call this script "Celebrate Your Success!"

After induction:

Now imagine yourself in your own safe place... You may come here in your mind whenever you wish to experience peace within...

Imagine beautiful sights, sounds, and feelings which make you feel at one with nature. This is a journey of imagination. In the rehearsal room of your mind, you may rehearse or relive anything you choose. You may travel through time or space simply by imagining. In an instant you may imagine yourself in your favorite vacation spot... You may now return just as quickly to your own safe place... and as you imagine that inner peace, it becomes real...

In the storehouse of your mind is a record of everything you've ever experienced, including your successes and your triumphs... And as you allow my voice to be your guide, your inner creative mind will find that it is easy to re-create your accomplishments as you go deeper and deeper into the soothing state of hypnotic relaxation...

Now go back in time to an academic accomplishment and relive it in your imagination... Enjoy the accomplishment and appreciate the recognition... Activate your power point as you feel the feelings... Go to your winner's area...

Wait until client activates power point. If there is no response, give suggestions to choose a power point at this time. Ask for ideo-motor response to indicate that this has been done, in case the trigger for peak performance involves something you cannot observe.

Now come back to your place of peace, and take a deep breath and go deeper...deeper and deeper. You are responding very well as you allow my voice to be your guide...

For your next journey you may choose a time when you enjoyed either an athletic or artistic accomplishment--a sports success or an artistic success... RE-LIVE the experience with as many of your five senses as possible... Activate your power point as you feel the sensations of satisfaction and you create an attitude of gratitude...

Wait for client response with power point.

Go to your winner's area... and now come back to your place of peace, and enjoy the increasing awareness that you may recall and relive your successes whenever you choose...

Now go back to a social success--a time when you were appreciated by other people... Activate your power point as you feel the appreciation... go deeper into the feelings of appreciation and into the awareness that it is good for you also to appreciate yourself... Go to your winner's area...

Wait for client response with power point.

Now come back to your safe place once again, and take a deep breath and go deeper... deeper and deeper...

Now take a journey to a success involving job or career... Just BE THERE and relive the time of triumph... Activate your power point and go to your winner's area as you feel your increasing confidence...

Wait for client response with power point.

This VICTORY is ALSO a part of who you are, and you may remember your time of triumph whenever you choose...

As you come back to your place of peace once again, you realize that we all appreciate a moment of special love or friendship from a friend or loved one. I want you now to go back to a totally pleasant experience when you appreciated an act of love... As you relive this experience, activate your power point and realize that you are worthy of love...

Wait for client response with power point.

We are asked to love our neighbor as we love ourselves, and that means it is good for us to love ourselves too... As you come back to your safe place of peace, go deeper into the realization that you deserve to love yourself... Feel the wonderful power of love transforming you into the best that you can be...

Now project yourself into whatever success you choose to imagine, and activate your power point... and imagine MAXIMUM SUCCESS!

Wait for client to activate power point.

Feel the power of love as you know that through the power of love you are free to celebrate your success! By loving yourself more, you love others more--and you find your life filled with greater love. By loving yourself more, you find yourself becoming more and more aware of your successes--both big ones and little ones... And all these suggestions are going into the storehouse of your mind, as you remember to remember your successes.

Say the following with feeling and conviction:

You have the freedom to enjoy even more successes. You have the freedom to love yourself enough to celebrate your successes... freedom to love yourself enough to be the person you choose to be...

The power of choice is yours, and like a muscle that's used becomes stronger with use, your power of choice becomes stronger with use... know it... feel it... OWN it! You love your power of choice, and this gives you greater confidence as you become more empowered to be the person you choose to be... free to be the best you can be... free to love yourself as you love others!

And so it is.

Awaken slowly and gently.

If you wish to order hypnosis tapes with a script similar to the above, please visit my website (www.royhunter.com) and click on the box for *tapes*. You may order online.

Post Hypnosis Discussion

I ask clients how many successes they were able to recall, and whether they could easily tap into some positive feelings. The answers may provide good clues both to the present progress as well as to what may need to be accomplished in future sessions.

Often a client is astounded at how good it feels to remember successes that have long been forgotten. In some cases the tissue box has quickly found its way into a client's lap. Not all is peaches and cream, however, as some clients need so much help with their own self-esteem that they remember very little at all the first time. Sometimes I give a client the self-hypnosis tape "Celebrate Your Success" (similar to the above script) and suggest that it be heard several times before the next session. Then I may question the client at the start of the following session as to any additional progress.

Who Can Benefit?

Virtually every client seeing me for business motivation will spend at least one session on peak performance. The reason should be obvious to anyone intelligent enough to read and understand this book. I also incorporate this for clients with other goals whenever more confidence and self-esteem are important for progress. Often it is appropriate to include this session for clients seeing me for weight management, as self-esteem and confidence are often helpful in strengthening the power of choice. In some cases I may also offer this to a client seeing me for something like smoking cessation. Since every person is different, there is no set rule.

Personally, I believe that everybody can benefit from this; however, this opinion must be balanced with professionalism. A few clients that I've suggested this to have simply told me that they don't want to spend the extra time or money. That is their choice.

I do suggest that you, as a practicing hypnotherapist, experience this for yourself. Even if there is no hypnotherapist near you, ask your mate (or a trusted friend) simply to read the script to you after you put yourself into a state of self-hypnosis. You may be amazed at what you remember!

For a fee, I will facilitate this for a group of people. If interested, you may contact me at the address mentioned above, call me at (253) 927-8888, or you may e-mail me at (*rhunter@halcyon.com*).

Or you may wish to learn it from the person who taught me, Richard Zarro (Futureshaping Technologies, Inc., PO Box 489, Woodstock, NY, 12498). If you wish, you may reach him by phone at: (914) 679-7655.

Doing It!

At the conclusion of a session for establishing personal power points, I remind each client that a trigger for peak performance is only good if it is used; so it is wise to choose to use it.

In addition, let's realize that professional "burnout" is much easier to prevent than it is to deal with once it occurs. Therefore, we should all balance our work time with play time. I discuss this with all clients who see me for business motivation, even recommending that they establish personal rewards for various degrees of success.

Most of us prefer warm fuzzies rather than caustic criticism; so let's start looking for the good that we accomplish. As we find the good in our work, we may anchor all our successes with our personal power points. Then when there is a need to be at peak performance, we may activate our power points to trigger our best abilities and confidence.

Let's *celebrate our successes!*

Chapter 15

Motivation Mapping

Some of the precious gems of the subconscious mind given to us by Charles Tebbetts were touched on in the very first chapter of his book, *Self-Hypnosis and Other Mind Expanding Techniques*. Shining brilliantly among them we may find what my mentor referred to as "The Five Principles of Convincing the Subconscious"--which he also called the five methods of subconscious programming. I expand upon them in Chapter 6 of my book, *Master the Power of Self-Hypnosis* (Sterling Publishing, 1998), and did so in my first self-hypnosis book published back in 1987 by Westwood Publishing.

Today I refer to them as the five methods of subconscious motivation, and have successfully incorporated them into my *benefits approach* for motivation and habit control--and most specifically into an individualized consulting session which I have developed and refined over a period of several years. I call it *motivation mapping*.

Done properly, it is easy for clients to appreciate and understand. Some of my clients have actually expressed their belief that motivation mapping alone was worth the investment in an entire series of sessions! Yet as easy as it is to facilitate for clients in a simplistic way, I've discovered that it is much more challenging to teach the facilitator; so my students must now wait until the third quarter of classes before learning how to use this valuable consulting technique.

I've actually tried out several different charts during the years for this rather complex information-gathering process. In so doing, I've found that if I design a format that is easy to teach, it seems confusing to the client--and consequently un-appreciated. Yet when I make it simple for the client, it be-comes more complicated to teach. Why? Because there are certain questions that must be asked in order to maximize the benefits. And from the client's viewpoint, he/she needs only those questions asked that are relevant to his/her goal.

Regardless of the packaging, however, motivation map-ping revolves around one simple concept: *how the subcon-scious is motivated.* I may change the packaging even after this book is printed, looking for better ways to teach and facilitate this concept.

The Five Subconscious Motivators

Before beginning the client survey (or map) of subcon-scious motivation, I spend three to five minutes summarizing each of the five subconscious motivators--so let's do that here. I also call them the five gateways to the subconscious.

1. Repetition

This is the slow, hard way of reaching the subconscious; but nonetheless, once the subconscious learns to respond to a given trigger, a habit is formed. Smokers frequently light up when the telephone rings even when they are not consciously desiring a cigarette, simply because it triggers an old habit. Some people eat so fast out of habit that they almost inhale their food.

2. Authority

Ideas presented by authority figures often create either *automatic acceptance* or *rebellion* at a subconscious level. Al-though Mr. Tebbetts taught that this often occurs more often in childhood than in adult years, this is not necessarily so. The "rebel button" can be pushed even by someone who is not an authority over us no matter how old we are.

Smokers, for example, often are motivated to quit for health reasons--because of a desire to obey the laws of health. Yet some of the same people wanting health benefits wish to *rebel* when advised by a physician to quit smoking-- while others might stop suddenly and permanently after medical advice to quit.

3. Desire for identity (ego)

Charles Tebbetts taught that we all have a desire to belong and/or to conform. We are vulnerable to peers. And we have as well the desire to belong to a group and/or culture class. Furthermore we often tend to identify with a hero. My teacher called this *identification.*

I've expanded on this concept. All of us have an "inner child" who wants love, acceptance, belonging, recognition, and/or attention. We prefer "warm fuzzies" over caustic criticism or rejection. And just as some of us have a desire to conform, a few people desire to be non-conformists as part of their need for attention. This influences our habits and behavior!

4. Hypnosis/self-hypnosis

All forms of hypnosis or self-hypnosis open the subconscious to motivation and/or new programming, regardless of whether or not it is called hypnosis.

Charles Tebbetts said on page 17 of *Self-Hypnosis and Other Mind Expanding Techniques* (3rd Edition):

> *Hypnosis is a more practical and the most effective method for subconscious change. Since the subconscious has no power of discernment, it believes anything it is told.*

When we get engrossed in a good movie or television show, we actually enter a hypnotic trance state. (This is why I am concerned about the excessive violence in movies and television. I believe this has contributed to today's violence among youth.) In my opinion **it is of the utmost importance** that we *bring hypnosis out of the closet once and for all!* We must let people know that any hypnotic trance is *still hypnosis* regardless of what name it is called by--and regardless of whether the hypnotist is a hypnotherapist (or other professional), a minister, a television set, a CD player, or a video game! How many young people are filling their minds with violence while experiencing deep hypnosis?

By helping others become more aware of the many ways we enter the hypnotic trance, it is my hope that people can be more careful about what they let into their subconscious minds. And if this awareness were multiplied by every hypnotherapist and psychologist in the country, would it make a difference on our planet?

5. Emotion

While imagination is the language of the subconscious, emotion is the motivating power. We frequently hear emotion mentioned as energy, and it is!

On page 16 of *Self-Hypnosis and Other Mind Expanding Techniques* (3rd Edition), Charles Tebbetts wrote:

> *Intense emotion opens up the corridor to the subconscious because the conscious mind is inhibited by emotion. If a child is badly frightened by a dog, he may fear dogs for the rest of his life, in spite of his conscious reasoning that the average dog is not only harmless, but friendly.*

Just think about the logic of an intelligent adult who is afraid of elevators or afraid of needles, etc., and it becomes easy to understand how an emotional experience can energize a mental block in the subconscious mind.

Let's also consider that negative emotions do not have to create negative results, nor do positive emotions always guarantee positive results. How can this be?

While negative emotions can frequently hurt or hinder us, if directed properly they can motivate us as well. Even fear can quickly motivate someone to get out of harm's way; and someone could get just angry enough at a cigarette that he/she throws the habit away forever. Also, the desire for positive emotional satisfaction can motivate a person to eat too much candy, etc., or get into an unwise relationship.

Objectives of Motivation Mapping

Some therapists might wonder just what I expect to accomplish through motivation mapping--so let's briefly discuss the objectives before moving on into the survey itself.

First, I wish to help my clients discover sources of subconscious motivation that could make them vulnerable to backsliding. It is easier to avoid a pit than it is to get out of one, so I provide my clients with important information on which potential pitfalls to avoid and how to avoid them. Furthermore, by helping my clients become aware of sources of subconscious motivation for success in their desired goals, they are in a better position to use the power of choice.

Armed with awareness of how we can outsmart the subconscious, the chances of long-term success are greatly enhanced. Remember, a smoker seeing me to quit smoking isn't just interested in going into hypnotic trance. He/she is interested in quitting smoking--and hypnosis is just one vehicle to help achieve the desired goal. So by adding the motivation mapping, I am giving my clients more tools to help them stay on track.

In addition to providing my clients with valuable insight, motivation mapping gives me a better idea of the potential difficulties as well as the potential needs for more advanced hypnotherapy techniques in future sessions. You could say that motivation mapping is one of the techniques I personally use to help uncover causes, even though it is accomplished outside of the trance state. So in addition to being a certified hypnotherapist, I am also a motivation consultant.

Since this technique is optional, you may skip both this chapter and the next if you don't wish to use it. If this book is in your library, you know where to find the information if and when you change your mind. However, even if you don't use it, I believe that the awareness of the five methods of subconscious motivation can benefit your practice if you help people overcome undesired behavior.

When Is Motivation Mapping Used?

I use this technique with most clients who see me for smoking cessation and weight management. It is also very appropriate for any goal involving motivation, including professional or business motivation.

It would be inappropriate for phobias, pain management, or client objectives that are not of a motivational nature. These include habits or behaviors that spring from negative experiences or anxiety, such as biting fingernails.

Normally I use motivation mapping in conjunction with the benefits approach. In rare instances, however, I may skip motivation mapping even when the benefits approach is used--such as in helping clients overcome the use of marijuana.

Which Session Is Best?

Experience has taught me to facilitate the benefits approach at the customary first session, and to wait until the second or third session before using motivation mapping. When I first developed this technique, I normally used it on a client's first session and followed it with hypnosis. This created some problems, however, as my intake sessions often lasted two hours or more. Furthermore, most clients were getting too much information on a first visit--diluting some of the value because of information overload.

If a very analytical client is willing to wait until the second session for hypnosis, I will complete the motivation mapping as part of the intake session. Most clients, however, want to be hypnotized on their first visit; and I do my best to comply with the wishes of my clients, within reason. (Obviously a client wishing to have four sessions for the price of one will not get that wish granted!)

Completing the Map

Examine the blank mapping forms on pages 250-251 (un-numbered so you may copy them). Compare them with the samples of completed forms for a smoker on pages 252-253.

Notice that the forms resemble a filing cabinet with five drawers. Each source of motivation obtained in my survey is listed as though it represents a file in a drawer (or you may liken it to a file in a subdirectory of a computer) and is written into the method of subconscious motivation that most closely fits. Most clients find it much easier to follow along by visualizing filing cabinets or subdirectories in a computer.

I ask a series of questions relating to the particular goal of my client in order to create a profile, or "map" of potential sources of subconscious motivation for success or failure, much like mapping or identifying the files of a directory in a computer. (I liken the subconscious to a computer.) The questions relate to the five methods of subconscious motivation described previously in this chapter. When a question is answered in the affirmative, an appropriate "file" is recorded on the client survey form. The questions for smokers are always the same. Likewise, the questions for overeaters are also the same, even though different from those I ask smokers. The exact wording used for each "file" may vary from client to client, which is why there are only blank lines on the forms. And since the "motivation map" is *subjective*, I may sometimes combine two files into one (or not list one), depending on the client's perceived degree of sensitivity.

Once I've completed the questions and mapped the sources of subconscious motivation on the mapping forms, the results are scored. In the example shown for the smoker on pages 252-253, note that Bill scored "9" for the *smoker* on the *FORMER YOU* page, and "5" for the *non-smoker* on the *NEW YOU* page.

The next step is to disclose the score to the client (should you choose to do so) and explain what it means. Although I prefer to use scoring, that is optional--but my clients seem to like it. (I used to use a picture of a scale or balance.)

Now we can review each source of motivation and discuss what can be done to delete a file when possible or to avoid getting caught in an active negative one. Furthermore, some enhancements may be made on the *NEW YOU* page to increase positive motivation. Chapter 16 lists the more common motivation source files, and provides some suggestions for your consideration so that you might give some intelligent ideas to your clients. Finally, the "best case scenario" for the immediate future is summarized and scored. Refer to Bill's example on pages 254-255. His chances of permanently remaining a non-smoker are excellent if he follows all of the suggestions.

Now let's step through the questions I ask a smoker, followed by the questions I ask a client seeing me for weight management.

Mapping a Smoker

Once again, refer to the blank mapping forms on pages 250-251. You may feel free to photocopy these for your own use, provided you copy them EXACTLY (enlargement permitted) as shown--along with the appropriate credit to me at the bottom.

Let's categorize the questions and explore the logic behind them. Remember to list the "files" under the appropriate categories on the applicable page.

Repetition

For smokers, I ask only one question in this category:

Do you light up often without consciously deciding to, simply out of habit?

If YES, write "Old triggers" on the top line in this category on the FORMER YOU page.

This is the only source file listed under repetition for smokers. I do not list details about *old triggers*. I simply consider that people who light up a cigarette automatically when the phone rings, or when putting the key into the ignition, or when picking up a beverage cup, etc., are smoking at such times without a conscious decision to do so simply because the act of lighting up has become triggered so often that it has simply become a conditioned reflex through repetition. (Bill, our sample smoker, has a file here.)

There is normally no existing positive motivation source for smokers under *repetition* on the *NEW YOU* page.

Authority

The following questions should be asked:

1. Is part of your decision to quit smoking related to your health?

If YES, record "Health benefits" in this category on the NEW YOU page of the mapping form. Explain that accepting the authority of proven health statistics for a better expectation of improved health as a non-smoker is a positive motivation file.

2. This is a two-part question. First, have you ever been personally advised or encouraged by a physician or health professional to quit smoking? *[If YES, continue...]* **When you were given this advice, which of the following would best describe your reaction: were you, (a) more motivated to quit? (b) motivated to rebel and light up? (c) both of the above? or (d) neither of the above?**

The (a) answer indicates a file on the NEW YOU page called "Medical advice." The (b) answer indicates a file on the FORMER YOU page called "Rebel button." The (c) answer indicates both files, while the (d) answer indicates none.

3. Do you have an active "rebel button" that sometimes motivates a desire to smoke?

If YES, list it on the FORMER YOU page if it was not listed after asking the second question under the authority category. (You may skip the third question if "Rebel button" is already listed.)

4. Do you have any religious beliefs that are influencing your decision to quit smoking? *[If YES, continue...]* **Do these beliefs motivate you to quit, push your "rebel" button, both, or neither?**

List "Religious beliefs," "body = temple of God," or "Prayer," etc., on the NEW YOU page if appropriate. Also, if appropriate, list "Rebel button" on the FORMER YOU page unless it is already listed.

5. Are there any other past or present encounters with authority figures or authority imprints which might have influenced either your desire to smoke or your desire to quit?

If YES, list "Authority imprint" on the appropriate page. You may give more descriptive names to these files, such as

"Non-smoking job," "Encounter with Dad," or "Military orders," etc. Find out whether it is a FORMER YOU (negative) influence or a NEW YOU (positive) motivator--such as a "Non-smoking job," which could trigger a desire to obey, a desire to rebel, or both. If the client is not certain of the answer, explain that sometimes there are "hidden files" which may or may not hinder--or help--the motivation to change; and that only the obvious ones will be mapped. Hidden files can be uncovered and dealt with in future sessions only if it becomes necessary.

Bill answered YES to the first question, (a) to the second, YES to the third, NO to the fourth, and YES to the fifth (non-smoking work environment increased his desire to quit).

Desire for identity (ego)

Most smokers started smoking because of peer pressure-- in order to gain acceptance by friends and/or siblings, or because they wanted to project a more grown-up image, etc. Although there are some exceptions, I sometimes hear some interesting stories! There are other aspects of ego involved with the smoking habit as well.

1. Did you start smoking because of either peer pressure or the desire to feel more mature?

If YES, list "Peer pressure" or "Mature look" on the FORMER YOU page.

2. Here is another multiple choice question. Society today is favoring the non-smokers and ostracizing the smokers. Which of these four statements most applies to you? (a) Are you more motivated to quit to gain greater social acceptance? (b) Do you resent the peer pressure to quit? (c) Are both of the above true? or (d) Is what society thinks irrelevant to you?

If (a) is answered, list "Greater social acceptance" on the NEW YOU page. If (b) is chosen, list "Resent pressure to quit" on the FORMER YOU page. If (c) is chosen, list both. If (d) is chosen, just move on to the next question.

3. Have you frequently smoked either as a reward or a way of giving yourself some attention?

If YES, list "Cig. as rewards" on the FORMER YOU page.

4. Have you felt a sense of pride with your identity as a smoker or as a member of the remaining minority of smokers?

If YES, list "Smoker's identity" or "Smokers' minority" on the FORMER YOU page.

5. Is part of your decision to quit related to your self-image, family image, parental pride, social image, or professional image?

If YES, list the one most applicable on the NEW YOU page. If more than one are chosen, list "Better self-image."

6. Will it give you a sense of personal pride or satisfaction just to win at quitting? *[If YES, continue...]* **How would you best describe this? ...pride of success? ...pride of accomplishment? ...sense of success? ...winning? ...or what?**

List according to client's wishes on the NEW YOU page.

7. Do you seek out the company of smokers so that you may "light-up" and follow the crowd?

List "Follow others" on the FORMER YOU page.

Bill answered YES to the first, third, and sixth question. He answered (d) to the second question.

Hypnosis/self-hypnosis

If the motivation mapping is done at the first session, begin with the second question--otherwise start with Question #1.

1. Are you listening to the hypnosis tape I gave you at the first session?

If YES, list "Hypnotherapy" on the NEW YOU page. If NO, you may still list this file if the client has evidenced improvement as a result of his/her previous visit(s).

2. The most prevalent hypnotist in the country is television. Do you frequently smoke while watching television or while reading?

If YES, list "TV smoking" or "Smoking while reading" on the FORMER YOU page. If both are listed, this will still count only as one file when scoring--and you may list it as "Smoke w/TV + reading."

3. Road hypnosis is not just slang. We can literally trance out while driving, even while responding to traffic and road conditions. Do you smoke continuously while driving?

If YES, list "Smoking while driving" on the FORMER YOU page.

4. We have to pass through the alpha state on the way to and from sleep every night. Do you smoke in bed? *[If NO, then continue...]* **If you wake up at night, do you usually have to have a "smoke" before going back to sleep?**

List either "Smoking in bed" or "Midnight smoking" on the FORMER YOU page if applicable.

5. Have you experienced success with hypnotherapy in the past with any goal or objective?

If YES, list "Past success" on the NEW YOU page.

Bill answered YES to the second and third questions (this was his first session).

Emotion

Remember to remind the client that emotion is the motivating power of the mind.

1. Do you still enjoy the habit of smoking?

If YES, list "Enjoy the habit" on the FORMER YOU page. If client is uncertain, leave it blank.

2. Do you feel compelled to smoke as a way of coping with stress?

If YES, list two files on the FORMER YOU page: "Past stress smoking" and "Recent stress smoking." If OCCASIONALLY, list only "Occasional stress smoking."

3. Have you frequently felt guilty or embarrassed for smoking, or a sense of shame for needing help to quit?

If YES, list "Guilt" or "Shame" on the FORMER YOU page.

4. Are you emotionally excited about your benefits for making this decision?

If YES, list "Love the benefits" or "Emotional excitement" on the NEW YOU page--whichever wording the client prefers.

Bill answered YES to the second, third and fourth questions.

Final question:

5. Are there any obvious sources of motivation that we might have missed?

If YES, discuss them and list as appropriate in the applicable categories.

Bill answered NO to this question.

Our sample client

Now review pages 252-253 to see how all Bill's files were recorded and scored.

Next, refer to Chapter 16 for some potential solutions and possible new files for the *NEW YOU* page.

Third, refer to pages 254-255 to review my suggestions for Bill to consider. Note that source files which may be easily removed are lined through. Those which are potential pitfalls have one asterisk by them. Those which are trouble spots that may require hypnotherapy have two asterisks.

Finally, compare Bill's suggested score with his actual score, and note the difference. Also be aware of how hypnotherapy may help in desensitizing both the obvious source files on the *FORMER YOU* page as well as in uncovering and releasing Bill from any "hidden files."

Mapping for Weight Management

Let's categorize the questions and explore the logic behind them. Remember to list the "files" under the appropriate categories on the applicable page.

Repetition

There are several conditioned habits that could be relevant with weight management:

1. Do you snack frequently, just out of habit?

If YES, write "Frequent snacks" on the top line in this category on the FORMER YOU page.

2. Do you eat too fast?

If YES, write "Fast eating" on the FORMER YOU page.

3. Do you habitually clean your plate?

If YES, write "Clean plate club" on the FORMER YOU page.

4. Do you drink water frequently instead of snacking?

If YES, write "Drinks water" on the NEW YOU page.

5. Do you exercise regularly as a matter of habit?

If YES, write "Regular exercise" on the NEW YOU page. Remember NOT to offer advice about exercise unless you are professionally qualified to do so!

Authority

The following questions should be asked:

1. Is part of your decision to reduce related to your health?

If YES, record "Health benefits" in this category on the NEW YOU page. Explain that accepting the authority of proven laws of health is a positive motivation file.

2. This is a two-part question. First, have you ever been personally advised or encouraged by a physician or health professional to reduce? [If YES, continue...] When you were given this advice, which of the following would best describe your reaction: were you, (a) more motivated to reduce? (b) motivated to rebel and indulge in continued excess eating? (c) both of the above? or (d) neither of the above?

The (a) answer indicates a file on the NEW YOU page called "Medical advice." The (b) answer indicates a file on the FORMER YOU page called "Rebel button." The (c) answer indicates both files, while the (d) answer indicates none.

3. Do you have an active "rebel button" that gets pushed whenever you are reminded about calories?

If YES, list it on the FORMER YOU page if it was not listed after asking the second question under the authority category. (You may skip this question if "Rebel button" is already listed.)

4. Do you have any religious beliefs that are influencing your decision to control your weight? [If YES, continue...] Do these beliefs motivate you to reduce, push your "rebel" button, both, or neither?

List "Religious beliefs" or "Prayer," etc., on the NEW YOU page if appropriate. Also, if appropriate, list "Rebel button" on the FORMER YOU page unless it is already listed.

5. Did your parents give you dessert for cleaning your plate?

If YES, list "Clean plate = snacks" on the FORMER YOU page.

6. Are there any other past or present encounters with authority figures, or authority imprints, which might have influenced either your desire to gain or lose weight, or to binge?

If YES, list "Authority imprint" on the appropriate page. You may give more descriptive names to these files, such as "Domineering parent/spouse," "Encounter with Dad," or "Military requirement," etc. Find out whether it is a FORMER YOU (negative) influence or a NEW YOU (positive) motivator (such as "Military requirement") which could trigger a desire to obey, a desire to rebel, or both. If the client is not certain of the answer, explain that sometimes there are "hidden files" which may or may not hinder--or help--the motivation to change; and that only the obvious ones will be mapped. Hidden files can be uncovered and dealt with in future sessions if subconscious resistance indicates that it becomes necessary to do so.

Desire for identity (ego)

1. Do you wish to control your weight in order to look good, or to improve your self-image?

If YES, list "Better self-image" on the NEW YOU page. Sometimes the client may not relate looks to self-image, and may prefer that you list "Look good" instead.

2. Here is another multiple choice question. Society today is favoring the slim look. Which of these four statements best applies to you? (a) Are you more motivated to reduce in order to gain greater social acceptance? (b) Do you resent society's attitude towards heavy people? (c) Are both of the above true? or (d) Is what society thinks irrelevant to you?

If (a) is answered, list "Greater social acceptance" on the NEW YOU page. If (b) is chosen, list "Resent society's attitude" on the FORMER YOU page. If (c) is chosen, list both. If (d) is chosen, just move on to the next question.

3. Do you use food either as a reward or a way of giving yourself some attention?

If YES, list "Food as rewards" on the FORMER YOU page.

4. When you are with others, do you tend to go along with the crowd with your choices in food and drink?

If YES, list "Follow others" on the FORMER YOU page.

5. Is part of your decision to reduce related to your professional image?

If YES, list "Professional image." I consider this a part of one's professional identity, and is a stronger positive motivation than simply "Better self-image" alone. It is also interesting to note that some clients may be far more concerned with a better professional image than with a better social image.

6. Will it give you a sense of personal pride or satisfaction just to win at reducing? *[If YES, continue...]* How would you best describe this? ...pride of success? ...pride of accomplishment? ...sense of success? ...winning? ...or what?

List according to client's wishes on the NEW YOU page.

7. Besides what we've already discussed, are there any other obvious sources of motivation to eat or to reduce that you can think of which may impact your ego or identity of who you are?

List any that are appropriate. You may also gather additional helpful information that did not surface during the initial pre-induction interview.

Hypnosis/self-hypnosis

If the motivation mapping is done at the first session, begin with the second question--otherwise start with Question #1.

1. Are you listening to the hypnosis tape I gave you at the first session?

If YES, list "Hypnotherapy" on the NEW YOU page. If NO, you may still list this file if the client has evidenced improvement as a result of his/her previous visit(s).

2. The most common hypnotist in the country is television. Do you usually snack while watching television or while reading?

If YES, list "TV snacking" or "Snacking while reading" on the FORMER YOU page. If both are listed, this will still count only as one file when scoring--and you may list it as "Snacks w/TV + reading."

3. Road hypnosis is not just slang. We can literally trance out while driving, even while responding to traffic

and road conditions. Do you usually have to snack while driving?

If YES, list "Snacking while driving" on the FORMER YOU page.

4. We have to pass through the alpha state on the way to and from sleep every night. If you wake up at night, do you usually need a snack in order to go back to sleep?

List either "Snacking to sleep" or "Midnight snacks" on the FORMER YOU page if applicable.

5. Before drifting off to sleep, do you frequently replay mental "tapes" or memories of backsliding or worry about being too heavy?

If YES, list "Negative self-hypnosis" on the FORMER YOU page.

6. Do you frequently daydream yourself slim?

If YES, list "Positive daydreaming" on the NEW YOU page.

7. Have you experienced success with hypnotherapy in the past with any goal or objective?

If YES, list "Past success" on the NEW YOU page.

Emotion

Remember to remind the client that emotion is the motivating power of the mind.

1. Since all of us enjoy the tastes of certain foods, everybody gets a file called "Food tastes good."

List it on the FORMER YOU page.

2. Do you binge as a way of coping with stress?

If YES, list two files on the FORMER YOU page: "Past stress eating" and "Recent stress eating."

3. Have you frequently felt guilty or ashamed of being overweight, or guilty for needing help to reduce?

If YES, list "Guilt" on the FORMER YOU page.

4. Are you emotionally excited about your benefits of managing your weight?

If YES, list "Love the benefits" or "Emotional excitement" on the NEW YOU page--whichever wording the client prefers.

Final question:

5. Are there any obvious sources of motivation that we might have missed?

If YES, discuss them and list as appropriate in the applicable categories.

Mapping Other Habits

When you map the sources of motivation for weight management and for smokers enough to thoroughly understand the logic behind this valuable technique, you can follow the same concept and create questions to ask for each category.

If there is enough interest and someone to market the materials, I will design Motivation Mapping Kits for professional use--and include questions to ask for various uses of motivation mapping, along with appropriate client mapping forms. If you would be interested in purchasing such a kit, please e-mail me at rhunter@halcyon.com.

Scoring

Count up the number of motivation source files on the *FORMER YOU* page and record the number in the "Actual score" space. Do the same with the *NEW YOU* page. Now subtract the *FORMER YOU* page score from the *NEW YOU* page score and record this figure in the "Difference" space (+ or -). If the *NEW YOU* page score is greater than the *FORMER YOU* page score, the difference is recorded as a "plus" number. If vice versa, then the difference is recorded as a "minus."

So now what does this mean?

The page with the higher number of files represents where the dominant subconscious motivation exists. Now let's find out how to use this information for the client's benefit.

Medium to high PLUS score

If the dominant motivation is to change a habit, chances are slim that the client would have any reason to see a hypnotherapist.

A high PLUS score has never resulted with smokers on an intake interview, although it sometimes occurs if motivation mapping is done on a third session. The same holds true for clients seeing me for weight management, although in rare instances a score of +2 or +3 has occurred. In these instances, however, there were so many files mapped that the clients were experiencing inner conflicts and going up and down like the yo-yo effect.

Often a business owner or sales person seeing me for professional motivation receives a good positive score, however; and has chosen hypnotherapy to enhance what he/she is already doing successfully. Some of the results have been spectacular!

Even or close to even

Where there are relatively few files and the score is even or within one of being even, it is quite possible for the client to make progress on his or her own without any additional help or hypnotherapy--provided there is a strong level of commitment. This is especially true if motivation mapping was done at the intake rather than two or three sessions later.

The greater the number of files, however, the greater the potential for inner conflict; so even a client with a score of +1 might still benefit from hypnotherapy if there were five or six files on the *FORMER YOU* page.

As a general rule, clients with scores of -1, 0, or +1 will have a better chance of successfully responding to the *benefits approach* alone than someone with a higher negative score. But there are always exceptions, because we are *all different*. Or you could say motivation mapping is an art, and *not* an exact mathematical way of measuring motivation.

Medium negative score

A score of -2 or -3 on an intake would generally indicate that a person could temporarily make a change of habit during an emotional state of mind, or with emotional incentive. But unless something happens to change accidentally the motivation map, that person will most likely need professional help to enjoy lasting success.

If this score comes up two or three sessions after the intake, pay closer attention to any potential pitfalls. That client may need additional hypnotherapy sessions to uncover and remove subconscious sources of resistance.

If this score comes up on the intake session, there is still a good possibility of success with the *benefits approach* unless there are several trouble spots on the *FORMER YOU* page.

High negative score

A score of -4 or worse indicates a good possibility of the need for hypnotherapy techniques to accomplish all four hypnotherapeutic steps discussed at the end of Chapter 2.

Furthermore, if motivation mapping reveals a high negative score after hypnotherapy has begun, both you and your client can almost count on the need for additional sessions; however, once again, remember that there are always exceptions. Just as "hidden files" might exist that keep old habits active, there can also be "hidden files" that help motivate a person to change.

Now What?

Rephrasing what I wrote on the previous page, motivation mapping is not a science; it is a *subjective* way of mapping the more obvious sources of subconscious motivation so that we might be better able to help our clients help themselves. The analytical clients especially appreciate their motivation maps, as the concept of motivation mapping provides a logic that goes beyond hypnosis alone for subconscious motivation. Even the less analytical often find their maps helpful, as they reveal ways to help maintain long-term success. (Also remember that they help the therapist as well.)

There are no absolutes--and the possible "hidden files" could change the score. Also, a common negative motivation file may be much more difficult for one person than it is for another. Clients frequently express their appreciation for the self-awareness gained from this technique, however; so I plan to continue using motivation mapping. Hopefully you will find it equally useful.

If you have not yet done so, examine the motivation mapping sample suggestions for Bill on pages 254-255. Notice how some files are lined out. Others have one or two asterisks. There are also some client suggestions on the dotted lines. Where did this come from?

What I say to clients comes from years of experience. And the best way to share that experience with you is to organize it. That was my objective for writing Chapter 16 in its present format. You may use it for reference.

Also note that on actual client maps, I record the original source files in black, and then put my recommendations in *red*. This makes it is easy for the client to remember what his/her existing sources were, and it highlights just what the recommendations are. Then I record the new scores in the boxes marked "Suggested" and compute the "Potential difference." The usually significant difference between the original difference and the potential difference gives each client a greater *expectation* of success as well as a logical reason to *believe* in that success.

Remember our friends from the hypnotic formula (discussed in the second chapter of *The Art of Hypnosis*) belief and expectation? When added to imagination, they help to *convince* a client that success can be obtained--and this helps get results! In addition, the **client now has a motivation map** to follow on his or her journey to success.

The next six pages contain the mapping forms discussed earlier in this chapter.

Note that the first two, which are blank, do not have any page numbers at the top. As I mentioned earlier in this chapter, this is so that you may copy them if desired for your own use, as long as you reproduce them EXACTLY as printed, with my name and copyright printed at the bottom of the pages, along with my phone number and URL (except that you may enlarge them).

Note that pages 252-253 contain the completed first phase of Bill's motivation map, and pages 254-255 represent the second phase, along with written suggestions for Bill to consider. You may wish to compare these pages with what is written in Chapter 16, which follows the sample motivation map.

Mapping the Basic Subconscious Motivators

Motivation Mapping--the FORMER YOU:

Repetition (conditioned responses)

_____   - - - - - - - - - - - - - - - - -
_____   - - - - - - - - - - - - - - - - -
_____   - - - - - - - - - - - - - - - - -
_____   - - - - - - - - - - - - - - - - -
_____   - - - - - - - - - - - - - - - - -

Authority (to obey or rebel)

_____   - - - - - - - - - - - - - - - - -
_____   - - - - - - - - - - - - - - - - -
_____   - - - - - - - - - - - - - - - - -
_____   - - - - - - - - - - - - - - - - -
_____   - - - - - - - - - - - - - - - - -

Desire for Identity (ego)

_____   - - - - - - - - - - - - - - - - -
_____   - - - - - - - - - - - - - - - - -
_____   - - - - - - - - - - - - - - - - -
_____   - - - - - - - - - - - - - - - - -
_____   - - - - - - - - - - - - - - - - -

Hypnosis/self-hypnosis (all trance states)

_____   - - - - - - - - - - - - - - - - -
_____   - - - - - - - - - - - - - - - - -
_____   - - - - - - - - - - - - - - - - -
_____   - - - - - - - - - - - - - - - - -
_____   - - - - - - - - - - - - - - - - -

Emotion (the energy of the subconscious)

_____   - - - - - - - - - - - - - - - - -
_____   - - - - - - - - - - - - - - - - -
_____   - - - - - - - - - - - - - - - - -
_____   - - - - - - - - - - - - - - - - -
_____   - - - - - - - - - - - - - - - - -

Actual score:_____   Difference (+ or -): _____
Suggested: _____   Potential difference: _____

Mapping the Basic Subconscious Motivators

Motivation Mapping--the NEW YOU:

Repetition (conditioned responses)

Authority (to obey or rebel)

Desire for Identity (ego)

Hypnosis/self-hypnosis (all trance states)

Emotion (the energy of the subconscious)

Actual score: _____
Suggested: _____

Mapping the Basic Subconscious Motivators

Motivation Mapping--the FORMER YOU: **Bill, a former smoker**

Repetition (conditioned responses)
Old triggers

Authority (to obey or rebel)
Rebel button

Desire for Identity (ego)
Mature look
Cig. as rewards

Hypnosis/self-hypnosis (all trance states)
TV smoking
Smoking while driving

Emotion (the energy of the subconscious)
Past stress smoking
Recent stress smoking
Guilt

Actual score: __9__   Difference (+ or -) _-4_
Suggested: _____   Potential difference: _____

©1989 by Roy Hunter   30640 Pacific Hwy. S. #E
(253) 927-8888 * www.royhunter.com   Federal Way, WA 98003

Mapping the Basic Subconscious Motivators

Motivation Mapping--the NEW YOU: ***Bill, a NON-smoker***

Repetition (conditioned responses)

_____   - - - - - - - - - - - - - - - - -
_____   - - - - - - - - - - - - - - - - -
_____   - - - - - - - - - - - - - - - - -
_____   - - - - - - - - - - - - - - - - -
_____   - - - - - - - - - - - - - - - - -

Authority (to obey or rebel)
Health benefits   - - - - - - - - - - - - - - - - -
Medical advice   - - - - - - - - - - - - - - - - -
Job = non-smoking   - - - - - - - - - - - - - - - - -
_____   - - - - - - - - - - - - - - - - -

Desire for Identity (ego)
Pride of success   - - - - - - - - - - - - - - - - -
_____   - - - - - - - - - - - - - - - - -
_____   - - - - - - - - - - - - - - - - -
_____   - - - - - - - - - - - - - - - - -

Hypnosis/self-hypnosis (all trance states)

_____   - - - - - - - - - - - - - - - - -
_____   - - - - - - - - - - - - - - - - -
_____   - - - - - - - - - - - - - - - - -
_____   - - - - - - - - - - - - - - - - -
_____   - - - - - - - - - - - - - - - - -

Emotion (the energy of the subconscious)
Love the benefits   - - - - - - - - - - - - - - - - -
_____   - - - - - - - - - - - - - - - - -
_____   - - - - - - - - - - - - - - - - -
_____   - - - - - - - - - - - - - - - - -

Actual score: ___5___
Suggested: _____

Mapping the Basic Subconscious Motivators

*Motivation Mapping--the FORMER YOU: **Bill, a former smoker***

Repetition (conditioned responses)

~~Old triggers~~ _____ Make deep breath a habit _ _ _ _ _ _
_____ _ _(file moves to NEW YOU page) _
_____ _ _ _ _ _ _ _ _ _ _ _ _ _ _ _ _ _
_____ _ _ _ _ _ _ _ _ _ _ _ _ _ _ _ _ _
_____ _ _ _ _ _ _ _ _ _ _ _ _ _ _ _ _ _

Authority (to obey or rebel)

*~~Rebel button~~ _____ Claim your power of choice _ _ _ _ _
_____ _ _ _ _ _ _ _ _ _ _ _ _ _ _ _ _ _
_____ _ _ _ _ _ _ _ _ _ _ _ _ _ _ _ _ _
_____ _ _ _ _ _ _ _ _ _ _ _ _ _ _ _ _ _

Desire for Identity (ego)

~~Mature look~~ _____ Change the perception_ _ _ _ _ _ _ _
**Cig. as rewards_____ Choose alternate rewards _ _ _ _ _ _
_____ _ _ _ _ _ _ _ _ _ _ _ _ _ _ _ _ _
_____ _ _ _ _ _ _ _ _ _ _ _ _ _ _ _ _ _
_____ _ _ _ _ _ _ _ _ _ _ _ _ _ _ _ _ _

Hypnosis/self-hypnosis (all trance states)

*TV smoking_____ Water + beware what you IMAGINE
**Smoking while driving_____ Water, sugarless gum, mints, etc. _ _
_____ -- and beware what you IMAGINE
_____ _ _ _ _ _ _ _ _ _ _ _ _ _ _ _ _ _
_____ _ _ _ _ _ _ _ _ _ _ _ _ _ _ _ _ _

Emotion (the energy of the subconscious)

**Past stress smoking_____ Use stress coper + self-hypnosis _ _
*~~Recent stress smoking~~ _____ -- avoid negative fantasies _ _ _ _ _
~~Guilt~~ _____ Forgive yourself _ _ _ _ _ _ _ _ _ _ _
_____ _ _ _ _ _ _ _ _ _ _ _ _ _ _ _ _ _

* = Potential pitfall--heed advice!   ** = Trouble spot, may need hypnosis.

Actual score: _9_   Difference (+ or -): _-4_

Suggested: _4_   Potential difference: _+3_

©1989 by Roy Hunter   30640 Pacific Hwy. S. #E
(253) 927-8888 * www.royhunter.com   Federal Way, WA 98003

Mapping the Basic Subconscious Motivators

Motivation Mapping--the NEW YOU: ***Bill, a NON-smoker***

Repetition (conditioned responses)

NEW: Deep breath habit _____   When old triggers cause you to take _
_____   _deep breath automatically, you have
_____   _a new file _ _ _ _ _ _ _ _ _ _ _ _
_____   _ _ _ _ _ _ _ _ _ _ _ _ _ _ _ _ _ _

Authority (to obey or rebel)
Health benefits _____   _ _ _ _ _ _ _ _ _ _ _ _ _ _ _ _ _ _
Medical advice _____   _ _ _ _ _ _ _ _ _ _ _ _ _ _ _ _ _ _
Job = non-smoking _____   Be careful of REBEL button _ _ _ _
_____   _ _ _ _ _ _ _ _ _ _ _ _ _ _ _ _ _ _

Desire for Identity (ego)
Pride of success _____   Reward yourself for your success _ _
_____   Other files to consider here: _ _ _ _
_____   _ parental pride, professional image
_____   _ _ _ _ _ _ _ _ _ _ _ _ _ _ _ _ _ _

Hypnosis/self-hypnosis (all trance states)
NEW: Hypnotherapy _____   Listen to tape often_ _ _ _ _ _ _ _ _ _
_____   _ _ _ _ _ _ _ _ _ _ _ _ _ _ _ _ _ _
_____   _ _ _ _ _ _ _ _ _ _ _ _ _ _ _ _ _ _
_____   _ _ _ _ _ _ _ _ _ _ _ _ _ _ _ _ _ _

Emotion (the energy of the subconscious)
Love the benefits _____   Imagine them often _ _ _ _ _ _ _ _ _
_____   Another file to consider here: _ _ _ _
_____   make rewards fun _ _ _ _ _ _ _ _ _
_____   _ _ _ _ _ _ _ _ _ _ _ _ _ _ _ _ _ _

Actual score: __5__
Suggested:__7__

Chapter 16

Sources of Subconscious Motivation

This chapter is here primarily for reference. Before using the information in this chapter, please read Chapter 15 thoroughly and be sure you understand the concept of motivation mapping. This will provide much more meaning to the information presented here.

The following pages contain a glossary of frequently appearing motivation source files. Rather than alphabetized, they are categorized in accordance with the five methods of subconscious motivation and further separated by *FORMER* and *NEW*. Those that apply only to smokers are preceded with (s), while those that apply only to weight management are preceded with (w).

Those that can be mostly neutralized have descriptions that begin with "Delete"--and may be lined out on the *FORMER YOU* page (see p. 254). Those that are more difficult to deal with have one or two asterisks (or *stars*), depending on both the file and the client's situation. Note that we may recommended appropriate *new* files to help the client strengthen his or her motivating desire to change!

Recommendations and/or guidelines following each file shown are based on over a decade's experience. Again, since I am not a scientific researcher, please accept my comments as subjective; besides, there are no absolutes when it comes to the art of hypnotherapy. Also, since personalities vary, you may wish to customize your recommendations for each client based on that person's unique situation.

Until you become familiar with what to recommend for the various source files, you may wish to split the motivation mapping into two sessions. And just because I may specify a probable need for parts therapy or other hypnothreapy for a volatile file does not necessarily mean that will be true in every case. Some people make wonderful progress in spite of some potential trouble spots.

Repetition

FORMER you

(s) **Old triggers:** Delete. On the dotted lines I write: *make deep breath a habit.* It is easier to replace a habit than it is to erase one, so I suggest that my clients replace the former act of lighting up with one deep breath of air as the new replacement habit. (This suggestion is also on the hypnosis tape I give to clients to listen to at home.) A deep breath has no calories and no side effects; and I encourage my clients to get into the habit of doing this whenever an old trigger occurs, even if they no longer have a smoking urge.

(w) **Frequent snacks:** Delete and place one star (*). Write: drink sufficient water or whatever else is appropriate. Most of us don't drink enough water. Since it is much easier to replace a habit than it is to erase it, a few sips of water can replace a snack urge whenever chosen. The client is always free to make the conscious choice to eat if there is a physical need for nourishment. If the motivating desire is strong, the benefits approach and hypnosis tape may be sufficient to help. In the case of subconscious resistance, use one or more of the techniques in Chapter 6 to uncover the cause--and proceed accordingly. On the dotted line,

(w) **Fast eating:** Delete. Write: *eat slowly.* This is usually easy to correct with client awareness and programmed imagery during hypnosis, along with post-hypnotic suggestion to eat slowly enough to enjoy the flavor of each bite.

(w) **Clean plate club:** Delete. Write: *push plate away.* This is also usually easy to correct with client awareness and a recommendation to do what Charles Tebbetts used to call the "pushaway" exercise. I also use programmed imagery for the "pushaway" during hypnosis, along with post-hypnotic suggestions such as:

> **When you eat, you eat slowly enough to enjoy the flavor of each bite. PAY ATTENTION to each bite of food. You will HARMONIZE your physical and emotional appetite, and your body will let you know when you have had enough to eat. Then, just set your silverware on your plate, and ever so slightly PUSH the plate away. This sends a signal to your subconscious that it is O.K. to push away the excess food, and push away the excess pounds. RELEASE the excess food, and RELEASE the excess pounds...**

NEW you

(s) **Deep breath habit:** I write this in red as a suggested "NEW" file. I explain to my clients that once the deep breath becomes an automatic response to the former old triggers, there will be a significant reduction in the frequency of urges. Notice that just following this one recommendation changes the difference by two points.

(w) **Drinks water:** *If this file does not already exist, I write it in red and suggest--both before and during hypnosis--drinking sufficient amounts of water. Also see notes on frequent snacks.*

(w) **Regular exercise:** If this file is already present, I leave it alone with little or no discussion unless initiated by the client. If the file does not exist, I avoid discussing exercise unless the client asks--in which case I remind them that I am neither licensed to recommend for nor against specific exercises. The client must choose wisely and accept responsibility for choosing those exercises that are appropriate for his/her health. Why? What if you recommended an exercise that results in illness or injury? I do not want that responsibility! If a client still asks me to give an opinion, my response is: "If you choose an exercise that is FUN, you will most likely find it easier to be self-motivated to do it regularly. But whatever you choose to do, make sure it is appropriate for your health; and if you have any questions in this regard, consult with your physician or an appropriate health professional."

Authority

FORMER you

Rebel button: Delete and place one star (*). Write: *claim your power of choice.* Internalizing this is a quick way of desensitizing the "rebel button." One of my clients said that she would have quit smoking two years earlier if her husband hadn't incessantly tried to make her quit. Once she realized that she was allowing his attitude to manipulate her into continue smoking, she decided to quit--not because he told her, but because it was her *choice* to quit! If the client is unable to work through this by simple awareness, some self-empowering may be necessary through techniques to accomplish all four hypnotherapeutic steps.

Authority imprint, encounter with parents, military requirement, non-smoking job, etc.: Delete and place one star (*). Depending on the situation, I may write *forgive* on the dotted line, and/or *possible hypnosis.* If motivation mapping reveals a workable difference between positive and negative files and/or there is strong client motivation to change, the benefits approach may be sufficient. In some cases, regression or parts therapy or other techniques for releasing and relearning may be needed--including cognitive counseling.

(w) Clean plate = snacks: Delete. Write: *push plate away.* Release from the need to clean the plate could actually make it easier for the client to avoid snacks as a result of this authority imprint. See notes for "Clean plate club" under *Repetition (FORMER you).*

NEW you

Health benefits: Write: *appreciate!* Encourage client to be aware of increasing health benefits, and to imagine them often. It is pointless to recommend this as a NEW file if the client did not respond appropriately during the motivation mapping questions, as a person who already feels healthy might have resentment if advised to enjoy better health benefits for quitting smoking or reducing.

Medical advice: Focus on benefits of reducing rather than penalties of excess weight. Same notes apply as for *Health benefits*.

Religious beliefs, body = temple of God, prayer: Tactfully get past this topic as quickly as possible. Work within the framework of your client's spiritual beliefs without trying to change them. It is usually wise to avoid giving recommendations in this area, or recommending it as a NEW file if it does not already exist.

Authority imprint: A positive imprint is just one more trump card to work with, provided there are no negative "hidden files" associated with it (such as a "rebel button").

(s) Non-smoking job: Ask your client if he/she finds it easy to work without smoking--in which case you can add more power to the post-hypnotic suggestions with words such as:

Just as you find it easy to be a non-smoker on the job, you find it easier and easier to be a non-smoker elsewhere because you CHOOSE. Your subconscious already knows how to allow you to be comfortable in a non-smoking environment, and you realize this every time you go to work. Now YOUR ENTIRE BODY is a non-smoking environment!

Desire for Identity (ego)

FORMER you

(s) Peer pressure, mature look: Delete. Write: *fades with time* and/or *change the perception*. I explain to my clients that as long as they are smoking even occasionally, there is a risk of the subconscious clinging to the idea that it is still mature to smoke. This has been confirmed during parts therapy with more than one backsliding client. Also, it is my own opinion--based on feedback from successful clients--that the energy surrounding this file fades quickly AFTER the last cigarette. For some people it may be days or weeks; for others, perhaps only hours or even minutes.

(s) **Resent pressure to quit:** Delete and place one star (*).
Write: *claim power of choice.* If there is a "Rebel button"
recorded, you may draw a red arrow up to that file and link
the two together. The same recommendations apply.

(s) **Cig. as rewards:** Place two stars (**). Write: *choose different
(or alternate) rewards.* This is an active file that can be a
potential trouble spot if the recommendations are not followed, resulting in nagging urges that could last for many
months. Specific hypnotherapy may be required to help the
client experiencing difficulty with this, including parts
therapy and/or other techniques--depending on the situation.
(If the motivating desire is strong enough, direct suggestion
to choose alternate rewards may be sufficient.) This is just
one example of why so many people fail in the one-session
group stop-smoking seminars!

(s) **Smoker's identity, smokers' minority:** Place two stars (**).
Write: *hypnotherapy likely--CHOICE!* This is a very volatile
file. Specific work during hypnotherapy will often be necessary for release and relearning, including possible parts
therapy and/or other techniques. Remind your client that
quitting totally must be a matter of CHOICE, because the
benefits of quitting must be more important than any perceived benefits of smoking. If the client balks--or resists advanced techniques--it is better to offer a smoking reduction
approach rather than to let the client fail totally. If he/she
MUST quit but still resists, psychotherapy may be needed.

(w) **Food as rewards:** Place two stars (**). Write: *choose different rewards.* This is an active file that can be a potential
trouble spot if the recommendations are not followed; and
specific work during hypnotherapy may be required to help
the client, including possible follow up--depending on the
client's situation.

(w) **Resent society's attitude:** Delete and place one star (*).
Write: *claim power of choice.* If there is a "Rebel button"
recorded, you may draw a red arrow up to that file and link
the two together. The same recommendations apply.

Follow others: Delete. Write: *claim power of choice.* Some suggestions for confidence and self-empowerment may be

beneficial here. There is also a potential for some confidence building and/or self-esteem work if client has difficulty with making his/her own choices. Help the client *imagine* success around others. Help the client *believe* in the power of choice. Help build the *expectation* of success, and *convince* the client that he/she has the choice!

NEW you

(w) **Look good:** If this file is present, write: *appreciate yourself!* Most of us appreciate "warm fuzzies" from others; but if a client becomes dependent on a compliment from someone, he/she is giving some personal power away!

Greater social acceptance: If this file is present, write: *recognize your own success!*

Pride of success, pride of accomplishment, sense of success, winning: Suggest that your client imagine already enjoying the sense of accomplishment, etc.

Better self-image, family image, parental pride, social image: Ask your client during hypnosis to imagine what that means personally.

Professional image: Ask your client during hypnosis to imagine what that means professionally.

Reward your success: Suggest this as a NEW file unless one of the two above files is present--in which case you may add these comments as recommendations. Suggest that the smoker reward himself or herself three days after quitting, and one week, one month, three months, and one year later. Suggest that the client reducing plan rewards every five pounds, with nicer rewards at the mid-point and at goal fulfillment. The client may then fantasize these rewards during self-hypnosis.

Hypnosis/Self-hypnosis

FORMER you

(s) TV smoking, smoking while reading, smoke w/TV + reading: Place two stars (**). Write: *sip water + beware what you im-*

agine. This active file can be a potential trouble spot if the recommendations are not followed. Additional hypnotherapy may be required, depending on the client's situation.

(s) **Smoking while driving:** Place two stars (**). Write: *water, sugarless gum, mints, etc. + beware what you imagine.* This is a very active file that troubles the frequent driver. Specific hypnotherapy may be required to help some clients, especially those who drive professionally.

(s) **Smoking in bed, midnight smoking:** Place two stars (**). Write: *use self-hypnosis to sleep + be very careful what you imagine.* This is a potent file that is almost always a trouble spot if the recommendations are not followed. Specific work during hypnotherapy will likely be required to help the client, including possible follow up--depending on the client's situation. It may be beneficial to teach your client a self-hypnosis technique for inducing slumber and reinforce it with posthypnotic suggestion.

(w) **TV snacking, snacking while reading, snacks w/TV + reading:** Place two stars (**). Write: *sip water + beware what you imagine.* This is an active file that can be a potential trouble spot if the recommendations are not followed; but once the subconscious gets comfortable sipping on water while watching TV or reading, the client may be surprised at the results.

(w) **Snacking while driving:** Place two stars (**). Write: *sip water or chew sugarless gum + beware what you imagine.* This is an active file that can be a potential trouble spot if the recommendations are not followed. Remember that it's easier to replace than to erase. Specific hypnotherapy may be required to help some clients, especially those who drive professionally.

(w) **Snacking to sleep, midnight snacks:** Place two stars (**). Write: *use self-hypnosis to sleep + be very careful what you imagine.* This is an active file that can be a potential trouble spot if the recommendations are not followed. It may be beneficial to teach your client a self-hypnosis technique for inducing slumber.

Negative self-hypnosis: Delete and place one star (*). Write: *im-*

agine results rather than problems. Teach your client self-hypnosis. Give or sell him/her a copy of my book, *Master the Power of Self-Hypnosis* (Sterling Publishing).

NEW you

Hypnotherapy: If this file already exists, write: *listen to hypnosis tape.* If this is the intake session, list this as a NEW file, and on the dotted line, write: *sessions as needed.* Motivation mapping makes it obvious that hypnosis cannot be used as a quick fix when the negative motivation files outnumber the positive ones.

Self-hypnosis, positive daydreaming: Write: *Imagine benefits often.*

Past success: Ask what client believes helped him/her the most. A past success helps with belief, imagination, conviction and expectation, our friendly ingredients of the hypnotic formula (covered in Chapter 2 of *The Art of Hypnosis*).

Emotion

FORMER you

(s) **Enjoy the habit:** Place two stars (**). Write: *Hypnotherapy needed.* This is the worst negative file possible for smokers. Specific hypnotherapy is almost always necessary to accomplish all four hypnotherapeutic steps. Often it is necessary for the client to go through a temporary smoking reduction phase before being able to quit totally.

(s) **Past stress smoking *and* Recent stress smoking:** Place two stars (**) by the first one. Write: *Use stress coper.* Mastering the coping technique through self-hypnosis will help minimize temptation to light up during moments of stress, so you may strike through the *recent stress smoking* file. The *past stress smoking* file can be a source of future trouble, however, if the client does not learn to allow his/her power of choice to become a better way of managing stress. Since stress buttons cause more backsliding than all other reasons combined, I devote one entire session to stress management for every smoker wishing to quit.

(s) Occasional stress smoking: Delete and place one star (*). Write: *Practice stress coper.* See my notes above.

(w) Food tastes good: Write: *Accept this fact.* This is why the benefits must become important emotionally.

(w) Past stress eating *and* Recent stress eating: Place two stars (**) by the first one. Mastering the coping technique through self-hypnosis will help minimize temptation to eat during moments of stress, so you may strike through the *recent stress eating* file. This file can be a source of future trouble, however, if the client does not learn to allow his/her power of choice become a better way of managing stress. When these files are present, I devote one entire session to teaching self-hypnosis for stress management.

Guilt or shame: Delete. Write: *Forgive yourself.* Now that the client has an understanding of the sources of subconscious motivation, perhaps he/she can easily forgive himself or herself. If necessary, this can be addressed with hypnotherapy.

Past emotional hurts: Delete and place one star (*). Write: *Forgive.* If client is unable to do this, regression therapy may be appropriate, and/or traditional cognitive counseling.

NEW you

Love the benefits, emotional excitement: Write: *Imagine them often.* Remind your client that emotion is the motivating power of the mind. If this file is not present, it should be written in as a NEW file. Emotional involvement in the benefits is almost always essential for any lasting success.

Positive emotional experiences: If applicable, your client is fortunate to have these to draw upon.

Make rewards fun: This can be written as a NEW file. Remind the client that the subconscious is the child inside that loves fun and games. We all can benefit from learning how to be nicer to ourselves!

Chapter 17

Common Potential Applications of Hypnotherapy

Now I wish to discuss some of the common potential uses of hypnotherapy which I have encountered during my years of practice. In addition, I'll share with you some potentially useful suggestions to consider in your selection of initial hypnotic techniques; and conclude with a section on training.

Please realize that there is more than one effective way to help an individual--and personalities vary greatly. In light of this, my first choice may be your second or third choice. Nonetheless, if you know in advance what goal your client wishes to accomplish, you may find what I share in this chapter to be helpful as a reference guide. Then, based on the needs and unique personality of your own client, please be willing to change techniques as appropriate. Be intuitive as well as flexible with your client. The best hypnotherapist is the one who works as an *artist* rather than as a scientist. That being said, the artist must also have an understanding of the disciplines of the art, and not rely on intuition alone.

To make it easy for the professional, the chapter sections in this chapter appear in alphabetical order. (Some have subsections.) If you don't find a topic quickly, use the index.

Anger and Stress Management

There are three basic ways of dealing with stress and/or anger. I'll write a paragraph about each--although there are entire books written about these subjects.

First, a person may take the stress prevention route, doing whatever is possible to reduce the vulnerability of allowing buttons to be pushed in the first place. Traditional counseling will frequently be the best choice for learning techniques to improve communication skills, whether at work or home. I explain to clients that there are people with outstanding academic credentials, including psychologists, psychotherapists, vocational counselors, family counselors, pastoral counselors, and others who can assist in managing stress through stress prevention.

Second, there is the aftermath of stress. The same group of professionals can help with post trauma stress. Add hypnotherapists to this group, along with travel agents, massage therapists, racquetball courts, golf courses, cocktail lounges, and other less desirable methods of coping with the aftermath of stressful events. Since the causes of anger and/or stress can be as varied as the birds in the sky, it's important to fit the technique to the client rather than the other way around. If I believe I can help with hypnotherapy for post trauma stress and/or anger management, I disclose my training and qualifications--as well as my limitations--to the client. Then I use regression therapy with Gestalt, along with the informed child technique when appropriate, with special emphasis on forgiveness, release, and verbalizing for relearning. I tell a client before beginning hypnosis, "You cannot control what someone else does, but you--and *you alone*--can control your reactions to other people, places, events and things." Also, I'm very quick to refer to other professionals when appropriate. This is especially true for someone who is filled with anger, as there may be numerous unresolved issues requiring cognitive couseling or other psychological help. Facilitating a regression on a person filled with anger can be like opening Pandorra's box. You might get more than you bargained for, especially if there is hardware damage.

Now let's talk about the third area, the moment stress occurs. The most significant part of managing stress is learning to cope right at the moment stress buttons are activated; because no matter what we do to try to prevent stress, there is usually someone who can always manage to push our buttons anyway! If we can stay in control of ourselves during times of stress, there will be less intensity to any aftermath.

So how do I help clients better cope with stress? I teach them the peaceful place meditation (discussed at the end of Chapter 5) and anchor the peaceful place trigger. Also, I teach self-hypnosis. There is more information on this in Chapter 10 of *The Art of Hypnosis.*

Confidence and/or Self-esteem

Self-esteem is near and dear to my heart, so allow me to get somewhat wordy in this chapter section--and share what worked for me personally in rebuilding my own self-esteem.

Many of us get so caught up in the quest for perfection that we sometimes forget to recognize ourselves for our positive accomplishments. We seem to dodge darts everywhere-- from the little things at home, to career concerns coming at us on the job. In addition we are often vulnerable to fears caused by financial frustrations, and/or guilt over inability to change undesired habits. These frequently take a heavy toll on self-esteem.

Why do I say "WE" instead of simply referring to our clients? The reason is simple: *this chapter section is meant for all of us!* We have a far greater ability to help another person build self-esteem if we are making progress in that area ourselves. My own experience has proven this to me.

When helping a client build confidence and self-esteem, I frequently begin with a pleasant session--the one described in the chapter on *Peak Performance* (Chapter 14). Everyone has at least some past successes stored somewhere in the subconscious, and skillful use of hypnotic regression can help a client remember them. From there, I give my client some positive suggestions for building confidence. Sometimes I include one of Arthur Winkler's scripts after a few regressions into past successes. I also use open screen imagery as well as programmed imagery to ask my client to *image* using his/her *power point for peak (or maximum) performance.*

Sometimes, however, there may be a major subconscious block to positive suggestions. When this happens, the course of future hypnotherapy depends on what emerges as well as client feedback the following week. One male client actually failed to remember any former successes, and cried instead-- because nothing he did could please his perfectionist father. That session ended up being regression therapy and Gestalt, since his parents had found fault with everything he did when he was a child. He had a lot of forgiving and releasing to do. Another businessman was afraid of success because of an incident that happened at age 25. Usually it's beneficial to facilitate self-forgiveness as well as release of emotional hurts if there is resistance to the script for *Celebrate Your Success!* I also spend one session teaching self-hypnosis for managing stress, as discussed in Chapter 10 of *The Art of Hypnosis.*

In a few cases I've suggested cognitive counseling, particularly when dysfunctional family members are ongoing sources of continuing damage to the self-esteem. See Chapter 11 for some case summaries.

Depression

Avoid making bold promises about what hypnosis can do! Give the prospective client a *complimentary consultation* to determine whether the client believes his/her depression is purely an emotional response to circumstances, or whether there could be any possibility of physical or serious mental problems--in which case it would be wise to refer to either a medical or mental health professional.

Assuming the depression is not an organic problem, gather enough information to determine whether or not to *refer to a psychologist* and/or other professional for cognitive counseling. Find out whether the person is currently seeing another professional for depression, and whether or not that professional knows hypnotherapy is being considered. You may need a written referral in some instances (for your own protection).

If both you and the client are satisfied that you might be able to assist, then use the uncovering techniques explained in Chapter 6 of this book and proceed accordingly. The best techniques will depend on the combination of the client's particular needs as well as what emerges. Be sure to give your client a *safe place* trigger before using any advanced hypnotherapy techniques.

Forensic Hypnosis

Use *extreme caution* here!!! (I cannot emphasize this enough.)

Even with all my years of experience in the full-time practice of hypnotherapy, I usually avoid involvement with the use of hypnosis with victims of crime or in the investigation of such. If you are interested in this area, I urge you to pursue independent study and obtain whatever specialized training is available. Any regressions to help victims or witnesses remember events or details could result in the testimony being thrown out of court, because of the danger of false memories resulting from hypnosis.

In the few cases where crime victims have asked me for hypnotherapy to help them get on with life, each client has been advised to obtain legal counsel as to the impact hypnosis may have on the case; and I've also asked the client to note in writing that such advice was given.

One civil case I was asked to help with involved regressing

a client to remember where certain records were stored; and since the written information substantiated the claim more than the verbal testimony did, my client won his case. His attorney had recommended the use of hypnosis for the purpose intended.

Contact the National Guild of Hypnotists to find out how, when and where you may obtain specialized training in this area--where professionalism is a must!

Grief Therapy

Although I do not specialize in grief therapy, this has sometimes been the unexpected result of regression therapy for another issue.

I have found Gestalt therapy during the trance state to be a very powerful benefit to my clients. Sometimes the client regresses back to the last living encounter with the deceased relative; but I normally use a form of open screen imagery and guide the client to a scene of his or her choice and suggest that the departed loved one be there. I suggest that my client speak directly to the desired relative; and then the client takes on the role of the departed person and responds. Usually the dialogue is filled with emotion and healing. I ask my client to let me know when there is love and release.

In a few cases this has been done as a variation of silent abreaction in a client's safe place--without me knowing what the dialogue is. I can still ask questions with ideomotor responses to let me know when there is release.

Verbalizing can allow the client to use guided autosuggestion to improve life and benefit from the release. Often a client makes a statement such as, "My mother's love is always with me, but I know now that she wants me to get on with my life. It was her time to go, and I know that now." Charles Tebbetts would call this *facilitating adult understanding at a subconscious level--where it gets results.*

There are some case summaries in Chapter 11. Regardless of which technique you use, be sure to have a supply of tissues handy!

Habit Control

Besides the two most obvious uses of hypnotherapy, weight management and smoking cessation, let's explore some of the other potential applications of the art for habit control.

There is a basic guideline I follow with all clients who see me for help in breaking an undesirable habit: *it is much easier to replace a habit than it is to erase it.* So whenever possible, I attempt to give my client an alternative response to triggers. Also, with changes of habit, I usually use the benefits approach (except for nail biting or other nervous habits). For case summaries, check the index listings for the specific habits you wish to look up.

Beer drinking

Look in the subsection on *alcohol* under the chapter section entitled: "Substance Abuse."

Biting fingernails

Unlike other habits, my normal starting point for nail biters is to spend the first session teaching the client self-hypnosis for managing stress. (See Chapter 10 of *The Art of Hypnosis.*) The reason is that someone who bites his or her fingernails will almost always do so immediately when a stress button is pushed, or as a response to any nervousness or anxiety. Since the stress response is one deep breath of air, which becomes a self-empowering trigger for choice, the client has a greater chance of accepting one deep breath as a replacement for putting the fingernails into the mouth. When another trigger is needed (as is often the case), I have the client touch the thumb to a finger (explained below).

Normally I skip the benefits approach and use regression therapy on the second session (and/or other uncovering techniques) to find out when and why this habit started. If the client is resistant and only goes into a light state of hypnosis, then I may use imagery and suggestion alone--suggesting the practice of self-hypnosis so that the client becomes more responsive to a deeper state of trance on the third visit. It is normally after releasing the core cause that I suggest touching the thumb and finger together briefly as a replacement for biting nails, just in case the deep breath is not sufficient.

Chewing

My approach is very similar to smoking cessation, except that those who chew seem to be far more addicted than those who smoke. Because of this, gum seems to be a more acceptable replacement to chewing tobacco (or snuff) than a deep breath of air.

I use the benefits approach on the first visit, followed by motivation mapping on the second (or vice versa). After this, I simply deal with what emerges and choose whatever techniques seem appropriate. Whether or not a stress management session is included depends on the client.

The success rate is significantly less than for smoking cessation; so before I even accept the client's money, I do my best to ascertain that the decision is being made of the client's *own free will.* There must be a total commitment to success, or the client will be wasting his time and money. (I use the pronoun "his" here because I have never seen a female for chewing!)

Also, let me add that no client has ever yet asked me to help break the habit of chewing gum. If that request ever comes my way, I'll use the benefits approach and go from there intuitively.

Coffee Consumption

Use caution here! Caffeine withdrawals can be intense if a person stops drinking coffee suddenly. Withdrawals are much easier to manage by gradually decreasing one's coffee consumption. Once, when I found myself drinking too much coffee, I stopped quickly...it was an unwise choice! Not only did hypnosis prove ineffective for easing my headaches, neither did any over-the-counter headache medication help me. The next time I found it necessary to reduce my coffee consumption, I did so gradually.

Although nobody has ever seen me just for this one habit alone, several clients seeing me for other habits have asked to include suggestions for cutting down on coffee consumption. By sharing my own story, it usually takes only one session with the benefits approach and/or direct suggestion to help them.

Drugs or alcohol

See the chapter section entitled: "Substance Abuse."

Marijuana (pot)

Refer to the subsection on *marijuana* under the chapter section entitled: "Substance Abuse."

Soft-drink addiction

Only three clients have seen me for this. I used the benefits approach, gradually replacing cola with water. As far as I know, two of the three were successful. The third had some other issues to deal with, and I suggested cognitive counseling.

Use caution here! Cola contains caffeine. See my comments above under the subsection about coffee.

Impotence

Upon the request of others, this topic is included in my current revision. First, the therapist needs to find out whether the client has been examined for a possible medical cause, as hypnosis might not provide adequate help for someone with a medical condition. Once it is ascertained that there is a subconscious cause rather than a physical one, we must use all four of the hypnotherapeutic steps to facilitate change. There are several choices of available techniques to start with to discover the cause(s).

Normally I begin by using ideomotor responding. Based on the responses, I will then choose between regression therapy or parts therapy. On some occasions, depending on information gathered during the intake session (such as when a client says he feels guilty about sex), I might skip the finger response questions and go straight into regression therapy.

Gil Boyne, in *Transforming Therapy* (Westwood Publishing, 1989), wrote about a case where he used verbalizing to have the client spell out his fear (G-I-R-L-S); and he then used the feeling connection (affect bridge) to regress the client back to an earlier time when he felt that fear. Within one week, the client reported success.

Although guilt might be very common in the cause(s) of impotence, don't go looking for it.

Marijuana (pot)

Refer to the subsection on *marijuana* under the chapter section entitled: "Substance Abuse."

Medical Uses of Hypnosis

A licensed physician told me that he would like to see greater acceptance of the hypnotherapy profession by the medical community, including open cooperation. But again I repeat the warning given by Charles Tebbetts--pain means something is wrong with the body, and the cause needs to be discovered. He urged his students to require a written referral from the client's examining physician. Assuming you have such referral, then there are numerous techniques that may be used, which are described in Chapter 9. (Check the index for references to pain control and disease.)

Childbirth

I believe there is virtually an untapped market here. Although I've only been involved in two cases, both were profound professional experiences for me as well as for my clients. Both were also handled with the physician's consent. In one case, I was with the patient through delivery, suggesting that contractions simply be felt as pressure. (I also gave her considerable guided imagery during her nine hours of labor to keep her mind on pleasant thoughts.) With my other case, I taught a few simple hypnosis techniques to my client's husband, and provided a script for his use before and during labor. Since he took an active part in her pregnancy, this seemed to work out quite well. I would suggest that any hypnotherapist interested in this market seek specialized training wherever available. For additional information, go to the HypnoBirthing website (www.hypnobirthing.com).

Disease and illness

For disease or catastrophic illness, you may wish to begin with some of the techniques described in Chapter 6 to uncover any possible subconscious causes that might have made the client vulnerable to attracting the disease and/or lowering the immune system--and then use other techniques as appropriate based on what emerges. Imagery seems to be very effective, however, based on the research of others.

Give your client a safe, peaceful place to go to inside the

imagination (see Chapter 5)--and to be there with a *healthy body*. Post-hypnotic suggestion to use self-hypnosis to return to the safe place often might also be beneficial. Ask the client to practice frequent self-hypnosis (or meditation) with imagery of good health. If stress is compounding the illness, teach the client self-hypnosis for managing stress. And be careful to stay within the medical boundaries approved by the examining physician. For example, helping a client control headaches would be unprofessional if the referral is for pain of arthritis.

One of my former hypnotherapy students, a woman by the name of Ella Tate, worked off and on for several years with an AIDS patient. He had only a few weeks to live when she first saw him. I met him in 1993 and he looked as healthy as any normal person. Mrs. Tate has carefully documented this case, and hopefully will publish it sometime. But what is equally astounding in this case is the physician's reluctance to meet with the hypnotherapist to discuss his patient's profound recovery. The reluctance to accept hypnotherapy as a benefit for AIDS patients unfortunately is not limited to a few skeptical physicians, as there are some organizations dedicated to helping AIDS patients that still are not open to the use of hypnotherapy. It is my belief that hypnosis may prove to be the best treatment available today for patients of AIDS.

If you wish to work with disease, be sure to read *Love, Medicine and Miracles* by Bernie Siegel, M.D. There is other reading available for any hypnotherapist wishing to work with disease and pain management, including *Hypnosis in the Relief of Pain* (Hilgard/Hilgard), *Hypnosis in Skin and Allergic Disease* (M. J. Scott), and *Clinical and Experimental Hypnosis in Medicine, Dentistry and Psychology* (William S. Kroger, M.D.).

Perhaps our profession might build a respectable bridge

between the artistic and scientific communities. The International Medical and Dental Hypnotherapy Association has paved a few roads leading to those bridges. Their website address is: www.infinityinst.com/aboutim.html

Headaches

Charles Tebbetts believed that we should use uncovering techniques to find any possible subconscious cause if the headaches are migraine. Refer to the case summary in Chapter 11, contained in a subsection: *Harry, a multifaceted approach.*

For those that are not migraines, but have been professionally verified as not related to a serious condition requiring referral, he wrote a script which I have paraphrased here:

> **Now that you are completely relaxed, and in a deep hypnotic sleep, let go, all over, once again. Sooooo relaxed... Sooooo calm... Now all the muscles in your forehead are relaxing. They are getting more and more comfortable, relaxed and at peace. This pleasant, relaxed feeling spreads to your eyes... Your eyes are so relaxed, so comfortable. Your forehead is calm, and all the muscles are relaxed and at peace. Your eyes are calm and relaxed. The calm feeling goes over the top of your head, and your whole scalp feels a peaceful sensation. You feel better and better. Now all the muscles in the neck let go... calm and tranquil... relaxed and comfortable. The base of your skull is calm and relaxed. You feel so good! Better and better! You feel much better, relaxing more and more. Your neck muscles are now completely relaxed and comfortable. Your whole head is relaxed and comfortable. You feel wonderful! Your whole head is relaxed and comfortable. This wonderful feeling keeps on spreading. You feel more wonderful with every moment! Your head and neck feel clear. You feel good. You feel absolutely wonderful! All the muscles and nerves in your head and neck are completely relaxed and you feel fine. When you awaken you will continue to feel better and better**

with each passing minute. You will feel better and better for the rest of the day. You feel absolutely perfect! All of your neck and head muscles and nerves are completely relaxed.

According to my mentor, most people will find the headache gone either upon awakening or within twenty minutes afterward.

Hypnodontics

If a client has a phobia of going to the dentist, then traditional hypnotherapeutic techniques may be necessary to uncover the cause and facilitate release. Several of my students, however, have found it very beneficial to simply use self-hypnosis and imagery of a peaceful place. As for me, a former dental phobic, I am comfortable with both the gas and my peaceful place meditation! Before I learned the art of hypnosis, the gas actually made me more uncomfortable, because my focus was drawn towards the discomfort rather than away from it. Emphasize to your client the importance of keeping mental focus AWAY from the dentist's activities rather than trying to pay attention to what's happening. Self-hypnosis makes it much easier to accomplish this objective. If the peaceful place meditation is not a sufficient distraction, the client can re-live a happy vacation inside the imagination.

Pain management

For pain management, Charles Tebbetts normally used object projection, followed by the white light healing technique--also discussed in Chapter 9. There are numerous other hypnotic pain control techniques, some of which are summarized below:

Displacement of pain (pain transference): The pain may be moved from one location to another, and then modified and reduced.

Glove anesthesia: The objective is to make one of the

hands completely numb, allowing the client to then transfer the numbness to the appropriate part of the body. One way to accomplish this is to have the client imagine putting the hand in a bucket of ice or cold water until there is numbness. Another is to simply suggest an increasing numbness, as though the hand were shot with novocaine. Be sure to give a suggestion for normalizing the hand before awakening.

Gradual pain reduction: This is a good alternative if total pain removal is resisted by the subconscious, or if the nature of the pain makes it unwise to mask it totally. Suggest a partial reduction of the pain, even if only 5% per day, until the acceptable reduction is reached. An arthritis patient referred to me by her physician was able to reduce her pain by 50% and cut her pain medication down by over half, saving her $70 monthly--not to mention the much more tolerable level of pain.

Ideomotor exploration & turning pain off at unconscious level: Ask questions of the subconscious to identify the source and/or the "on-off switch" of the pain. If appropriate, you may ask for ideo-motor responding about secondary gain and/or other psychodynamics (see Chapter 6); then deal with what emerges.

Inner advisor: Ask client to imagine an inner advisor (of his/her choosing) who will modify or release the pain. If desired, client may be allowed to verbalize appropriate suggestions to help facilitate the process.

Object imagery: This is another name for object projection, described in Chapter 9.

Protective shield: Client may imagine a protective force around the body providing a shield from additional pain and/or unpleasant feelings. This shield may be in the form of a white light, or whatever the client desires to use for a shield.

Time and body dissociation (safe place): Escape to enjoyment of a pleasant past event while healthy, and/or escape to a peaceful place. (This is the peaceful place meditation, described in Chapter 5.)

Memory and Study Habits

Charles Tebbetts used regression therapy, verbalizing, and imagery with a student who had a perceived learning disorder. The case is summarized in Chapter 11 in the chapter section entitled, "Increased Learning Ability." My work in this area is limited. In those few cases I've worked with, I've employed the use of direct and indirect suggestion--and have provided a self-hypnosis tape for reinforcement. If motivation is part of the problem, that issue must also be addressed as well with techniques that fit the client.

Here are some sample suggestions you may find helpful:

Your mind records everything you see, hear and feel. Like a computer, your mind has a storehouse of memories.

Whenever you read or hear material you wish to remember, you find you are increasingly able to recall and present that information whenever required or desired. Your work shows increasing accuracy and understanding. Your comprehension and recall improve daily. Your mind is calm, efficient, and orderly.

You have an increasing ability to study when you choose, excluding all common distractions, with an increasing ability to focus.

Whenever desired or required, you can present that information easily and quickly, whether orally, in written form, or by demonstration.

Your memory improves daily.

My most profound success was a high school student whom I hypnotized only one time, giving her suggestions such as what is above. Her grades went from a D average to an A- average! Another was a college student struggling with one particular class; and she became one of the best students in the class after three sessions incorporating self-hypnosis, stress management, imagery and peak performance, along with suggestions such as the ones listed above. However, I've had two clients who saw me for only one session, claiming no improvement. Whether or not a second session might have made a difference is a matter of speculation. One of those failures was someone who was not motivated to study, and just wanted a magic hypnotic "quick fix" to get good grades without spending any effort to learn the material.

For test anxiety, see my comments in that chapter section.

Multiple Personalities

It is my own opinion that the most qualified therapist to help a person with multiple personalities would most likely be *EITHER* a psychiatrist, psychologist, or mental health professional who is *also* trained in hypnotherapy and parts therapy, *OR* an *integrated* hypnotherapist who became whole and cured from multiple personalities as a result of parts therapy. This opinion comes from lengthy conversations with two hypnotherapists who have experienced the benefits of integration of former personalities through hypnotherapy, as well as a psychotherapist experienced with MPD's who took my hypnosis course.

One of the hypnotherapists I spoke with at a national hypnosis convention informed me that her personalities split as a result of childhood trauma. It was her opinion that what were originally just personality parts simply walled themselves off to protect her from going totally insane or killing herself when her father, a minister, had molested her and *blamed her* for his actions. She had seen two psychiatrists and several psychologists over a period of more than a decade--*without any improvement.* Apparently two of the professionals she had seen knew enough about hypnotic regression to regress her numerous times over a period of a couple of years; but rather than experiencing release and integration, she simply became the subject of their research--at her own time and expense. Finally she was referred to a psychologist who had also been trained in the art of hypnotherapy by the hypnotherapy profession, and became *fully integrated* within a period of several months! She told me that as a fully integrated person, she now had conscious memories of playing the role of all of her former "personalities." Her success motivated her to change careers and become a hypnotherapist.

The other hypnotherapist also believes that her personality "parts" during childhood walled themselves off into separate personalities as a result of trauma; and that parts therapy had done more to integrate than anything else. She informed me that she has facilitated several workshops for small groups of mental health counselors and psychologists as a result of her success with hypnotherapy.

In my 17+ years of practicing hypnotherapy, I have not knowingly worked with multiple personalities. Furthermore, I have no immediate plans to do so, unless it is in cooperation with a psychologist or qualified mental health counselor willing to supervise the client's progress and provide appropriate cognitive counseling. I would suggest that you follow my example unless you are professionally qualified to do otherwise.

Phobias

Chapter 10 is devoted exclusively to phobias. Please read it carefully before attempting to help any clients release them. Remember that complex phobias may require cognitive counseling.

Public Speaking

This is the one phobia resulting in my use of systematic

desensitization rather than implosive desensitization; however, I begin with the script for peak performance first. Once my client has established his/her power point as a trigger for peak performance, I use programmed imagery to have the client imagine various speaking situations. A trigger for stress release is also helpful (see Chapter 10 of *The Art of Hypnosis*). In fact, when I am personally being introduced for a speaking engagement, I use my own trigger for stress release as well as my power point for peak performance.

Since I have professional speaking experience, and have been a member of National Speakers Association for over a decade, I feel qualified to add the element of some of my own cognitive counseling on certain techniques to improve public speaking skills. It is my opinion, however, that a hypnotherapist who is afraid to speak in public might have a more difficult time working with a client wishing to overcome this phobia (or *anxiety*, as some prefer to call it)--so if you have that fear yourself, please refer this client to another hypnotherapist with speaking experience if there is one in your area.

Remembering Lost Items

Regression to a specific event is the best way to help a client remember the location of a lost or misplaced item. I usually begin the regression at the point where my client consciously remembers having (or seeing) the item for the last time--and proceed from there. Usually it takes only one session.

It is extremely important that you know the difference between guiding and leading! Refer to the chapter section in Chapter 7 which discusses this--and also contains an example of a session I facilitated for a man who misplaced some cash.

Sales & Business Motivation

This is my specialty. Because of my ten years of experience in both sales and sales management prior to entering the hypnotherapy profession, I feel well qualified to blend some motivational consulting into hypnotherapy to help business people become better at what they do. My clients go through a series of sessions covering--but not limited to--what is written in my book, *Success Through Mind Power*. I teach self-hypnosis for managing stress. Confidence and self-esteem are frequently needed. The benefits approach is used as well. I also employ motivation mapping. Depending on what emerges, additional sessions are included for those I consult with privately. Several of my clients have reached six-digit incomes after going through a series of sessions with me. Others have become much happier, even if their incomes have only increased slightly.

Nothing qualifies a sales consultant more than sales experience! A hypnotherapist with a sales background will be far more accepted than one who has none--regardless of whether there is a college degree, post-graduate degree, or simply a high school diploma. My sales experience qualifies me in this department far more than my Master's degree does, as most professional sales people do not believe *anyone* lacking in sales experience is qualified to give specific advice directly relating to sales productivity. Even if lip service is given out of respect to a therapist with an advanced degree, there will usually be a credibility problem--whether expressed or not.

If you have no sales experience, and there is no hypnotherapst in your area who does, then I suggest you recognize the fact that *we sell self-help!* You may explain to your client that your sales experience is limited to your years of selling self-help as a hypnotherapist; but you know what has worked for others. Then proceed from there. Most salespeople will respect your honesty about this--and the few that don't are likely to be the ones you may not wish to work with in a professional relationship.

It is my desire to facilitate more group sessions in this specialty area. Naturally, any local hypnotherapists in the area would benefit from possible spinoff business. If you wish to promote a workshop, please contact me at (253) 927-8888, or e-mail me (rhunter@halcyon.com). My saying is, "Have voice, will travel!"

Sexual Abuse

If someone is living in a situation where an abuser is a *present* threat to him/her or others, then traditional counseling and/or legal counseling would virtually always be *essential* in this scenario. The hypnotherapist would be wise to proceed with **extreme caution** unless also qualified to provide other professional help--or unless working in conjunction with another qualified professional. If confrontive measures are considered, the *potential consequences* of such confrontation should be considered as well. Let the hypnotherapist beware: the victim of current abuse needs more than hypnotherapy!

If the prospective client is a recent rape victim, there could be some potential problems with court testimony--so you might suggest your client consider legal advice on how hypnotherapy might impact the legal outcome before you proceed.

If the abuse is in the past, there are some *important points to consider.* Although hypnotherapy may be valuable in helping people heal from former sexual abuse, caution must be used here because of the increasing public concern over false memory syndrome. The hypnotherapist must be working from a totally objective position, with the goal of helping the client *heal* rather than staying angry and trying to lay blame.

By no means am I an expert in this area; my work has been very limited. However, one of the most profound client successes of my career was with a woman who was originally referred to me for professional confidence. Parts therapy revealed that the cause of her low self-esteem was due to numerous sexual abuses committed by her stepfather when she was in her teens. She had not disclosed this to me previously, but confirmed consciously that these were real memories she had carried for years.

This woman saw me several times before this emerged. I then explained that I had not done any work in this area, but she insisted that I be the one to help her. She told me that traditional counseling had been a waste of time. In a series of regressions, using the informed child technique and Gestalt therapy, she was able to understand her deceased stepfather. She eventually forgave him without condoning his actions, and then she forgave herself. She is the one I mentioned earlier, in the first chapter of this book, who approached me in a public place and thanked me for "giving her life back" to her. I was literally touched to tears by her gratitude. This woman looked five years younger, and her eyes had a sparkle that I had not seen in any of her therapy sessions.

A former hypnotherapy student who was the victim of sexual abuse complained that the therapists she saw wanted to *lay blame* on her for "hanging on to the hurt" rather than help her forgive and get on with her life. She was actually advised by one therapist that she would not be able to heal unless she confronted her father! Can you believe this? Shouldn't we look for solutions instead of compounding the problems?

I previously disclosed that I myself suffered sexual abuse by a relative during my childhood. Thank God I refused to believe that I would be scarred for life. It is my strong opinion--personally, professionally, and spiritually--that forgiveness and release were vital to my own healing. Yet a psychotherapist advised me that I needed to get angry and confront that relative in order to fully claim my power back.

Absolutely NOTHING would be gained by confronting that relative today! It would only hurt *me* if I wallowed around in anger or self-pity over what happened in my childhood.

If you wish to do some reading, the list of books on victims of abuse and dysfunctional families is almost endless. My advice is that you consider everything you read with a grain of rock salt. Too many people spend too much energy wallowing around in self-pity, blaming others for their problems so that they can justify hanging onto their grudges and bitterness. Had I been among them--and I easily could have been--you would not be reading this book.

Let's find the healing power of forgiveness so we can *get on with life!* To me, this is personal...very personal, in that I've walked the talk.

Sports Enhancement

Although my professional experience in this area is somewhat limited, it is profoundly successful in almost every case. My approach is to create a trigger for peak performance in the desired sport, and to use both open screen imagery and programmed imagery to strengthen it.

A professional golfer saw me twice before a tournament. During hypnosis, I took him through 18 holes of golf. On his second session I taught him self-hypnosis and took him through the holes he said were most likely to cause problems. His name must remain confidential.

A semi-professional bowler improved his average by 17 pins after only four sessions through the same techniques.

A swimmer who saw me won a medal in the Senior Olympics. This name must also remain confidential, although he has told several people about me.

I would *love* to do more work in this area. (Any professional team and/or sports association is welcome to make an offer!)

Stress

See the chapter section entitled: Anger Management and Stress.

Stuttering

Over the years, I've only seen two clients with this problem. One was successful; one failed. (The failure resisted both parts therapy and regression therapy.) I used regression therapy with the successful client.

Charles Tebbetts worked with several clients who stuttered, using regression therapy. Gil Boyne has also worked with a number of stutterers over the years, including one that he worked with in my presence at a hypnosis convention. I personally talked with the former stutterer a year later, and he spoke quite clearly! Mr. Boyne also included a case history on stuttering in *Transforming Therapy* (Westwood Publishing, 1989). He employed parts therapy, regression therapy, and several other techniques.

Substance Abuse

Be careful here! Unless you have training and experience in working with people addicted to drugs or alcohol, you may be wasting someone's time and money. The exception might be for people who smoke pot, provided there is total commitment to change.

Several substance abuse counselors have taken my hypnotherapy course, and have informed me that hypnotherapy is a valuable addition to their tool kit. But if you are not good at spotting a lie, the addict may lead you down the rosy trail. Let's consider three basic areas.

Alcohol

My success rate has been very low for those few clients

who have persuaded me to work with them for a drinking problem. In the first place, I am not trained to know the difference between someone who has a chemical dependency and someone who is simply drinking too much as a habit which could be controlled.

Several years ago a man tried to convince me that his problem with drinking excessive beer was due to stress and habit. Although he liked the benefits approach, he resisted parts therapy. He convinced me that simply learning to manage stress would reduce the desire for beer, and help him easily replace the beer with something else. When I suggested water, he said he preferred orange juice because of its Vitamin C content. After three sessions he was bragging about his success. Two months later his wife saw me for something different. She tried to get me to break client confidentiality, and I would not. Instead, I simply sat quietly without responding when she said, "I bet my husband told you he was replacing his beer with orange juice." After a brief pause, she continued with, "I bet he failed to tell you that he puts Vodka in the orange juice!"

One of my few successes was with a person who was apparently accurate in his belief that his subconscious could help him drink only on holidays and special occasions--and without getting intoxicated. It took parts therapy to help accomplish this. Another success was with a person seeing me for a different issue but who also wanted to stay sober. He convinced me his decision to quit drinking was genuine. He was involved in cognitive counseling, but his counselor did not believe in hypnosis--and he needed to get his subconscious to accept his decision to remain sober. I used an excellent script with Ericksonian metaphors written by Dr. Arthur Winkler, and the client responded quite well. His commitment was so strong that parts therapy was not necessary.

One amazing success was a person who saw me to *quit*

smoking--and failed. Almost two years later he called me to go through my smoking cessation a second time, at which time he disclosed to me the fact that every time he heard me say "non-smoker," he modified the suggestion to "non-drinker!" He had not touched a drop in all that time. Needless to say, he quit smoking the second time around. Along this same line is the astounding success of Scott Lamb, detailed in Chapter 12 of this book, who quit drinking after successful parts therapy.

The bottom line is that I normally recommend traditional counseling with someone trained in substance abuse. If a client insists on seeing me, it is legal for me to do so (as long as I explain my limitations); but the client must convince me that he/she is making the choice willingly to quit drinking. There must be a total commitment to success, or I will not accept the client.

Drugs (except pot)

In every case that I know of where someone has seen me for hypnotherapy to overcome cocaine or other hard drugs, the client has failed (except for marijuana). All of those I've worked with for drugs have resisted getting past the light state of trance. Apparently many still believe that hypnosis can just remove the desire by magic. (Or did they resist deep trance because they were afraid hypnosis just might succeed?) The last two people who convinced me to work with them failed to even show up for subsequent sessions, and they also failed to return my phone calls--so I am inclined to assume they went back to the substance.

Again, however, I believe that appropriate use of uncovering techniques and/or parts therapy can make a real difference for a trained substance abuse counselor, provided the client is willing to make a commitment to success.

Marijuana (pot)

My track record in this department is about 40%. It is my belief that it would be higher if I had done a better job of screening during the first few years of my practice.

Just as with alcoholism, there must be a total commitment to success--otherwise the client can tell others that hypnosis doesn't work.

When I accept a client for pot addiction, I use the benefits approach and give suggestions for vivid imagery through the use of self-hypnosis. (Parts therapy and/or other techniques may be used if necessary.) Some clients have informed me that they can enjoy their favorite music and duplicate the feeling of pot without the use of the substance--except that they can awaken immediately from their self-induced trance states into fully alert conscious awareness.

One example of success is discussed in Chapter 11 (on pages 173-174), about a teenager who quit smoking pot. His father contacted me two years later and informed me that his son had not smoked once since his first session with me, and had also been accepted into the Navy.

Success

See the chapter section entitled: "Sales Motivation and Business Motivation."

Suicidal

I'm not qualified to give an opinion in this area. The only time I ever used hypnotherapy with someone who was suicidal was when a friend called me at home one night to tell me he was going to kill himself unless I could give him a reason to keep on living. He refused to call the crisis line, so I broke speed limits to get to him as quickly as possible. After two hours in hypnotic trance, with the help of parts therapy I was able to get his parts to agree to seek psychological help to put his life back together again. He had experienced extreme abuse as a child, hated his father, and had never worked through those issues.

Even though I don't choose to work in this area, my friend told me that the help provided that night saved his life. I don't know whether or not he actually would have taken his own life had I not responded to him, but I'm glad that I never had to find out.

Test Anxiety

Find out whether the difficulty with taking tests is due to improper preparation, lack of motivation, or due to actual anxiety itself. If the study habits need improvement, work on that area. (See my notes in that section.)

Some people have a tendency to get stressed whenever taking exams, even though they have studied the material. When this is the case, I spend the first session teaching self-hypnosis for stress management. By anchoring the peaceful place into the trigger of one deep breath, a client can relax into a light state of self-hypnosis just before an exam. I also suggest a trigger for mental focus: being able to think with a clear mind, using the best wisdom, knowledge, understanding and training. The client is then asked to imagine being in the test environment, ready to begin. The deep breath trigger is suggested, along with the trigger for mental focus. You may also find some additional positive suggestions are helpful, such as the ones in the chapter section on memory and study habits. At the cognitive level, the client may wish to complete the easy questions first, and then come back to the more challenging ones. This may be helpful in preventing one difficult question from causing unwanted early anxiety.

A couple of my former clients who have had deeper subconscious causes of test anxiety (or delay in progress) have been referred to a psychotherapist who is also a certified hypnotherapist. She specializes in learning disorders, and can provide cognitive counseling as appropriate to supplement the help provided through hypnosis.

Tinnitus

No hypnotherapy text can be complete without a few words about a condition that impacts millions of adults: tinnitus, a ringing (or roaring) in the ears.

Until I met Kevin Hogan, Ph.D., only one client had ever seen me for tinnitus, and she was not successful. There is much more to helping a client with this condition than simply reading hypnotic scripts and giving suggestions.

Dr. Hogan has written an outstanding book entitled, *Tinnitus: Turning the Volume Down* (Network 3000 Publishing, 1998). If you plan on working in this arena, this book is a "must purchase" for your library. First, there are medical concerns that must be addressed before hypnotherapy even begins. Once those concerns are properly addressed, all the causes must be uncovered from the subconscious. The client will most likely require several sessions involving both parts therapy and regression therapy to facilitate all four hypnotherapeutic objectives.

One personal success of mine took place in June of 1999, while teaching a parts therapy workshop for the Irish School of Ethical and Analytical Hypnotherapy. The presenting problem had no apparent connection to tinnitus, but a seemingly simple inner conflict was linked to unresoved grief. When the old grief emerged and was released, a reduction of the ringing in the ears was a fringe benefit discovered only after the session concluded.

Ongoing Training and Specialty Courses

I actually use the tools to help teach the tools, working

with both the right brain and the left brain in the training process. Group hypnosis is common in my classroom. Also, as my students practice with each other, they are asked to give frequent suggestions to each other for improving confidence and competence in the art of hypnosis. Practicing hypnotherapists also ask me to facilitate sessions as well. Additionally, I have asked other hypnotherapists to work with me whenever situations have resulted in my getting into a negative frame of mind. We can all take advantage of the tools we use to help us be our best.

In addition to working with the right brain, we can work with the left brain by participating in ongoing continuing education. There are numerous annual hypnosis conventions held around the country, as well as workshops and occasional specialty training opportunities. The National Guild of Hypnotists offers one of the best annual conventions available.

Also, when the first version of this book was completed, several advanced specialty courses in hypnotherapy were added to the hypnotherapy program at Tacoma Community College, including the following:

A licensed clinical psychologist specializing in substance abuse agreed to teach an advanced specialty course in *hypnosis and substance abuse* at the college. He has built a bridge of cooperation between the scientific community and the hypnotherapy profession through active involvement with the Washington Hypnosis Association. I have also attempted to find a qualified medical professional teach a class designed to help hypnotherapists work cooperatively with the medical community by using medical applications of hypnosis. Hypno-Birthing was taught until my instructor left the country. More recently, a counselor (certified as a hypnotherapist) has offered a course on healing from abuse.

Furthermore, there are several hypnotherapy instructors teaching my course in other colleges, including a fully accredited college.

This active cooperation helps bridge the great gulf between the scientific community and the artistic community, providing both needed recognition and valuable training for professional hypnotherapists. It is history in the making! Hopefully other advanced specialty classes will be added in the years ahead to enhance the hypnotic journey.

Chapter 18

The Journey Continues...

When you've learned enough to become professionally certified, will your journey of hypnotism training finally end? Is the journey *ever* over? Do we ever learn all there is to know about hypnosis? Where do we go from here?

Do we ever achieve *perfection?* I don't think so. No therapist has a 100% success rate, but a competent hypnotherapist may be able to help most of the people most of the time. If we do our job to the best of our abilities, we do not need to accept responsibility for a client who is unwilling to change, nor do we need to buy into a client's desire to blame others for his or her problems.

Sometimes a client complains about another therapist because of a previous failure to respond to hypnotherapy. While I endeavor to be a good listener, I do my best to consider that there are always two sides to an issue; so I listen with a grain of salt.

In one instance, the target of the complaint happened to be a very competent hypnotherapist who had personally helped *me,* so I have first-hand knowledge of her competency. In certain other instances, I knew personally of successes facilitated by the targets of the criticism.

I know for a fact that not everyone who sees me reaches his or her goal. Also, since people often would rather blame anyone but themselves for their problems, I'll be surprised if there haven't been a few criticisms behind my back as well. Bear this all in mind whenever you hear a client complaining about another hypnotherapist--because one of your former clients may be doing likewise in another therapist's office!

This being said, some of the criticism I've heard from clients is the result of a previous therapist receiving inadequate training. If your client is not successful, be willing to refer whether you have ten weeks or ten years of experience. If you need more training, however, make the investment; and if you know others using hypnosis who have received only minimal training in the art, please encourage them to pursue more adequate training and education. This will benefit their own careers as well as the entire hypnotherapy profession. Make your best better.

I am not perfect, but I endeavor to do my best at giving my clients what I believe would help me if the roles were reversed. I'm still growing. The longer I'm in this profession, the more I realize that there is always something new to learn; and where my knowledge might be considered excellent in some areas, it seems lacking in other areas. All of us can actually be both students and teachers to each other in our ongoing journey of life.

* * *

These are the ongoing voyages of the hypnotherapy profession. THE MISSION: to explore many new ways of helping people become self-empowered; to seek out new clients and open-minded professionals; to boldly go where few have gone before...

* * *

Some may wonder why a man in his fifties would compare hypnotherapy to a theme out of Star Trek. Perhaps it's because there are lessons from that phenomenally successful science fiction series that can apply to all of us... or perhaps it's simply because I love adventure, and this adventurous soul chose an adventurous profession which can help people reach their full potentials.

It is also both my personal and professional opinion that we need to experience the tools in order to appreciate the tools. If you have not yet done so, *experience hypnotherapy for yourself.*

I have shared openly the fact that hypnotherapy helped me personally to heal from hurts of the past, making my life easier and happier. This has two upsides! The *professional* upside of this is a firm conviction of the benefits of using **diversified client-centered hypnotherapy.** When I look into the eyes of a client, there is total sincerity in my statements about the benefits of hypnosis; and it is my opinion that clients pick up intuitively on that fact. My *personal* upside of hypnosis is so profound that I find it difficult to put into words. It can best be defined as experiencing the difference between peace and turmoil, happiness and bitterness, and learning to love life instead of simply surviving life--or learning to love myself as much as my neighbor.

The healing power of forgiveness, enhanced through hypnotherapy, helped me find an inner peace that goes beyond what organized religion ever provided. The freedom obtained by releasing past emotional baggage makes it easier to continue on my own journey through life and find greater happiness along the way. Claiming my own power of choice has helped me gain greater self-empowerment, making my mission to others a personal matter. I thank God that modern psychology was unable to deny me the profound healing obtained through hypnotherapy; yet if certain licensed professionals had gotten their way, I might be a client of psychotherapy even today for issues that have long since been healed.

My original mission statement was to help people claim the power of choice. My current statement is to **help people attain their ideal empowerment;** I endeavor to empower clients to facilitate subconscious acceptance of their choices.

When I wrote my first book, *Success Through Mind Power,* I was struggling financially; and it seemed that my subconscious was talking to *me* through those printed pages just as much as to my readers. By applying what was written in that self-help book, my career has taken me lightyears beyond my original expectations. My former mentor also spoke highly of my self-hypnosis book; and out of all the students that ever studied under Charles Tebbetts, he chose *me* to carry his torch. To say that his choice has touched my life is putting it mildly!

Charlie has gone where none of us will go until our time is up. Yet even from beyond this life he is still reaching out through his teachings and touching people's lives. Each and every successful client leaving my office has been indirectly influenced by Charles Tebbetts. It's also very satisfying to know that my students carry both *his* teachings as well as mine into their practices and their lives.

Whether you have personally taken my hypnosis training course, or simply invested time reading my two books about hypnotism, your journey is not complete--*especially* if you plan on using a client-centered approach to hypnosis.

This hypnosis course is only the *beginning* of a long journey which will continue as long as you choose to practice the art of hypnotherapy. I encourage all my students to be willing to learn new techniques and use them when appropriate so that they may grow beyond the basic training of **Diversified Client-Centered Hypnosis.**

By mastering the art of hypnotherapy, how many lives can each of us influence in a beneficial way? If enough of us spread the light of truth about who actually has the power during hypnosis, can we finally keep hypnotism out of the dark ages once and for all?

Can we continue to grow as a profession without being restricted by the scientific community? Can we encourage other hypnotherapists to seek adequate training if their initial training was insufficient? Yet in so doing, can we critique the *performance* when necessary rather than negatively criticizing or attacking the person? Can we create tolerance of each other within the profession so that we don't have to endure criticism from both inside and outside?

Can we create enough unity and self-regulation that there will be no need for anyone else even to try to regulate us? Can we work cooperatively with the scientific community without letting them dictate what we can and cannot do? Can we collectively turn their skepticism into respect through skilled use of diversified client-centered hypnosis? Can we build a bridge of credibility with the various other health care professions?

Can we also work on our own issues so that we will come from a *love center* with our clients as well as with each other? Can we actually create enough positive energy to help propel the hypnotherapy profession into the new millenium at warp speed? Can hypnotherapy become a profound way to help heal this planet?

Let's *make it so!*

The journey is ongoing....

Suggested Reading

These books come recommended by several well-known and highly respected people in the hypnotherapy profession:

Counseling Hypnotherapy: The Synergism of Psychotherapy and Hypnotherapy
  Charles J. Francis (National Guild of Hypnotists)

Creative Visualization
  Shakti Gawain (Bantam Books; 1983)

Embracing Each Other
  Hal Stone & Sidra Winkelman (New World Library; 1992)

Essentials of Hypnosis
  Michael D. Yapko (Brunner/Mazel Trade; 1994)

Hypnosis for Change
  Hadley & Staudacher (Ballantine Books; 1987)

Hypnosis Induction Technics
  Myron Teitelbaum (Charles C. Thomas; 1969)

Hypnosis: The Induction of Conviction
  John C. Hughes (National Guild of Hypnotists)

Hypnotherapy
  Dave Elman (Westwood Publishing; 1984)

Hypnotic Inductions & Prescriptions
  (Arthur E. Winkler) Publisher: St. John's University Publications

Hypnotic Investigation of Psychodynamic Processes
  Milton Erickson; ed. by Ernest Rossi (Irvington; 1980)

*Hypnotic Realities
  Erickson & Rossi (Irvington) Out of print.

Hypnotism & Meditation
  Ormond McGill (Westwood Publishing; 1984)

Introducing Neuro-Linguistic Programming
  O'Connor & Seymour (Thorsons; 1993)

Love, Medicine & Miracles
    Bernie S. Siegel (Harperperrenial Library; 1990)

Master the Power of Self-Hypnosis
    Roy Hunter (Sterling Publishing; 1998)

Mind Probe Hypnosis
    Irene Hickman (Hickman Systems; 1983)

*Miracles on Demand, 2nd edition
    Charles Tebbetts (self-published; NO LONGER IN PRINT)

*Psychosemantic Parenthetics
    James F. Russell (Institute of Hypnotechnology)

Self-Hypnosis and Other Mind Expanding Techniques
    Charles Tebbetts (Westwood Publishing; 1977)

Success Through Mind Power
    Roy Hunter (Westwood Publishing; 1987)

TimeLine Therapy and the Basis of Personality
    Tad James (Meta Publications Inc.; 1988)

Tinnitus: Turning the Volume Down
    Kevin Hogan, Ph.D. (Network 3000 Publishing; 1998)

Transforming Therapy: A New Approach to Hypnotherapy
    Gil Boyne (Westwood Publishing; 1989)

You'll See It When You Believe It
    Wayne W. Dyer (William Morrow and Company Inc.

*Most out-of-print recommendations appearing in earlier versions of my book were deleted from this list, except for the starred (*) ones, which are worth finding if possible.

There are other good books besides those listed...

Go online to *http://www.royhunter.com* and click on "Other Books." You may also click on the FAQ, and then click on the Resource Guide.

Index

Have you read the first volume yet?

The *Art of Hypnosis:*
Mastering Basic Techniques

by *C. Roy Hunter, M.S., C.Ht.*

with Preface by *Ormond McGill, Ph.D.*

Kendall/Hunt Publishing; ISBN 0-7872-7068-7

*Obtain your copy from the same vendor where you
obtained this book; or you may order directly from
Kendall/Hunt Publishing by calling 1-800-228-0810.*